W9-BUO-814

OBEDIENCE—THE GREATEST FREEDOM

OBEDIENCE -
the Greatest Freedom

In the Words of Alberione
Ambrose
Aquinas
Augustine
Basil
Chiesa
Cushing
de Liguori
de Lubac
Giaccardo
Gregory the Great
Häring
Ignatius Loyola
John Neumann
John of the Cross
John XXIII
à Kempis
Lagrange
Larraona
Leeming
Leo XIII
Paul VI
Pius XI
Pius XII
Rahner
Royo
Sacred Scripture
Sheen
Tanquerey
Teresa of Avila
Vatican II
Wright

ST. PAUL EDITIONS

Compiled by the Daughters of St. Paul

IMPRIMATUR:

✝ Richard Cardinal Cushing

Archbishop of Boston

June 30, 1966

THE DAUGHTERS OF ST. PAUL *are grateful to the following publishers for their kind permission to reprint the selections appearing in this book. The sources of the quotations are footnoted on the first page of each selection.*

America Press, 106 W. 56th Street, New York, N.Y. 10019

Alba House, a division of St. Paul Publications, Staten Island, New York

B. Herder Book Company, 15 & 17 South Broadway, St. Louis, Missouri

Benziger Brothers, Inc., 7 East 51st St., New York, N.Y. 10022

The Catholic University of America Press, 620 Michigan Ave., N.E., Washington, D.C. 20017

The Critic, 180 N. Wabash Avenue, Chicago, Illinois 60601

Cross Currents, a quarterly review, West Nyack, N.Y. 10994

Desclée & Co., Piazza Grazioli N. 4, Rome

McGraw-Hill Book Company, 330 West 42nd St., New York, N.Y. 10036

The Newman Press, Westminster, Maryland

The Priory Press, 2570 Asbury Road, Dubuque, Iowa

Redemptorist Fathers, 5 E. 74th St., New York, N.Y. 10021

Sheed & Ward Inc., 64 University Place, New York, N.Y. 10003

Library of Congress Catalog Card Number: 66-28123

TO

JESUS DIVINE MASTER
"OBEDIENT UNTO DEATH"

TO

MARY MOST HOLY
WHOSE WHOLE LIFE WAS A CONTINUOUS
"BEHOLD THE HANDMAID OF THE LORD"

TO

ST. PAUL THE APOSTLE
WHO FOUND THE FULFILLMENT
OF HIS PERSONALITY IN CHRIST
THE MOMENT HE RESPONDED AND LIVED HIS
"LORD, WHAT WILL YOU HAVE ME DO?"

FOREWORD

"Your life is an imitation of Christ, bringing to full development the consecration received in Holy Baptism, as the Council states in the Dogmatic Constitution on the Church: 'The religious state faithfully imitates and continuously represents in the Church that way of life which the Son of God embraced, when He came into the world to do His Father's Will, and which He proposed to His disciples.' And again: 'Through you the Church presents Christ to both believers and non-believers. Through you it portrays Christ in contemplation on the mountain, proclaiming the Kingdom of God to the multitudes, healing the sick and maimed, converting sinners to a better life, blessing children and doing good to all men, always obedient to the Will of the Father Who sent Him.'

"In the light of this imitation of Christ one comprehends the significance of perfection, attained and to be attained, which is a continuous tending towards Him according to the Pauline thought: 'For love of Him I have renounced everything and reputed it as refuse so that I might gain Christ and be found united to Him. . . . In order that I might know Him and the power of His resurrection I will participate in His sorrows and be transformed into the image of His death. Not that I have reached the goal and attained perfection, but I follow after in order to conquer it so that in the end I may be conquered by Christ Jesus' (Phil. 3:8-12)."

These words were addressed by Pope Paul VI on May 17, 1966, to an assembly of religious who had met in Rome to study the Conciliar decree, Perfectae Caritatis. *The Holy Father explained at this meeting that his words were to be considered an exhortation to all religious throughout the world.*

11

The present volume responds to the expectation of the Holy Father by reason of the witness it bears to one of the fundamental subjects of our day—obedience.

An in-depth presentation of obedience, under its theological, mystical, and philosophical aspects is given by Augustine, Aquinas, Ignatius Loyola, de Liguori, Lagrange, Royo, de Lubac, Häring, Rahner, Larraona, and many more.

While they remind us that obedience in religious life retains all its importance in our day, these renowned writers also guide us as to the manner of presenting this virtue and of practicing it out of convictions—convictions that win the mind and bend the will.

Obedience is treated herein under its various aspects: as imitation of Christ, as a means of formation, as moral security, as the expression and actualization of the life of love, as ecstatic virtue, as continual communion with God.

Father Elio Gambari, in exalting the dignity and grandeur of religious obedience, says:

"Religious obedience is participation in and communion with the fundamental attitude of Christ toward His Father: 'Behold, I come . . . to do thy will, O God' (Heb. 10:7). Hence the practice of obedience is the most intimate union between the soul and Christ. It is the continuation of the sacrifice consummated by Jesus on the cross which is renewed on the altar and is completed in the members of the Mystical Christ. As a result, for the religious, every act is swept up into the sacrifice of Christ.

OBEDIENCE—THE GREATEST FREEDOM *will be read with special interest and above all with special advantage by both superiors and subjects, by both men and women religious.*

CONTENTS

13

SECTION 7

NOT MY WILL BUT YOURS

SECTION 8

OBEDIENCE IN THE PLAN OF SALVATION

Section 1

Oboedientia et pax

OBOEDIENTIA ET PAX *
John XXIII

THE DUTIES of my life are all contained in these three words. This is all I have to do: to know, love, and serve God, always and at all costs; God's will must be mine and I must seek it only, even in the slightest things. This is the first and fundamental principle.   *April* 1-10, 1903

HOWEVER THINGS may go, in rain or sunlight, cold or heat, and however my greater or lesser superiors may dispose of me, I must always stay in the same frame of mind: never a word of complaint or disapproval, in public or in private; my smile must be cheerful, frank and friendly; I must not let my head be turned in good fortune nor let myself be soured by the bitter moments of life.

This does not mean denying that the senses or the impulses of nature exist. The enjoyment of God's love, the sweet and total abandonment to His will must absorb all else in me or, rather, transform and sublimate all the desires of my lower nature.

To practice this principle must be the work of my every moment, whatever the place or circum-

* From *Journal of a Soul* by Pope John XXIII. Copyright 1965 by Geoffrey Chapman Ltd. Used by permission of the publisher, McGraw-Hill Book Company.

stances, and one of the chief points of enquiry in my examinations of conscience. *April* 1-10, 1903

THE GOLDEN and sublime conclusion of all the meditations of this first day is the great principle of detachment. In theory I succeed in this remarkably well, but in practice I am the man who abides least by this principle. When something happens here which even indirectly affects me personally, my imagination and my pride torment me to an extraordinary degree. Yet the keystone of the spiritual edifice is just this: to do not my own will but God's, to be habitually disposed to accept anything at all, however repugnant to my feelings and my pride.

In important matters there is no difficulty; I will do nothing more or less than what my superiors and spiritual father require. The crux of the matter lies not in doing what I have to do, under obedience, but in conforming my understanding and my will to the wishes and advice of my superiors, setting aside my own personal views—even if apparently fine and holy—the flights of my imagination and my other self.

No anxiety then, no castle in the air; few ideas, but they must be sound and serious, and fewer desires. "One thing is needful" (Luke 10:42). Golden dreams of working in one way rather than another, highly colored plans of what I hope to be able to do tomorrow or next year or later: away with all these!

I shall be what the Lord wants me to be. It is hard for me to think of a hidden life, neglected, perhaps despised by all, known to God alone; this is repugnant to my pride. And yet, until I succeed in doing such violence to my own likes and dislikes that this obscurity becomes not only indifferent but welcome and enjoyable, I shall never do what God wants from me.   *December* 9-18, 1903

I WANT TO GUARD my faith carefully, like a sacred treasure. Most of all I want to be true to that spirit of faith which is gradually being whittled away before the so-called requirements of criticism, in the atmosphere and light of modern times. If the Lord should grant me a long life and the opportunity of being a useful priest in His Church, I want it to be said of me, and I shall be prouder of this than of any other title, that I was a priest of lively simple faith, solidly behind the pope and for the pope, always, even in matters not yet officially defined, in every detail of seeing and feeling. I want to be like those good old Bergamasque priests of old, of blessed memory, who neither saw nor desired to see further than could be seen by the pope, the bishops, common sense and the mind of the Church.

It will always be my principle, in all spheres of religious knowledge and in all theological or biblical questions, to find out first of all the traditional teaching of the Church, and on this basis to judge the findings of contemporary scholarship. I do not despise criticism and I shall be most careful not to think ill of critics or treat them with disrespect. On the contrary, I love it. I shall be glad to keep up with the most recent findings, I shall study the new systems of thought and their continual evolution and their trends; criticism for me is light, is truth, and there is only one truth, which is sacred. But I shall always try to introduce into these discussions, in which too often ill-considered enthusiasms and deceitful appearances have too much to say, a great moderation, harmony, balance and serenity of judgment, allied to a prudent and cautious broad-mindedness. On very doubtful points I shall prefer to keep silent, like one who does not know, rather than hazard propositions which might differ in the slightest degree from the right judgment of the Church. I will not be surprised at anything, even if certain conclusions, while preserving intact the sacred deposit of faith, turn out to be rather unexpected. Surprise is the daughter of ignorance. On the contrary, I shall rejoice to see God doing all this in order to make the pure treasure of his revelation more crystal clear and free from dross.

In general, it will be my rule to listen to everything and everyone, to think and study much, to be very slow to judge, neither to talk too much nor to try to attract attention, and not to deviate by one jot or tittle from the mind of the Church. As Cicero said: "Time destroys the invention of public opinion; truth remains and grows ever stronger, and lives and lasts forever." *December 9-18, 1903*

Is IT NOT TRUE that the saints, in their early years, appeared to set out on a road quite different from the one which their natural gifts and brilliant qualities had seemed to indicate? Yet they became saints, and such saints! Reformers of society, founders of famous orders! They practiced holy detachment: they were willing to listen to the voice of God who spoke to them as He speaks to me; they did not measure what they had to do by considering their pride, but cast themselves blindly into all that God wanted them to do. "Look then, my boy, look and make it according to the pattern" (Exodus 25:40) and this means in everything. All my wanting to do and say is nothing but pride, there is no other word for it; if I go on in my own way I shall work and sweat over it ... and in the end ... what shall I be? ... a wind bag!

If I want to be really great, a great priest, I must be stripped of everything, like Jesus on His cross; I must judge everything that happens in my life, and the decisions of my superiors concerning me, in the light of faith. God forbid we should carry criticism into this field! O blessed simplicity!

August 1-10, 1904

I AM ABOUT TO ENTER the thirty-second year of my life. The thought of the past makes me humble and ashamed; the thought of the present is consoling because mercy is still being shown to me; the thought of the future encourages me in the hope of making up for lost time. How much future will there be? Perhaps a very short one. But long or short as it may be, O Lord, once more I tell you that it is all yours.

I must not try to find or follow new ways of doing good. I live under obedience, and obedience has already overburdened me with so many occupations that my shoulders are sagging under the weight. But I am willing to bear this and other burdens, if the Lord so desires. My rest will be in heaven. These are the years for hard work.

October 13-19, 1912

THIS IS THE SEVENTH TIME that I have withdrawn to this dear and holy place to think of my soul. My overwhelming obligation is always the same: to bless the Lord who continues to show me his love, to preserve me from grave faults and make me feel ashamed of my own unworthiness.

I feel I need add no more, except in confirmation of all that I have written and proposed in earlier years. I say only this to the Lord: here I am, ready for everything, sufferings as well as joys. "For me to live is Christ and to die is gain" (Phil. 1:21). I wanted to rid myself of some of the burden of my responsibilities and to indicate which of these I would prefer to retain. But I have decided not to do anything about it. My superiors know everything, and that is enough. As I have not been asked about this I will be careful not to show my preference for one kind of work rather than another. I must proceed, as my spiritual director tells me, with my head in the sack of Divine Providence.

October 19-25, 1913

THE CHURCH IS making me a bishop in order to send me to Bulgaria, to fulfill there as Apostolic Visitor, a mission of peace. Perhaps I shall find many difficulties awaiting me. With the Lord's help, I feel ready for everything. I do not seek, I do not desire, the glory of this world; I look forward to greater glory in heaven.

I INSERT in my coat of arms the words *Oboedientia et pax* (Obedience and Peace) which Cesare Baronius used to say every day, when he kissed the Apostle's foot in St. Peter's. These words are in a way my own history and my life. O may they be the glorification of my humble name through the centuries!   March 13-17, 1925

IT IS NOT DIFFICULT for me now to understand that the beginning of sanctity lies in my total abandonment to the Lord's holy will, even in little things, and that is why I must insist on this. I do not wish or ask for anything beyond obedience to the dispositions, instructions, and wishes of the Holy Father and the Holy See.

I will never take any step, direct or indirect, to bring about any change or alteration in my situation, but I will in all things and at all times live from day to day, letting others say and do, and suffering whoever so desires to pass ahead of me, without preoccupying myself about my future. *December 20-24, 1928*

WITH THE GRACE OF GOD, I feel, I want to feel, truly indifferent to all that the Lord may decide for me, as regards my future. Worldly gossip about my affairs makes no impression on me. I am willing to live like this even if the present state of things were to remain unchanged for years and years. I will never even express the desire or the slightest inclination to change, however much this may cost me in my heart.

Oboedientia et pax. That is my episcopal motto. I want to die with the satisfaction of having always, even in the smallest things, honored my obligation.

In truth, were I to ask myself what I would desire or do, other than what I am doing now, I would not know how to answer. *April 28-May 4, 1930*

MY WORK IN TURKEY is not easy, but it is coming along well and gives me great consolation. I see the charity of the Lord here, and the clergy united among themselves and with their humble pastor. The political situation does not allow me to do much, but it seems to me there is something gained if at least I do not worsen it through my own fault.

My mission in Greece, on the other hand, is so full of vexations! For this very reason I love it even more and intend to go on working there with heart and soul, forcing myself to overcome all my repugnance. For me it is an order: therefore it requires obedience. I confess I would not mind if it were entrusted to someone else, but while it is mine I want to honor the obligation at all costs. "They who sow in tears shall reap in joy." It matters little to me that others will reap.   *November* 12-18, 1939

READINESS FOR SELF-SACRIFICE, such as the Lord wants from every one of us, and in the measure He requires, this must present a great lesson and warning for me. This is what loyal and sincere devotion means. Not just shedding consoling tears during prayer but preparing a ready will for God's service, whatever it may be. "My heart is ready, O God, my heart is ready," for much or for little, to do what God wants of me and understand what He does not want, which therefore must not be done. So frequently we are deceived about this. We take pleasure in fashioning for ourselves ways of serving the Lord which really are simply ways of expressing our own taste, our own ambition, our own caprice. "The pride of your heart has deceived you, you who dwell in the clefts of the rock." You hardly know how to take in God's service, one step outside your hole, in which like a tarantula, you take refuge from the storms that rage, and yet you like to persuade yourself that you could fly like an eagle if you receive a call from beyond the mountains and beyond the seas. In your piety you have unwittingly deceived yourself. Let the readiness of your will be seen in works done to carry out the will of the Lord, as this is made known to you day by day, and do not show this readiness merely by heaving fervent sighs. *November* 30, 1940

Good Friday: my present

MY PRESENT is spent in faithful service to Christ, who was obedient and was crucified, words I repeat so often at this season: "Christ was made obedient." So I must be meek and humble like Him, glowing with divine charity, ready for sacrifice or for death, for Him or for His Church.

Good Friday, 1950

AFTER MY FIRST MASS over the tomb of St. Peter I felt the hands of the Holy Father Pius X laid on my head in a blessing full of good augury for me and for the priestly life I was just entering upon; and after more than half a century (fifty-seven years precisely) here are my own hands extended in a blessing for the Catholics, and not only the Catholics, of the whole world, in a gesture of universal fatherhood. I am successor to this same Pius X who has been proclaimed a saint, and I am still living in the same priestly service as he, his predecessors and his successors, all placed like St. Peter at the head of the whole Church of Christ, one, holy, Catholic and apostolic.

THIS PARTICULAR WAY of sanctification, which is the right way for me, has once again been shown to me here at Castel Gandolfo, in a passage in a book and in a picture.

The passage I came across unexpectedly in a little volume: *La perfezione cristiana. Pagine di ascetica* by Antonio Rosmini: "In what does sanctity consist?"

"Reflect on this thought, that sanctity consists in being willing to be opposed and humiliated, rightly or wrongly; in being willing to obey; in being willing to wait, with perfect serenity; in doing the will of your superiors without regard for your own will; in acknowledging all the benefits you receive and your own unworthiness; in feeling a great gratitude to others, and especially to God's ministers; in sincere love; in tranquillity, resignation, gentleness and the desire to do good to all, and in unceasing work. I am about to leave and can say no more, but this is enough."

I find it comforting to note that these are simply the applications of my own special motto, which I took from Baronius: *Oboedientia et Pax.* Jesus, this shows me that you are always with me! I thank you for this doctrine, which seems to follow me wherever I go.   *August* 10-15, 1961

CONCERNING OBEDIENCE. I have never felt any temptation against obedience and I thank the Lord that He has never permitted me to feel this even when obedience was a great effort, as it still is now that I am made 'the servant of the servants of God.'

August 11, 1961

MY OWN PERSONAL serenity, which makes such an impression on people, derives from this: the obedience in which I have always lived, so that I do not desire or beg to live longer, even a day beyond that hour in which the Angel of Death will come to call me and take me, as I trust, to paradise.

December, 1961

Section 2

The Voice of the Church on Obedience

LEO XIII *

THE MASTER and Model of all sanctity is Christ; it is on this model that all who desire to find a place among the blessed must fashion themselves. Now Christ does not change with the passing of the centuries, but "he is the same, yesterday, and today, and the same forever." It is therefore to the men of every age that are addressed the words "Learn of me that I am meek and humble of heart." There is no period in which Christ does not show himself to us as "being made obedient even unto death." And this word of the Apostle is also valid for all time: "And they that are Christ's have crucified their flesh, with the vices and concupiscences."

Would to God that these virtues were practiced today by a larger number and with as much perfection as by the saints of past ages. They by their humility, their obedience, their austerity, were "mighty in word and work" for the greater good not only of religion but also of their fellow-citizens and their country. *To Cardinal Gibbons, 1899*

* The above and following passages are from the *States of Perfection,* papal teachings selected and arranged by the Benedictine Monks of Solesmes. Copyright by the Daughters of St. Paul, 1966.

33

PIUS XI

BEFORE ALL ELSE, We exhort religious never to lose sight of the examples of their founder and lawgiver if they wish to be certain they are sharing in the abundant graces of their vocation. When these chosen men created their Institutes, did they do otherwise than obey an inspiration from God? That is why all those who reproduce in themselves the characteristic with which each founder wished to mark his religious family, surely do not depart from the spirit of their origins. Consequently, their disciples, like the best of sons, will take it to heart to give glory to their father by observing his rule and his counsels and by penetrating themselves with his spirit; they will be faithful to the duties of their state as long as they walk in the footsteps of their founder.

To the Superiors General of Religious Orders, 1924

PIUS XII

YOU MUST BE FIRM in your fidelity to your Constitutions and to all they prescribe. . . . Let obedience be your characteristic, your glory, your strength. It must aim as much as possible at making you perfectly submissive to the will of superiors, without complaint, without murmuring, without that blameworthy spirit of criticism which is the malady of our times, wasting strength, rendering apostolic enterprises fruitless and without stamina. The offices which an austere obedience will impose upon you will become light under the action of charity. When it is present, God Himself is present, since God is charity. May it be in you, therefore, this charity which springs "from a pure heart, and a good conscience, and an unfeigned faith" (I Tim. 1:5).

To the Tertian Masters of the Society of Jesus, 1946

IF GOD'S VOICE draws a man by certain signs towards the summits of evangelical perfection, one should propose to him without the slightest hesitation, that to realize this sublime plan he should freely sacrifice his liberty as the vow of obedience requires, this vow which the Church, in the course of so many centuries has appreciated, experienced, defined, and approved. Let none be urged against his will to make this consecration of self; but if a man desire it, let none dissuade him from it, still less prevent him.   *To members of the General Congress of Religious Orders,*
Congregations, Societies and Secular Institutes, 1950

YOU WOULD NOW like to receive from Our lips some points which have to do with the profession of the vows of religion and the training which is suitable for novices. In the program of matters to be discussed We read on this score: "Formation for religious obedience: exercise of authority and respect for the personality of the subject." Certainly, in religious houses supernatural obedience, which maintains the ardor of charity towards God, must at all costs flourish and be firmly and assiduously cultivated, generously, and in conformity with the established rules. Is it not here that we find the solid basis of discipline and the religious life?

Is it not true that the great enterprises which religious have successfully carried out and which they will carry out in the future, have obtained and will obtain their happy results only by reason of the union of forces in obedience? Recognize, therefore, and respect, and be willing to accept the salutary yoke of obedience as the burden of the strong. However, in our day, when the machine is everywhere in command, when technique invades all things, impregnates all things, and fashions all things to its own image, let those who command be careful not to treat those subject to their will as so many pieces of merchandise or as parts of a machine, and let them always respect in them the human personality.

To Discalced Carmelite Professors, 1951

MAY YOUR OBEDIENCE be founded on unshakable motives: those which make you behold God Himself in your superiors. Disobedience, that scourge peculiar to our times, dissipates strength and renders apostolic enterprises weak and sterile.

To the Friars Preachers, 1955

LET ALL THOSE who have taken the vow to seek evangelical perfection remember this fact, then; let them weigh it in the sight of God: to fulfill their obligation it is not enough for them to avoid grave sin, or even, with God's help, to avoid venial sin, nor materially to obey the orders of superiors, their vows and obligations in conscience, or even their particular constitutions according to which, as the Church lays down in the sacred canons, "each and every religious, superiors as well as subjects, must ... model their lives and so tend to the perfection of their state" (C.I.C., can. 593). All these things religious must accomplish with their whole heart and with ardent love, not merely out of necessity, "but also for conscience' sake" (Rom. 13:5), since in order to reach the heights of sanctity and to be for all men so many well-springs of Christian charity, they must be devoured by an ardent love for God and neighbor and full of every virtue.

Apostolic Constitution, "Sedes Sapientiae," 1956

How DEAR to the Church has always been entire and prompt obedience to religious superiors, the faithful observance of regular discipline, humble submission, even of the judgment, with respect to those whom the Vicar of Christ has placed over you, according to your institute, so often and so solemnly approved by him and his predecessors.

In fact, it is in conformity with Catholic understanding, this virtue sanctioned, with the approbation of the Apostolic See, by the constant tradition of the ancient and venerable religious families, the description of which St. Ignatius has left you in his famous "Letter on the Virtue of Obedience." It is an error far removed from the truth to think that the teaching of this Letter should henceforth be abandoned, and that for hierarchical and religious obedience should be substituted a certain 'democratic' equality according to which the subject would debate with his superior what is to be done until both reach an agreement.

To the Society of Jesus, 1957

AGAINST THE SPIRIT of pride and independence, with which very many are tainted today, you must keep intact the virtue of true humility which makes you pleasing to God and to men; the virtue of universal abnegation, by which you show yourselves disciples of him who "became obedient even unto death" (Phil. 2:8). Would he be worthy of Christ his Head who fled from the austerity of religious life and sought to live in religion like a layman, seeking according to his own whim what is useful, pleasing, and comfortable for himself? Those who pretend, under the vain and henceforth shopworn term of 'formalism' to empty religious discipline of meaning, must know that they contravene the wishes and thoughts of this Apostolic See, and that they are under an illusion when they appeal to the law of charity to cover a false liberty, freed from the yoke of obedience; what would that charity be which would neglect the good pleasure of God our Lord, which they have vowed to realize in religious life? *To the Society of Jesus,* 1957

To COME to the present difficulties in the way of religious obedience, it has been noticed that the movement of adaptation has brought about in this area a certain tension; not that there is any lack of sincere desire to tend to perfection by means of obedience, but that certain characteristics of obedience are being accentuated today which even serious religious with delicate consciences would wish to see disappear. In particular, it is said that the human and religious dignity of the person is being jeopardized, the development of the personality is being interfered with, the orientation to God alone is being hindered. These objections, it would seem, find their support in certain illusions experienced by individuals or noticed in individuals and appeal also for different juridical considerations.

In order to dispel a feeling of sadness stemming from an erroneous interpretation of the principles which govern religious life or from practical errors in their application, we must first recall the Lord's words: "Come to me, all you who labor and are burdened, and I will give you rest. ... Learn from me, for I am meek and humble of heart; and you will find rest for your souls" (Matt. 11:28-29). If the Lord thus exhorts men to take up His yoke, it is to teach them that beyond the legal observance, which may easily become difficult and hard to bear, they have to discover the meaning of true submission and Christian humility. Far from offending the dignity of the man who submits to it, they free him interiorly, they represent to him the acceptance of his state of subjection not as a constraint imposed from without, but as a deliverance of self into the hands of God whose will is expressed by the visible authority of those who have the mission to command. On his side, the superior will exercise his powers in the same spirit of the Gospel: "Let him who is greatest among you, become as the youngest; and him who is the chief, as the servant" (Luke 22:26). Therefore, the necessary firmness of the command will always be accompanied with the profound respect and the delicacy of a father's heart.

To Participants in the Second Congress on the States of Perfection, 1957

AN ARGUMENT against obedience is deduced from the fact that man's dependence on a superior is opposed to the supreme and direct control of God over the conscience. To hold that one man depends upon another even in his personal life and activity, is this not to confer upon superiors the prerogatives which are reserved for God alone?

In fact, the Church has never either defended or approved such a proposition. She looks upon obedience as a means of leading man to God. Because the motive which inspires it is that of union with God, and because it is ordained in the last analysis to the increase of charity, the superior in no way constitutes an obstacle placed between God and the subject, deflecting in his own interest the homage addressed to God alone. The superior can only command in God's name and in virtue of the powers of his office, and the subject should obey only out of love for Christ and not for human motives of utility or suitableness, still less out of pure constraint. In this way he will keep, in the most perfect submission, the joyous eagerness of the one who ratifies, by the concrete commitment of each day, the total gift of self to the unique Master.

To Participants in the Second Congress
on the States of Perfection, 1957

RELIGIOUS SHOULD NOT desire what is pleasing, what is agreeable, what is convenient, but God alone; and they will not find Him except by unceasingly curbing their senses and their wills; their wills by humility and submissive obedience; their senses by austerity of life and mortification of the body freely accepted. Without these means, recommended by the Old and New Testaments and the whole tradition of the Church, a Christian soul flatters itself in vain that it can arrive at the love of God and the love of neighbor for the love of God.

To Major Superiors of Religious Institutes, 1958

HUMAN NATURE is attracted by ease and it has always found disagreeable the discipline comprised in life in religion stemming from the rule; and this is naturally more disagreeable to men of our day, accustomed as they have been to a freer life before embracing the religious state. Even if, on some unessential points, you have rightly adapted the rule and are adapting it to the possibilities of those who present themselves to you, it would be inadmissible for you to demean it and still less to abandon it. The word of Proverbs is as true today as in the past: "Hold fast to instruction, never let her go; keep her, for she is your life" (Prov. 4:13). What the divinely inspired author states on the subject of discipline which each one willingly imposes upon himself, can we not say also, with every reason, of that particular discipline to which, by the profession of a more perfect life, one obliges oneself and which one promises to observe? "Those whom love urges on the road to eternal life, for the same motive enter straightway on the narrow path; ... no longer guided by their own judgment, not obeying their desires and their satisfactions, but walking according to the judgment and command of another, they wish nothing else, in entering the monastery, than to be subject to the Abbot" (Rule of St. Benedict, c.5).

To Religious, 1958

INTERNATIONAL CONGRESS
ON THE STATES OF PERFECTION *

The True and Unique Foundation
of Religious Obedience

TODAY THE CULT personality is fashionable, and in its name one can be tempted to consider less the authority of the one who commands in the name of the Lord and the legitimacy of his orders than their solid foundation, their reasonable aspect.

Today it is the democratic spirit that is honored. And even a religious soul can deceive himself and pretend that between him and the superior there are, so to say, democratic relations, that is to say, relations of trust and, as it were, of equality, where the subject, while recognizing himself as such, should prefer to be a collaborator, to whom all personal initiative is allowed, and who has the right to consider the motives of the orders given.

In particular cases the superior could give the reason for certain commands, for example, to new religious who have grown up that way, or to the young, not yet well trained and little inclined to

* From *For A Better Religious Life,* containing the essence of the proceedings of the International Congress on the States of Perfection, 1950, edited by P. Vitus Gaiani, O.F.M. Used by permission of Alba House, a division of St. Paul Publications.

obedience. But if this had to be done in all cases religious obedience would lose its supernatural aureola of free, conscious, unconditional, and filial adherence to the will of God, manifested by His representatives. There would be no more place for the exercise of the other virtues, such as faith, renouncement, humility, etc. And religious obedience would be reduced to a lay, external obedience without merit, based only, or in a predominant way, on the principles of natural character; on the necessity of a hierarchy, of rule or discipline in any human society; or on the qualities of the one who commands.

Extent of Religious Obedience

The religious who is seriously striving for perfection obeys his superiors not only when they command in virtue of holy obedience or its equivalent, but also when they express any order, desire, or counsel.

An ancient controversy remains unsolved today on the obligatory character of particular laws of every state of perfection, which are designated under the name of rule, constitution, etc. The question is this: "Does he who transgresses such rules commit sin or is he merely at fault in regard to purely directive norms, and in conscience must he only submit to the punishment provided for by the laws?"

The question has never been defined in a general way by the Church. And the various states of perfection, with a few exceptions, in practice adopt this principle suggested by the norms–No. 320– promulgated by the Holy See in 1901: "Of themselves constitutions do not oblige in conscience and hence the one who disobeys them does not sin, except when he transgresses through contempt, or in matter which concerns the observance of the vows, of the commandments of God, or of the Church."

The late Father Muzzarelli, who had been procurator general of the Society of St. Paul and consultor of the Sacred Congregation of Religious wrote: "Let it always be permissible to affirm that this principle is often badly interpreted, in such a way that many, in the practical application, are really led into error.... It seems that the principle that the constitutions do not bind, ought to be enunciated in a different way, more appropriately, more completely, and corresponding better to the actual concept of the constitutions (not an appendix to the rule, of secondary value, but a unique code, often of the particular legislation of a congregation). We reach this conclusion if the non-obligatory character of the constitutions is enunciated in the following or equivalent fashion:

1) The rules that relate to divine or ecclesiastical laws retain the obligation that they have of themselves.

2) The rules which concern the vows, that is, which tend to determine the remote or proximate

matter of the vows, receive this obligatory character from the vows themselves.

3) The prescriptions which regard government and define its necessary functions, the burdens and the offices that it implies, likewise those things which fix and consecrate the nature and the specific end of the congregation, oblige in conscience, according to the gravity of the matter.

4) The purely disciplinary or ascetic prescriptions, not comprised in the preceding, do not oblige, of themselves, under pain of sin. They oblige directly and in conscience that one accept the punishment for their violation, and no doubt they may constitute matter of the vow and of the virtue of obedience.

Moreover it is a fault to violate any rule, even the least out of contempt.

If one transgresses for a reason or purpose that is not right, for example, through laziness, through lack of necessary mortification, through an inordinate habit, or for any other bad reason; or if the fault gives scandal or contributes to laxity of the religious life; in all these cases the transgression implies a sin against the corresponding virtue." (I, 540)

The Duty of Superiors

SUPERIORS, commanding in the name of Our Lord, ought to imitate, in their governing, the qualities and virtues of the divine government.

How sweet and glorious is this virtue in which
other virtues are contained! Oh, obedience,
avigate without effort or danger and reach
fely! You conform to the only-begotten Word
mount the ship of the most holy cross to
the obedience of the Word, to not transgress
epart from its teachings. . . . You are great in
ng perseverance, and so great is your strength
heaven to earth that you open heaven's
(Dialogue, Ch. 155).

VI *

IS SUPREMELY important to cherish diligently
us obedience in your lives.

eligious obedience is and must remain a holo-
of one's own will which is offered to God. A
us makes this sacrifice of self with a view to
y obeying lawful superiors (whose author-
course, should always be exercised within
nfines of charity and with due regard for the
person), even though our times summon
us to the performance of many and heavy
ns, and to carrying out these duties more
fully and more promptly.   *To All Religious, 1964*

he following excerpts are from *To All Religious, To Women
*, and *Ecclesiam Suam,* published by the Daughters of St.
64.

The recently deceased Very Rev. John Bap-
tist Jansens, superior general of the Society of Jesus,
recalls the necessity of imitating, above all else, divine wisdom, striving to examine things carefully
before deciding, even asking the advice of the one
whom we know does not agree with us.

The superior ought to imitate the constancy of
our Creator, not changing his decision which has
been taken after mature deliberation, unless new
reasons come to light that have not been considered
before.

"But, above all," adds the Very Rev. Father,
"the superior, whether in the things he commands
or in the manner in which he does it, will strive to
imitate the incomparable delicacy of divine charity.
He will command with humility, with tact and
measure, putting himself in place of his subjects and
demanding from them only things that are reasonable, moderate, and normally possible.

"The subjects are not tools or machines: they
are human beings, endowed by the Creator, in
different degrees, with qualities of intellect and
heart, and provided by the divine liberality with
gifts of initiative, which vary from the little initiative of a capable cook to the vast initiative of a
founder. It enters into the plans of divine providence
that all these riches, which God distributes among
creatures return a hundred-fold or as much as possible. A superior who would try to smother under the
pretext of dependence, all initiative in his subjects,

would merit the reproach made by Our Divine Master to the servant who buried the talent entrusted to him. On the contrary, it is the highest art of superiors to utilize to the greatest measure humanly possible, all the resources of the subjects."

The Church has never admitted that all initiative must come from above; the approbation and decision, yes; the proposals, the experiences, the beginnings, no. . . .

Therefore, let the superiors seek to harmonize authority with the initiative of their subjects, leaving to them a fitting sphere of action.

JOHN XXIII *

THE APOSTLE St. Paul develops the concept of the humiliation of Jesus made obedient unto the death of the cross (Phil. 2:8). In order to follow better the Divine Master you have joined Him with the vow and promise of obedience.

This constant sacrifice of your 'ego,' this annihilation of self can cost much, but it is also true that herein lies the victory (Cf. Prov. 21:28), for heavenly graces correspond to this spiritual crucifixion for you and for all humanity.

The teaching of the Church on the inalienable rights of the human person is clear and precise.

* From *To Women Religious*, by Pope John XXIII, published by the Daughters of St. Paul, 1962.

The special gifts of every
duly developed in order th
to the gifts received from

But, if one passes fron
son to the exaltation of th
affirmation of personalisn
serious. May the words of
tion, *Menti Nostrae*, be o
for you:

"In an age like ours, i
authority is grievously di
necessary that the priest,
faith firmly in mind, shoul
cept this same authority, ne
the social and religious ord
dation of his personal sand

Here We address ou
duties of direction and resp

Demand a most gen
rules, but also be unders
sisters. Favor in each of th
natural aptitudes. The offic
obedience sweet and not
spect, still less to impose

Beloved daughters, W
according to the spirit of tl
ished by deep humility, b
ness and by complete detac
has become the program
can understand the words

IN THESE MATTERS [of apostolic zeal], let not the religious be left solely to their own initiative, since their work must always be subject to the vigilance of superiors, especially if it is a matter of work that has notable relevance to civil life.

To All Religious, 1964

THE CHOICE you have made is the best, the most difficult and at the same time the easiest. It is the closest to that of Mary Most Holy because, like hers, it is completely governed by a simple and total abandonment to the divine will: *Fiat mihi secundum Verbum tuum!* We will pray that she may make you strong; nowadays the religious life calls for strength. In times past it may have been a refuge for many weak and timid souls; today it is the workshop of souls that are strong, dependable and heroic.

To Women Religious, 1964

THE CHURCH's authority is instituted by Christ; it is indeed, representative of Him; it is the authorized channel of His word; it is the expression of His pastoral charity. Obedience, therefore is motivated by faith, develops into a school of evangelical humility, and links the obedient man to the wisdom, unity, constructiveness and charity by which the body of the Church is sustained. It confers upon him who imposes it and upon him who conforms himself to it the merit of being like Christ who was "made obedient unto death."

By obedience, therefore, in the context of dialogue, we mean the exercise of authority in the full awareness of its being a service and ministry of truth and charity, and we mean the observance of canonical regulations and respect for the government of legitimate superiors in the spirit of untroubled readiness as becomes free and loving children.

The spirit of independence, of criticism, of rebellion ill accords with the charity which gives life to the Church's solidarity, concord and peace, and easily transforms the dialogue into argument, dispute and disagreement. This most regrettable attitude, so easy, alas, to produce, is condemned by the Apostle Paul in his warning words: "Let there be no divisions among you" (1 Cor. 1:10).

Ecclesiam Suam, 1964

VATICAN II *

IN PROFESSING obedience, religious offer the full surrender of their own will as a sacrifice of themselves to God and so are united permanently and securely to God's salvific will.

After the example of Jesus Christ who came to do the will of the Father (cf. John 4:34; 5:30; Heb. 10:7; Ps. 39:9) and "assuming the nature of a slave"

* The following excerpts are from *The Sixteen Documents of Vatican II,* published by the Daughters of St. Paul, 1966.

(Phil. 2:7) learned obedience in the school of suffering (cf. Heb. 5:8), religious under the motion of the Holy Spirit, subject themselves in faith to their superiors who hold the place of God. Under their guidance they are led to serve all their brothers in Christ, just as Christ Himself in obedience to the Father served His brethren and laid down His life as a ransom for many (Cf. Matt. 20:28; John 10:14-18). So they are closely bound to the service of the Church and strive to attain the measure of the full manhood of Christ (Eph. 4:13).

Religious, therefore, in the spirit of faith and love for the divine will, should humbly obey their superiors according to their rules and constitutions. Realizing that they are contributing to building up the body of Christ according to God's plan, they should use both the forces of their intellect and will and the gifts of nature and grace to execute the commands and fulfill the duties entrusted to them. In this way religious obedience, far from lessening the dignity of the human person, by extending the freedom of the sons of God, leads it to maturity.

EVERYONE SHOULD KEEP in mind that the hope of renewal lies more in the faithful observance of the rules and constitutions than in multiplying laws.

Decree on the Adaptation and Renewal of Religious Life, 1965

THE DISCIPLINE of seminary life is to be reckoned not only as a strong safeguard of community life and of charity but also as a necessary part of the total whole training formation. For thereby self-mastery is acquired, solid personal maturity is promoted, and the other dispositions of mind are developed which very greatly aid the ordered and fruitful activity of the Church. Seminary discipline should be so maintained, however, that the students acquire an internal attitude whereby they accept the authority of superiors from personal conviction, that is to say, from a motive of conscience (Cf. Rom. 13:5), and for supernatural reasons. The norms of discipline are to be applied according to the age of the students so that they themselves, as they gradually learn self-mastery, may become accustomed to use freedom wisely, to act spontaneously and energetically, and to work together harmoniously with their fellows and with the laity.

Decree on Priestly Training, 1965

Section 3

The Education of Conscience

THE EDUCATION OF CONSCIENCE *
Pius XII

CONSCIENCE MAY BE CALLED the most personal and secret nucleus of man. There he takes refuge in absolute solitude with his spiritual faculties: alone with himself, or better, alone with God—whose voice conscience echoes—and with himself. There he makes up his mind, for good or for evil; there he makes his choice between the road to victory and the road to defeat. Even if he wanted to, man would never succeed in ridding himself of his conscience; with it—either as approving or condemning—he will proceed along the whole road of life, and likewise with it—a truthful and incorruptible witness—he will present himself before God's judgment.

. . . IT IS NECESSARY to refer to some fundamental concepts of Catholic doctrine to realize fully that conscience can and must be educated.

The divine Savior has brought His truth and grace to man, ignorant and feeble: truth to show him the way that leads to his goal, and grace to give him the strength to reach it.

---

* Allocutions of March 23 and April 18, 1952, of Pius XII from *Education,* papal teachings selected and arranged by the Benedictine Monks of Solesmes. Copyright by the Daughters of St. Paul, 1960.

To travel along that road means, in practice, to accept the will and commandments of Christ and to adapt one's life to them, that is, every individual action, both internal and external, that the human will chooses and determines. Now, what spiritual faculty is it that dictates to the will, in particular cases, so that it may choose and determine those acts that conform to the divine will, if not the conscience? It is therefore the faithful echo and the clear reflection of the divine rule of human actions. Such expressions as "the judgment of the Christian conscience," or "judge according to Christian conscience," have therefore this meaning: the rule for the final and personal decision of a moral act is to be taken from the word and will of Christ. He is in fact the Way, the Truth and the Life not only for all mankind as a whole, but for each individual person: as much for the adult, as for the child and youth.

... THE DIVINE SAVIOR has delivered His revelation, of which moral obligations are an essential part, not just to mere individual men but to His Church, to which He has entrusted the mission of leading souls to embrace faithfully that sacred duty.

"Morality according to the situation"

WE WISH TODAY to uncover the hidden sources of a "new morality." We might term it "ethical existentialism," "ethical individualism"—all understood in the restrictive sense of which We shall speak, and which has also been called "situation-ethics," or "morality according to the situation."

The distinctive mark of this morality is that it is not based in effect on universal moral laws, such as, for example, the Ten Commandments, but on the real and concrete conditions or circumstances in which men must act, and according to which the conscience of the individual must judge and choose. Such a state of affairs is unique and is applicable only once for every human action. That is why the decision of conscience, as the proposers of this ethic affirm, cannot be commanded by ideas, principles, and universal laws.

(*According to those who favor the new morality, conscience may make decisions contrary to the divine law, and even as regards God Himself, to violate this law.—For conscience, nothing exists other than God, the Father, and the ego of man, the child of God.—In this way, some Catholics think that they can soften the requirements of Christian living.*)

This is especially true of the negative obligations of the moral law, those which oblige us not to do something. The fundamental obligations of the Christian law, inasmuch as they supercede those of the natural law, and are based on the essence of the supernatural order established by the Divine Redeemer, do not apply only to the essence, the nature of man and his essential relationships, but to every sphere of his activity.

For the rest, against the "situation-ethics" We propose three considerations or maxims. The first: We grant that God wants, first and always, a right intention. But this is not enough; He also wants good work. A second principle is that it is not permitted to do evil in order that good may result (cf. Rom. 3:8). But this new ethic, perhaps without being aware of it, acts according to the principle that the end justifies the means. A third maxim is that there may be situations in which a man, and especially a Christian, must remember that it is necessary to sacrifice everything, even his life, in order to save his soul. We are reminded of this by all the martyrs, and they are very numerous, even in our time. The mother of the Machabees along with her sons; Saints Perpetua and Felicitas, notwithstanding their children; Maria Goretti, and thousands of others, men and women, whom the Church venerates—did they, in the face of the "situation" in which they found themselves, uselessly or even wrongly incur a bloody death? No, certainly not, and, by their blood they are the most explicit witnesses to the truth against the "new morality."

The Christian education of the conscience definitely does not neglect personality, even that of the young girl and the child, nor does it check its initiative. All sound education aims at rendering the educator unnecessary, little by little, and making the one educated independent within proper limits. This is also true of the education of the conscience by God and the Church. Its aim is, as the

Apostle says, "the perfect man, according to the measure of the fullness of the age of Christ," (Eph. 4:13-14) hence, a man who is of age, and who also has the courage which goes with responsibility.

But it is necessary that this maturity be on the right plane. By means of His Church, through which He continues to act, Jesus Christ remains the Lord, the Head, and the Master of every individual man, whatever be his age and state. The Christian, for his part, must assume the grave and sublime task of putting into practice in his personal life, his professional, social and public life, insofar as it may depend on him, the truth, the spirit, and the law of Christ. This is what We call Catholic morality, and it leaves a vast field of action for initiative and the personal responsibility of the Christian.

THE APPEAL TO CONSCIENCE *
Karl Rahner, S.J.

FIRST OF ALL, it goes without saying that a man must obey his conscience. For conscience is the most immediate giver of moral imperatives, and can never be passed over. Even if a conscience were objectively wrong about something, but in the concrete case the error could not be corrected, it would still have to be obeyed, because by its very nature it can never rightly be switched off or set aside or got round. Even in his obedience to his guiltlessly misinformed conscience, man is being obedient to God and paying homage to goodness. But it also goes without saying that the conscience is not automatically infallible; it can easily make mistakes and it is very difficult to distinguish *its* voice—the real voice of conscience—from the voice of precipitation, passion, convenience or self-will, or of a moral primitiveness which cannot see the finer distinctions or the more remote consequences of the act. And so man has a duty to do everything he can to conform his conscience to the objective moral law, to inform himself and let himself be taught and make himself prepared to accept (how difficult

* From *Nature and Grace,* by Karl Rahner, S.J. Copyright by Sheed and Ward, Inc., 1964

this often is!) instruction from the word of God, the magisterium of the Church and every just authority in its own sphere.

IF IT IS NOT TO DEGENERATE into a merely private subjective voice, the Christian conscience has the duty to order itself by the objective moral norms. And if the Christian knows that these objective norms are to be found in the teaching of the Church, and if he knows that his case too (like every similar case) is meant by the law, then it is not easy to see how a believing Christian can still logically and guiltlessly come to the conclusion that in his situation the 'case' is morally other than the universal law judges it to be. If in such cases he would at least admit that from human weakness he had offended against the law, which he was nevertheless bound to keep, then it would be easier to help him. But those who think that in their individual case they can still objectively justify their offence against the law by appealing to their situation with subtle theoretical excuses, or by appealing to their "conscience," or even to a private enlightenment from God, are in very serious and dangerous error. They can only succeed in deceiving themselves, for they are suppressing God's truth.

When a man has once realized (and in this age of psychoanalysis one would expect this realization to be widespread; unfortunately it isn't) how easily and in what refined ways he can deceive himself, how quickly what is desired by him appears also justified to him, how hidden and distorted the final standards are by which he in fact judges and values things, how 'obvious' something can seem to us when it is in fact a very dubious and problematic case, then he will be more careful in his appeals to a 'good conscience.' And anyone who has read the first chapter of St. Paul's Epistle to the Romans has read how God judges the doubtless very 'respectable' Jews and Gentiles (and where are there *no* people who think themselves very respectable?); and he will have been dismayed to find that the 'good conscience' of respectable people who know at once what God asks of them and what he 'naturally' can't expect of us, is only too often just the punishment and result of their blind but still responsible sinfulness: their real conscience has been muted leaving their heart to say what it will unhindered, and the Scripture says the heart of man is evil from his youth.

If we Christians, when faced with a moral decision, really realized that the world is under the cross on which God Himself hung nailed and pierced, that obedience to God's law can also entail man's death, that we may not do evil in order that good may come of it, that it is an error and heresy of this eudemonic modern age to hold that the morally right thing can never lead to a tragic situation from which in this world there is no way out; if we really realized that as Christians we must expect almost to take for granted that at some time in our life our Christianity will involve us in a situation in which we must either sacrifice everything or lose our soul, that we cannot expect always to avoid a 'heroic' situation, then there would indeed be fewer Christians who think that their situation requires a special ruling which is not so harsh as the laws proclaimed as God's laws by the Church, then there would be fewer confessors and spiritual advisers who, for fear of telling their penitent how strict is God's law, fail in their duty and tell him instead to follow his conscience, as if he had not asked, and done right to ask, *which* among all the many voices clamoring within him was the true voice of God, as if it were not for God's Church to try and distinguish it in accordance with His law, as if the true conscience could speak even when it had not been informed by God and the faith which comes from hearing.

A man who has learnt—by the grace of God!—to beware of man because he is a liar (*omnis homo mendax*) and so beware of himself because he is a man, will no longer be able to say so lightly: I will make this right with my conscience. Must we make the thing right 'with our conscience' or in fact—putting it more exactly and more honestly—with God? And doesn't God speak more clearly—precisely in complicated and difficult cases—by His own word through the mouth of His Church?—so we can only be certain that we are really hearing the voice of our conscience and not the voice of our own sinful inclinations when this voice agrees with the Church's teaching.

BUT IF THIS is the case, what has become of the freedom of the children of God? Does this not put us back under the rule of the letter which kills and is only the law of sin? (Cf. 1 Cor. 15:56) Isn't it true that we may "love and do what we will"? Is it true that where the Spirit of the Lord, who justifies, teaches and gives us divine life, moves a man, then he is no longer *under* the law, he is free from the law, the letter of which is imposed on him with binding force and reveals in him the helplessness of a man weakened and enslaved by sin; when the Spirit is strong and powerful within a man and binds him immediately to God above all law in a relationship of fully personal love, then the law 'superseded' by the inner law of the heart, the law of Christ in the power of which we not only know within us what is right but can have the strength freely to do it.

But in order to be free like this we must really have the Spirit; this Spirit can be lost; and man the liar can deceive himself that he has this Spirit when he really hasn't. We have not got the Spirit if we do not keep God's laws, and we can only keep these laws in the Holy Spirit in whom God's will and God's power are one, and in whom alone we can have true Christian freedom. He who boasts of the freedom of the children of God, when asked, Do we then overthrow the law? must answer with St. Paul: By no means, on the contrary we uphold the law (Rom. 3:31). He must know and live the Scripture; he who fulfills the law shall live (Gal.

3:12); the *doers* of the law will be justified before God (Rom. 2:13). The law has come to an end because it has been superseded, not by the arbitrary choices of our human will but by the power of the Holy Spirit. But the only way of knowing whether we have the Holy Spirit in us is precisely by whether we fulfill the law. And even the sinner, who flies to Christ's grace and finds therein salvation and justification, only really flies to Christ in his conversion if he confesses that he has become guilty precisely because the grace, which would have given the power to want and to do the will of God, has through his own fault remained ineffective, only really flies to Christ if he is truly prepared not only to seek forgiveness from God for the things he has left undone, but to do God's will henceforth; for "if any man says that God's commandments cannot be fulfilled even by those who have been justified and given grace, let him be anathema" (Council of Trent, sess. 6, can. 18).

To the free children of God also it is said (in the eternal freedom of God it will no longer need to be said; but now it must still be said because they are in danger of confusing their true freedom with the desires of their flesh): Do not deceive yourselves, neither the debauched, nor idolaters, nor adulterers, nor sodomites, nor thieves, nor misers, nor drunkards, nor revilers, nor extortioners will inherit the kingdom of God (1 Cor. 6:9). We can do 'everything' only when we love. But we are not loving if we do evil. Are there not today many 'good' Christians who study and dishonestly try and make the freedom of Christians a justification for a pact between right living and godlessness, light and darkness, Christ and Belial in their moral life, who do everything they want, good or evil, and then say they still love, instead of really loving (which calls for the greatest renunciation) and then doing everything which a man who really loves God may do?

And so it remains: The commandments of God come truly and plainly out of the mouth of the Church and they require obedience whether in this or that case they are easy to apply or not; they are the will of the living God who has spoken to us through Jesus Christ our Lord—the will of God—which is also for His children who are justified and living in grace and the freedom of the Holy Spirit. The Faith which justifies before God is the loving Faith which does God's will.

AN INNER VISION OF THE GOOD *
Bernard Häring, C.SS.R.

THERE EXISTS IN THE WORLD today a frightening kind of existentialism, absolutely inimical to law of any kind, which tries to undermine the authority behind even the most essential of commands; an unhealthy form of situation-ethics which would sacrifice the law, which was established by God to draw man to God, not only to a falsely understood spirit of the times, but which also wishes to bend the law itself to the will of a world aligned against God (St. Paul would say: aligned in the direction of 'the works of the flesh'). Moreover there are even among our average Christians, a great number of such 'juridically'-minded men. What is not commanded them in juridical form or under threat of punishment, does not exist for them. What is not written out in capital letters, does not touch them. The "juridicist" has no access to enlightening moral values. For him, such values have no splendor because he has too little love within his heart, because he has not become, through love, a man who truly sees. It is the task of those caring

---

* From *The Liberty of the Children of God,* by Bernard Haring, C.SS.R. Used by permission of Alba House, a division of St. Paul Publications.

for souls to educate them to a recognition of the good out of love for it. They, before God, must try to elevate their charges above that level of moral conduct in which they do only what is commanded by human superiors to a discovery of the infinite riches of the good behind these commands. Education to obedience demands not only that one bring to light the inner value of obedience as such, but, wherever it is possible, also the moral value of that which is commanded.

... We shall never arrive at a truly animated knowledge of the law, if the effort concerning moral knowledge is concentrated on the law or on human dictates and commands and nothing more. Superiors, including Church superiors, must do their best so that the subject is not left hanging to the letter of the law which is something external, but that he come to an inner vision of the good, both that demanded by the law and that which lies outside the law.

REFLECTIONS ON CONSCIENCE AND AUTHORITY *

John J. Wright, D.D.

IF I WERE to write a book of reflections on conscience and authority, . . . my first chapter would have to include a pointed explanation of one reason why there is so much seemingly tentative and even hesitant talk about the relations between conscience and authority. In fact, the problem is relatively modern in time and not even now universal in its geography, the contemporary statement of the problem of conscience being linked to recent and regional claims with respect to the sovereign independence of the individual person.

The orderly development of my subject would require that my second chapter concern itself, perhaps, with the history of the concept of conscience. This could be a book all by itself; indeed, many books have already been written on the concept of conscience in different times and places, even on the great changes in the concept of conscience within the Christian tradition from New Testament days down to our own times. I would point out that conscience is one of those words which everyone uses readily enough and which most think of as not only

* Reprinted from the April-May 1964 issue of *The Critic*. Copyright 1964 by the Thomas More Association, 180 N. Wabash Ave., Chicago, Ill. 60601.

basic but also very simple, though an invitation to define it usually reveals confusion and embarrassment. Fortunately, it is more easy and, indeed, better to have a good conscience than it is to define one, as Thomas à Kempis pointed out about compunction.

The contention of Father Bernard Häring, in his *The Law of Christ*, typically Catholic as distinct from "direct voice of God" concepts of conscience, is that God is indeed at work in the depths of conscience, at work as a person "who calls and invites, a judge, living, absolute, the source of the summons and the law," but that we ourselves contribute, out of our natures something which must be trained to play its part in the decisions of conscience. Even if we Catholics do not acknowledge the dictate of conscience as being the direct voice of God, as some others tend to do, we do speak of conscience as including somehow the voice of God. "It is the voice of God, but in the sense that we must contribute something of our own in the formation of the decision of a conscience which is right in God's sight. Error is possible in our decision, but we are able to trace it to its source." That source, and it operates commonly, is in ourselves, not God, and it is, of course, the presence and perils of it which so complicate the discussion of conscience itself and its relations with authority.

This is particularly true, as my chapter will point out, when there is talk of the freedom of conscience as that further concept is debated in our day. *The fact is that, contrary to a general but loose impression, conscience binds far more than it loosens.* Conscience is not something by which I am set free from obligations so much as it is something by which I am bound, controlled and on occasions sternly rebuked. It is necessary to get this unpleasant fact (if it is unpleasant) in clear focus at the outset of any discussion of conscience.

ON THE DECLINE in the prestige of authority and in the recognition of the constructive and noble elements of the virtue of obedience, another whole book could be written. I think it unlikely that any editor will be clamoring for it nowadays.

However, a plain, blunt man, I shall spell out some basic truths about authority, relying once again on the doctors of morals, dogma and laws *utriusque* to point out the premises and develop the corollaries of the Christian and human case for authority.

I shall emphasize that authority is not just a *word;* it is, as John Todd sagely notes, a *fact* whose manifestations everybody accepts or endures. [1] I shall follow, in this connection, Yves Simon in recalling that in every society, political and religious, public and private, necessary and voluntary, authority is essential as a cause of united action even in the smallest and most compact community; it is neces-

1. Footnotes, p. 84.

sary also for the very volition, let alone the attainment of the common good. Considered in its essential functions, therefore, authority is neither a necessary evil nor a lesser good, nor lesser evil nor the consequence of any evil or deficiency. It is, like nature and society, unqualifiedly good.

In accomplishing my task I shall be grateful to many authors, particularly to Romano Guardini for a brilliant essay in which he ... indicates how authority is bound up with the origins, divine and human, of our being. ...

Creation does not mean for many of our fellow men what it does for us in the Church; neither, therefore, does authority. But for those in the Church, the concept of authority on whatever level we encounter it will be shaped and hallowed by the mystery of creation, directly and fully in what pertains to God, analogously and proportionately in what pertains to anyone less than God. Christian doctrine will bring us to see that human authority is a phenomenon and service whose origin is in God's creative act. Everyone who exercises authority is invested therewith by God and will have to answer to God for the use he makes of it.

For this reason, it is established Christian doctrine that one who holds authority stands to his subjects in the place of God. But this must be understood in its most positive and fruitful sense; it must not be limited to meaning that the superior, natural or religious, only represents the authority of God in any merely negative or inhibiting sense. Understood as God, who works through the constitution of nature and the dispensations of grace, must intend it for the building up of His Kingdom, authority, communicated to others by God, must mean that he who holds it represents divine love not less than divine authority, divine mercy not less than divine justice and, in sum, the *life-giving* power of God.[2]

This means that authority is not only established to regulate, to order, to control and, on occasion, to forbid, all in analogy to God; it means also what is usually much more important and urgent, namely, that authority is given to inspire and to encourage the initiatives of others, as does God by His grace; to coordinate the purposeful lives, strivings, aspirations, undertakings and energies of others, to press forward, leading, directing and challenging others, as God, by His grace and through the voice of conscience, is constantly calling to new levels of excellence those subject to His sway and responsible to His authority, even as He sometimes, by a grace or a rebuke of conscience, dissuades, prohibits or overrules them.

HUMAN AUTHORITY needs always the spiritual disciplines and moral restraints that reason and revelation both inculcate; those who hold authority must, for their own salvation's sake, be mindful that they are, in themselves, not only the equals but the least of the brethren: "Each of you must have the humility to think others better men than himself, and study the welfare of others, not his own. Yours is to be the same mind which Christ Jesus showed..." (Phil. 2:3-7).

But while humility is essential to the salvation of one who holds authority, it is not enough for the achievement of that perfection of individuals and society for the service of which authority is given. These divine purposes require that human authority be not only Christ-like in humility but somehow God-like in its full and positive use of office to lead; Christ emptied Himself and became the equal of slaves, but not that they might remain slaves but that by adding His powers to their deepest desires, He might lift them to a level a little less than the angels, crowning them with glory and honor, giving *them* rule over God's handiwork. This is the purpose and office of authority, not contradiction and restraint only.

Nor can it be otherwise once it is recognized, as it must be, that authority in the Church is always a relative thing, a means necessary, under the present dispensation, to an end which is Love. Indeed, it is only in the Church that we can speak of authority as the servant of Love, rather than Justice, of which authority must elsewhere be the instrument. This is what Monsignor Journet means when he writes:

"The order of jurisdiction, necessary and of divine origin though it is, is not the noblest or most divine thing in the Church. All its greatness is derived from its purpose which is to be the servant of Love. Did not our Lord himself say that he had come to serve? . . ."

CHRISTIANS ARE IN ESSENCE and always a community; then [in the early centuries of Catholicism] they even lived as a community, wrote to each other as members of a community, were martyred as representatives of a community, prayed as a community. . . . In such a community the conscience of the Christian early acquired a formation which preserved it from individualism and moral solipsism.

On the side of authority, also, the situation was (and essentially is) such that Father Congar can write:

"In the early Church authority was that of men who were like princes in a community which was wholly sanctified, *plebs sancta,* and overshadowed by the Spirit of God. The Church leaders were all the more conscious of their authority in that they saw it as the vehicle of the mystery of salvation which God wishes to accomplish in his Church. They wanted to be, and knew that they were, moved by the Spirit, but they also knew that the Spirit inhabits the Christian community and in the exercise of their authority they remained closely linked to this community." [3]

But consciences, too, were moved by the same spirit; the formation of conscience was accomplished by a single spirit through the shared teachings of the single Mother Church, and this with the result that although conscience was warmly personal, as the Christian conscience must be, it was never sharply individualistic, as later influences have made the human conscience and most things else.

INDIVIDUAL CONSCIENCE is not always on the side of freedom, nor of life, nor of God, nor of man; "modern conscience" can mean moral solipsism, the arrogance and arbitrariness of which can be more horrendous, because more inaccessible to protest, than almost any despotism and certainly than any duly constituted authority which must function under written law—civil or canon.

Further, reflection on the deterioration of the sense of Christian community and the affect of this on both conscience and authority makes welcome the assurance of Westow [4]—an assurance that all who live in these exciting years of the Council deeply feel—that we are on the threshold of a new era of human and of Church history. In this era the concepts of both conscience and authority hopefully will be revitalized and reconciled anew within the Church, where alone they can achieve that synthesis which enables both to serve the person, the image of God in creation. This fresh vision, both of human history and of the Church, is characterized by an awareness of the human person as being not exclusively communal nor exclusively individual, but both; it sees the person as being responsible simultaneously for himself and for his society and as one who must, therefore, have the full resources of enlightened conscience and responsible authority to guide him. In such a vision, personal morality is not centered on self, nor on society, but on both at once within that *Christus Totus* of which Augustine spoke and of which the Church is at once the means, the instrument and the *Other Self* in history.

Within the Church, freshly appreciated and newly loved, those who hold authority will be more sensitive to the nature of their offices and what must be their spirit. In this new mood men may welcome more perceptively that *formation* of the enlightened conscience the need for which is, by all odds, our supreme need as we move from the fragmented age of individualism into a more organic society, consistent with and, please God, better serving the human person.

Accordingly, a chapter of our eventual book must consider the role of the Church in the formation of conscience.

FOR POPE PIUS XII conscience is: "that which is deepest and most intrinsic in man .... the innermost and most secret nucleus in man. It is there that he takes refuge with his spiritual faculties in absolute solitude: alone with himself, or, rather, alone with God—Whose voice sounds in conscience —and with himself. ...." [5]

How, then, can one talk of the education of conscience? We cannot do otherwise, of course, in the light of the Incarnation and claims of the Word of God in Christ and the consequent Christian obligation in matters of faith and morals to accept the will and the commandments of Christ and to conform one's life to them, i.e., each single act, inner or exterior, which the free human will chooses and decides upon. But what is the spiritual faculty, if not conscience, that, in each particular case, gives guidance to the will so that it may determine its actions in conformity with the divine will? Conscience, the Pope argued, must be the clear reflection of human action's divine pattern.

"Therefore, expressions such as 'the judgment of the Christian conscience,' or, 'to judge according to the Christian conscience,' mean this: that the *pattern* of the ultimate and personal decision for a moral action must be taken from the word and will of Christ. In fact, He is the way, the truth, and the life, not only for all men collectively, but for each single one; the mature man, the child, and the youth."

And so, the formation of the Christian conscience consists, above all, in illuminating the mind with respect to Christ's will, law and way; guiding it, also, so far as this can be done from outside, freely and constantly to execute the divine will. *This is the highest present task of moral education and moral education presupposes authority; it is the first con-*

tact between conscience and authority, that of the parent, of the teacher, above all, of those who teach divine law—and of all these within the Church. Nor is anything more consistent with the traditional Christian concept of conscience. For conscience, as Father Bernard Häring reminds us, since it is not an oracle which draws truth from its own obscure depths, by its very nature seeks illumination and guidance.

"God, the ultimate norm, the truth to which every conscience must conform . . . always instructs conscience in accordance with its nature: the natural conscience through the order of nature, the conscience endowed with the supernatural grace of faith through supernatural revelation. Just as it is not alien to natural conscience to draw from the natural revelation expressed in creation and to learn from the natural communities which correspond to it, so it is also 'according to nature' for the believing conscience elevated by grace and steeped in humility to harken to the word of revelation communicated to us in the Church . . . and only one with a totally perverted concept of the real nature and function of conscience could repudiate the infallible *magisterium* of the Church in the name of conscience. Only a conscience which itself enjoys creative plenitude of infallibility in its own native right could *a priori* reject as contradictory every intervention of objective authority."

Greater appreciation of this latter office of the Church in the formation of conscience would offset the temptation to pretend that the claims of authority to obedience have so stifled the initiative and freedom of devout consciences as to diminish the effectiveness of the Gospel and the Church. But Father Danielou proclaims the authentically heroic understanding of true obedience when he writes:

"Christianity would have had greater influence on social institutions if we had always had the courage to show that obedience to God, as an absolute duty, affects man's whole temporal, political, professional and family life. If Christians have not been more revolutionary, it is not because they lacked freedom but because they have not been sufficiently obedient. . . . This is problem number one and it involves fully relating conscience to authority, above all, the authority of God. How?" [6]

The answer to Father Danielou's "How?" is largely found in the study and experience behind Cardinal Newman's final judgment on the part of the Church in the formation of a Christian conscience. Newman was excruciatingly aware of the need for objective criteria for evaluating the dictates of conscience and no small part of his life was a search for such criteria in what pertained to the basic moral act, the act of faith. He could not find such criteria in unaided nature alone, particularly given the fallen state of man which was, of all dogmas, the one most clear to Newman. Neither could he consider Scripture in itself an adequate objective means to the formation of conscience nor norm for judging its dictates; . . . also Newman could find no adequate guide nor objective norm for conscience in tradition or the teachings of the Fathers and it is the point of his life that he could not find the rule of conscience in a National Church. The Universal Catholic Church, he decided, endowed with infallibility and teaching through divinely-appointed channels, must be the spiritual country in which authority brings supernatural doctrine to the direction of that conscience which is the herald of the Natural Law; the Catholic Church alone provides adequate objective criteria for the evaluation of those dictates of the sincere conscience which the upright man is bound to follow.

MY CHAPTER ON NEWMAN will have to point out that the English scholar, although the eager and unmistakable champion of conscience, was no partisan of "modern conscience" nor of moral liberalism. Like C. A. Pierce among recent Protestants and Bishop De Smedt in the Council, Newman must include in his defense of the rights of conscience a repudiation of its caricatures and counterfeits. He exposes the scientific and literary efforts to be rid of conscience entirely. . . .

He who faithfully follows the promptings of his conscience, his sense of right and wrong, Newman insists, will arrive at objective religious truth disposed to accept it and live by it. Brother Kaiser [7] summarizes from Newman's Oxford preaching five propositions setting forth this matter so vital to Newman. They are: (1) conscience consists in an habitual orientation of the whole man to God; (2) conscience develops in man a profound awareness of the presence of God; (3) conscience implies that a man desires to serve God with a perfect heart; (4) this orientation to God and perfect service will be manifested by consistency in conduct; (5) finally, conscience imposes the duty of habitual obedience.

. . . OURS IS AN AGE of great deference—must we not even say, in all honesty, of sometimes mistaken deference—to individual conscience; it is an age, alternately, of excessive expressions and excessive rejections of authority; above all, it is an age looking for terms in which it can express a dawning new love for the Church, a love such, as I think, as the twenty Christian centuries to date have not yet seen and precisely because it is sensed that in the Church and in the Church alone are reconciled human conscience made divine and divine authority made humane.

FOOTNOTES

1. John Todd, *Problems of Authority*, p.3
2. Corbishley, "Power and Authority," *The Way*, October, 1963, p. 285-293.
3. Yves Congar, O.P. *Problems of Authority*.
4. Theodore Westow, *The Variety of Catholic Attitudes*.
5. Radio broadcast, March 24, 1952.
6. Danielou, *The Christian Today*, Ch. 3.
7. Brother F. James Kaiser, *The Concept of Conscience According to John Henry Newman*, 1958.

Section 4

The Role of the Will

THE ROLE OF THE WILL *
James Alberione, S.S.P., S.T.D.

OUR WILL IS OUR sovereign faculty, queen of them all, of our internal and external senses, of our mental powers and of our passions.

Because it is free, it gives its own acts and the acts of the other faculties the liberty which entails either merit or demerit.

To regulate the will, therefore, means to regulate the whole man, body included.

The will is well-regulated if it is *strong*, on the one hand, so as to command and make itself obeyed by the powers and senses, and itself *docile*, on the other hand, so as to obey God's will always. Thus, the will has two functions to perform, we might say. Both are difficult, for the senses often revolt. Firmness, skill and divine grace are required, and before them even great enlightenment, conviction and faith. Moreover, because of its weakness, our will aspires to a certain autonomy or independence in respect to the will of God. The divine will cannot sanctify us without asking sacrifices of us, and often it happens that our will holds back when

---

* From *Alle Famiglie Paoline* by Very Rev. James Alberione, S.S.P., S.T.D., St. Paul Editions, 1954. Translated by the Daughters of St. Paul.

effort is required. This is the effect of original sin. The will rebelled against God and the senses rebelled against the will. Not being docile herself, she does not find docility in those beneath her.

God is good, but He made man free, just as He created the angels free. At a superficial glance, it could seem that everything went wrong for the Divine Maker when He took the risk of creating free beings. . . . But the wisdom, power and love of God provide quite different explanations!

Mankind was redeemed by the Son of God, the Divine Architect through whom "all things were made" (John 1:3). Redemption is a renewal of man in the order of nature and grace, according to God's original plan. Redemption of the will aims at making it queen of man once again.

In order that the will may be docile and at the same time strong, obstacles must be overcome and positive means put into play.

The *external* obstacles are *human respect,* which makes a man do good or evil out of respect for the opinions of others, and which is, therefore, voluntary slavery; *bad example* and *worldly views,* which have so much power over man because he is already drawn toward evil; and the *devil,* who made use of every opportunity against our first parents and who now acts likewise toward every soul of good will.

The *internal* obstacles are *lack of reflection,* which leads to a man's acting according to his feelings; and *neglect* and *laziness*, which spring from a lack of profound conviction.

The *positive means* may be summed up in a harmonious union of *intelligence, will* and *grace*. To proceed with intelligence and faith entails clearly knowing the goal and the means to obtain it. "Nothing can be willed before being known." To move the will effectively takes deep-rooted conviction, ample instruction, and a spirit of faith. These will work on the will, and the result will be resoluteness, firmness, and constancy, which will oppose all empty wishing and inconclusive dreaming.

Jesus Christ won grace for us. Through prayer and in particular, through the Holy Eucharist, we can in a certain sense regain the lost gift of integrity. Those who pray obtain the gift of actual grace, which strengthens the will and enlightens the mind, and which weakens the desires and concupiscence of the flesh. Holy Communion in particular cools passions and strengthens good tendencies. This is truly the bread of the elect, the wine of virgins, the viaticum for the hard journey of life.

"O Saving Victim, opening wide
The gates of heaven to man below...
Thine aid supply, Thy strength bestow."

Prayer is absolutely necessary. Jesus Christ is not only our light and our model: He is also our cooperator, our collaborator: "My strength and my courage is the Lord" (Ps. 117:14). With this strength that comes from God, we shall achieve submission to Him and the triumph of our will over feelings and passions.

The spirit of obedience presupposes:

—A meek, balanced, docile character;

—respect either natural or acquired, for superiors;

—sufficient mental capacity to understand the religious vow of obedience.

SELF-DISCIPLINE *
Fulton J. Sheen, Ph.D., D.D.

SELF-DISCIPLINE DOES NOT mean self-contempt or destruction of personality, but it rather aims at self-expression in the highest sense of the term. A train is not 'self-expressive' when it refuses to follow the roadway laid out for it by an engineer and jumps the track to its own self-destruction. A train is 'self-expressive' when it keeps its pressure within determined limits and follows the tracks.

. . . The purpose of self-discipline is, thus, not to destroy freedom but to perfect it. Freedom does not mean our right to do whatever we like, but to do whatever we ought; a man does not become free as he becomes licentious, but as he diminishes the traces of original sin. Self-denial is a denuding of the ego—it seeks to make the 'I' free to follow God. The more the ego knocks off the chains which bind it to things outside itself, the freer it is to be its own, its *I*. There is a potential nobility or even divinity in all of us, as there is a potential statue in a crude block of marble. But before the marble can ever reveal the image, it must be subjected to the

* From *Lift Up Your Heart,* by Most Rev. Fulton Sheen, Ph.D., D.D. Used by permission of the publisher, McGraw-Hill Book Company.

91

disciplinary actions of a chisel in the hands of a wise and loving Artist, who knocks off huge chunks of formless egotism until the new and beautiful image of Christ Himself appears.

. . . In studying painting, we view the work of masters rather than of dabblers—and so in studying self-discipline, the great artists of the spiritual life will have more to tell us than the psychologists.

. . . It requires great effort to make the will supple and responsive always to the highest ideals. Some people fail because they lack sufficient knowledge of what life is all about; never having disciplined their intellects to the way of truth, they are without markers on the roadway of life. Others start self-discipline too rigidly and with overeagerness, and fail as a result of too much hurry and the ensuing discouragement of finding that full sanctity is not achieved at once. (It is a generally accepted truth in religious societies that those postulants who complain about the want of opportunities for sacrifice are generally those who do not persevere). Others fail in their attempt to discipline the will because their ego is so strong that they cannot bear the thought of any failure. But any will can be trained; if there is genuine humility after a fall, and a renewed prayer for God's grace, then self-possession begins to be a habit, and the most difficult things become easy, in time. There comes a renewed sense of power and self-mastery and self-control, and the delightful realization that one at last has true freedom. One is no longer other-controlled, but self-controlled. Freedom is not so much a birthright, as it is an achievement. We are born with freedom of choice, but the way we use our choices makes us slaves or free men. Inner freedom of this kind is the last thing a man attains, and it is what St. Paul calls the 'glorious liberty of the children of God.'

Section 5

Obedience and Freedom

OBEDIENCE—
THE EASIEST WAY TO HOLINESS *
James Alberione, S.S.P., S.T.D.

RELIGIOUS ARE outstanding and effective in their vocation by reason of three valuable gems—chastity, poverty, and docility. History witnesses to this fact.

Whoever desires to lead men to ideals of holiness and eternal life must himself be poor in spirit. Whoever desires to lead men to purity of morals must himself be chaste, virginal. Whoever desires to lead men to good order in family living, in society, in the unity of the Church must himself be submissive.

Many have wanted to reform the Church, but not to reform themselves first of all. They had no mission, virtue, or true piety. Jesus Christ led by example, taught by oral preaching, and died to win grace for us.

EVERYONE IS TEMPTED by a threefold concupiscence: of the flesh, of the eyes, and of the pride of life. The first is checked by chastity, the second by poverty, and the third by obedience.

---

* From *Ut Perfectus Sit Homo Dei*. St. Paul Editions, Rome, 1960. Translated by the Daughters of St. Paul.

Through the three vows, the religious transforms passion into virtue and into an apostolic power. This is the secret of eternal happiness. In fact, poverty is the greatest wealth, for everything given up will be found in heaven, changed into pure gold: "They shall possess the kingdom of heaven." Chastity is the greatest love, for God and for souls, and joy will be in proportion to it: "Enter into the joy of thy Master" (Matt. 25:23). Obedience is the greatest freedom, for it gives us mastery over irregular passions and prepares us for the possession of God.

THE OVERWHELMING TRUTH is that this present life is directed toward eternal happiness, but to attain to it, we must know, love and serve the Lord, as His docile sons, following the Church. God will reward everything done in accord with His holy will. "In whatever you do, remember your last days, and you will never sin" (Sir. 7:36).

THE LORD CREATED US for the bliss of paradise, and He disposes or permits whatever will assure us of reaching this goal.

Obedience is the union of our will with the will of God. Hence it is the great means of salvation. It is entirely to our advantage to obey, for we elect to be led by the God of infinite wisdom and love, instead of by ourselves—deficient as we are in intelligence and blinded furthermore by passions, the world and the devil.

Obedience molds the truly wise soul. If Eve had obeyed God, she would not have set generations of men out on the road of error, sin, and death.

Obedience is the certain path of peace, of merit, of grace, and of God's blessings on our apostolate. Our Lord blesses solely what conforms to His will. Those who live by obedience unfailingly promote the glory of God and peace of men.

THE LORD MANIFESTS His will by His words through superiors, through events and other ways.

Manifestations by His word are the commandments of God, the evangelical counsels, the virtues recommended in Sacred Scripture.

Manifestations through superiors are the directives of the Church and of civil authorities. In the family, the parish, the school, the factory, the office, the club, the diocese, the community—everywhere we find duly authorized superiors. Obedience is also due the confessor in a number of cases.

Manifestations of the Lord's will through events and other ways include inconveniences of the season, sicknesses, misfortunes, ill-will, criticism, difficulties in our surroundings, persecution, even temptations, and a thousand different circumstances that fill up our years and our days. All are willed or permitted by God for our sanctification.

OBEDIENCE MAY BE viewed under three aspects: the vow, the virtue, and the spirit of obedience.

The vow, a sacred promise made to God, obliges us to submit to every superior who commands in virtue of holy obedience, that is, by the binding force of the vow.

The virtue bends the will to accept and carry out on a wider scale all the legitimate orders of superiors and the other manifestations of the divine will.

The spirit of obedience is the same virtue practiced with greater perfection, depth, and completeness. Through the spirit of obedience, the religious submits with his whole will and carries out the command both promptly and joyfully. Prudent, humble, and desirous of being submissive, he follows ordinary directives and advice, too. He willingly adapts himself to his elders, pleasing everyone in so far as possible, to avoid choosing and giving preference to what would be most to his own liking.

Obedience entails the sacrifice and holocaust of self to the Lord at every moment.

It is the great duty of the religious state.

It is the strength of an institution.

It is the virtue which safeguards the whole life of a congregation.

It is the practice that makes the attainment of sanctity easier.

It is the mother and guardian of every virtue.

It is a social virtue and yet also an individual one.

Self-will and independence are an attack on the life of an institute. Whoever makes a habit of following others rather than his superiors inexorably sets out on the road to ruin.

Rarely does the occasion of observing the vow of obedience arise, but by reason of the vow, every act of obedience becomes in very truth an act of religion. Thus, double merit is always earned. Life is constantly nourished by the spirit of obedience.

JESUS, Our Divine Master, sets us the example. He obeyed His Father from the moment of His Incarnation to His death on the cross, and then to His ascension into heaven. At every moment and in the smallest details, He could say "I do always the things that are pleasing to him" (John 8:29). His birth in the stable, His flight into Egypt, His life at Nazareth where He was subject to Mary and Joseph, His public life, His passion and death on the cross—St. Paul sums it all up in three words: "He humbled himself, becoming obedient to death, even to death on a cross." And he goes on to set forth the rewards of obedience: "Therefore God also has exalted him and has bestowed upon him the name that is above every name, so that at the name of Jesus every knee should bend of those in heaven, on earth and under the earth, and every tongue should confess that the Lord Jesus Christ is in the glory of God the Father" (Phil. 2:8-11).

In the Garden of Gethsemane, Jesus prayed over and over: "Father, not my will but thine be done; not what I will, but what thou willest" (Luke 22:42; Mark 14:36). He humbled Himself as far as it was possible to go, and so He was exalted to the right hand of the Father.

"Behold the handmaid of the Lord; be it done unto me according to your word" were the words of Our Lady.

Halted on his way to Damascus by Jesus Christ, St. Paul asked Him, "What will you have me do, Lord?" Being given the answer, he obeyed at once—and he obeyed always, down to the end of his life when, in response to the executioner's order, he bowed his head. This was the supreme act of obedience. After that came the 'crown of justice.'

There is no other way to sanctity and peace than "Thy will be done on earth as it is in heaven."

The religious state brings many blessings, but it also brings annoyances and dangers at every step. These constitute the 'uncertainties of the profession.' We could list the risks thus:

the risk of receiving annoying, painful, burdensome commands;

the risk of falling into the hands of a superior who is disagreeable and harsh, and among fellow-religious who are not too pleasant;

the risk of being misunderstood and left to one side—and how many undergo this trial...

the risk of being given posts demanding hardship, even with regard to one's health;

the risk of transferral, from one minute to the next;

the risk of being given an unpleasant duty, and one which may even be felt to be too much.

And what if the risk actually becomes a reality? Then we turn to Christ and say with Him: "Not my will but yours be done."

THE FOLLOWING make obedience difficult:

A lack of clear ideas on the part of superiors or subjects;

the rationalistic spirit, false principles;

age and temperament;

individualism, which tends to live a life of its own, like a little island or nest in the midst of the community;

superiors who do not give well-balanced commands;

tendencies of our modern world;

laxity and bad example.

TO BE COMPLETE, obedience must take in mind, heart and will.

Obedience of the mind entails understanding the meaning, the purpose, and the limits of the directive. For example, since a given amount of material is to be covered in a school year, a teacher has to prepare for his classes, explain the subject "with all patience and teaching" (2 Tim. 4:2), and require work from his students in accord with the most suitable method he knows, so as to be able to promote nearly all of them.

Obedience of the heart entails bringing love to one's assignment, to a task, to a duty. All this is to be loved because it is the will of God and the source of much merit. We ought to examine ourselves frequently in this regard.

Obedience of the will entails accepting our duty with full consent and full docility, applying all our spiritual and physical talents to each task, and much prayer for a successful outcome.

Half-hearted obedience is quite different. As far as the mind goes, it is marked by judgment, condemnation and contempt for the command, even though one carries it out because of external circumstances. While protesting obedience, such a religious criticizes.

With regard to the heart, there is no love. Submission in this case is like a flower with no fragrance. For there is nothing supernatural here. One obeys to win the superior to his side, so as to be given the position desired, or to satisfy self-love, self-interest and vanity. Instead, one should obey for love of God.

With regard to the will, a spirit of contradiction, laziness, malicious damage, carelessness, pharisaism, and the like hinder the good results the superior had in mind.

The foundation of obedience is threefold: authority, represented by the superior; religious profession, which is a giving of self to the point of being able to say, "I belong to the congregation, and no longer to myself"; and the vow, which is a sacred commitment.

IN CONCLUSION, let us recall St. John Berchman's confidential death-bed admission: "From the time I entered the society, I have never transgressed any rule." When one has lived thus, what remains for him to do? The supreme act of obedience to the invitation, "Come, good and faithful servant . . . enter into the joy of thy Master" (Matt. 25: 23), by responding, "Yes, Lord, I am coming!"

WHETHER OBEDIENCE BELONGS TO RELIGIOUS PERFECTION? *

St. Thomas Aquinas

OBJECTION 1. It would seem that obedience does not belong to religious perfection. For those things seemingly belong to religious perfection, which are works of supererogation and are not binding upon all. But all are bound to obey their superiors, according to the saying of the Apostle (Heb. 13:17), *Obey your prelates, and be subject to them.* Therefore it would seem that obedience does not belong to religious perfection.

OBJ. 2. Further, obedience would seem to belong properly to those who have to be guided by the sense of others, and such persons are lacking in discernment. Now the Apostle says (Heb. 5:14) that *strong meat is for the perfect, for them who by custom have their senses exercised to the discerning of good and evil.* Therefore it would seem that obedience does not belong to the state of the perfect.

OBJ. 3. Further, if obedience were requisite for religious perfection, it would follow that it is befitting to all religious. But it is not becoming to all;

* Quoted from the *Summa Theologica,* translated by the Fathers of the English Dominican Province; Benziger Brothers, New York, publishers and copyright owners.

since some religious lead a solitary life, and have no superior whom they obey. Again religious superiors apparently are not bound to obedience. Therefore obedience would seem not to pertain to religious perfection.

OBJ. 4. Further, if the vow of obedience were requisite for religion, it would follow that religious are bound to obey their superiors in all things, just as they are bound to abstain from all venery by their vow of continence. But they are not bound to obey them in all things, as stated above (Q. 104, A. 5), when we were treating of the virtue of obedience. Therefore the vow of obedience is not requisite for religion.

OBJ. 5. Further, those services are most acceptable to God which are done freely and not of necessity, according to 2 Cor. 9:7, *Not with sadness or of necessity.* Now that which is done out of obedience is done of necessity of precept. Therefore those good works are more deserving of praise which are done of one's own accord. Therefore the vow of obedience is unbecoming to religion whereby men seek to attain to that which is better.

ON THE CONTRARY, Religious perfection consists chiefly in the imitation of Christ, according to Matt. 19:21, *If thou wilt be perfect, go sell all* (Vulg.,—what) *thou hast, and give to the poor, and follow Me.* Now in Christ obedience is commended above all according to Philip 2:8, *He became* (Vulg., —becoming) *obedient unto death.* Therefore seemingly obedience belongs to religious perfection.

I answer that, As stated above (AA. 2, 3) the religious state is a school and exercise for tending to perfection. Now those who are being instructed or exercised in order to attain a certain end must needs follow the direction of someone under whose control they are instructed or exercised so as to attain that end as disciples under a master. Hence religious need to be placed under the instruction and command of someone as regards things pertaining to the religious life; wherefore it is said (VII, qu. i, can. *Hoc nequaquam*): *The monastic life denotes subjection and discipleship.* Now one man is subjected to another's command and instruction by obedience: and consequently obedience is requisite for religious perfection.

REPLY OBJ. 1. To obey one's superiors in matters that are essential to virtue is not a work of supererogation, but is common to all: whereas to obey in matters pertaining to the practice of perfection belongs properly to religious. This latter obedience is compared to the former as the universal to the particular. For those who live in the world, keep something for themselves, and offer something to God; and in the latter respect they are under obedience to their superiors: whereas those who live in religion give themselves wholly and their possessions to God, a stated above (AA. 1, 3). Hence their obedience is universal.

REPLY OBJ. 2. As the philosopher says (*Ethic. ii.* 1, 2), by performing actions we contract certain habits, and when we have acquired the habit we are best able to perform the actions. Accordingly those who have not attained to perfection, acquire perfection by obeying, while those who have already acquired perfection are most ready to obey, not as though they need to be directed to the acquisition of perfection, but as maintaining themselves by this means in that which belongs to perfection.

REPLY OBJ. 3. The subjection of religious is chiefly in reference to bishops, who are compared to them as perfecters to perfected, as Dionyius states (*Eccl. Hier.* vi), where he also says that the *monastic order is subjected to the perfecting virtues of the bishops, and is taught by their godlike enlightenment.* Hence neither hermits nor religious superiors are exempt from obedience to bishops; and if they be wholly or partly exempt from obedience to the bishop of the diocese, they are nevertheless bound to obey the Sovereign Pontiff, not only in matters affecting all in common, but also in those which pertain specially to religious discipline.

REPLY OBJ. 4. The vow of obedience taken by religious, extends to the disposition of a man's whole life, and in this way it has a certain universality, although it does not extend to all individual acts. For some of these do not belong to religion, through not being of those things that concern the love of God and of our neighbor, such as rubbing one's beard, lifting a stick from the ground and so forth, which do not come under a vow nor under obedience; and some are contrary to religion. Nor is there any comparison with continence whereby acts are excluded which are altogether contrary to religion.

REPLY OBJ. 5. The necessity of coercion makes an act involuntary and consequently deprives it of the character of praise or merit; whereas the necessity which is consequent upon obedience is a necessity not of coercion but of a free will, inasmuch as a man is willing to obey, although perhaps he would not be willing to do the thing commanded considered in itself. Wherefore since by the vow of obedience a man lays himself under the necessity of doing for God's sake certain things that are not pleasing in themselves, for this very reason that which he does is the more acceptable to God, though it be of less account, because man can give nothing greater to God, than by subjecting his will to another man's for God's sake. Hence in the Conferences of the Fathers (*Coll.* 18:7) it is stated that *the Sarabaitoe are the worst class of monks, because through providing for their own needs without being subject to superiors, they are free to do as they will; and yet day and night they are more busily occupied in work than those who live in monasteries.*

ADVANTAGES OF OBEDIENCE *
Servant of God, Canon Francesco Chiesa

WHAT FORTUNE, if we could know the will of God with certainty and precision in every case! Now, this benefit does indeed come to us from obedience. Did not Jesus say, "Come follow me"? (Matt. 19:21) and He has set up His representatives here on earth, declaring to them: "Who hears you, hears me; and who rejects you, rejects me" (Luke 10:16). If we obey these providential representatives of God, in certain circumstances, we are sure of not making a mistake. "Who follows me, does not walk in darkness" (John 8:12). But if we could spend our lives near them, so as to be able to listen to them in all the doubts that occur and in all our actions, would this not be the greatest good that one could desire in this regard? Always to be sure from morning to night that one is doing the will of God in all things and in every way! It was only natural, thus, that many souls felt strongly drawn by this attraction and conceived the desire of acquiring such a great blessing. And they obtained it, by irrevocably bind-

---

* From *Introduzione all' Ascetica,* by the Servant of God, Canon Francesco Chiesa, St. Paul Editions, Rome, 1954. Translated by the Daughters of St. Paul.

ing their will to the will of a representative of God. Hence they could exclaim with the spouse of the Canticles: "Come to me, delight of my soul; I will take you and never let you go" (Cant. 3:4). This, then, is the spiritual genesis of the vow of obedience.

With the vow of obedience we reproduce in our souls a more lively and more perfect image of Him who became, "obedient unto death, even unto death of the cross" (Phil. 2:8) and who said: "I came from heaven, not to do my will, but the will of Him who sent me ..." (John 6:38). "My food is to do the will of him who sent me" (John 4:34). "The things that are pleasing to him, I do always" (John 8:29). And even in His most trying hour, Christ was able to exclaim: "Not my will, but thine be done" (Luke 22:42). Does not our perfection consist precisely in the extension of this life of Jesus in us? "Therefore, let Christ be formed in you" (Gal. 4:19).

No matter how humble the role which he may be assigned, one who makes the vow of obedience is always a cooperator in a great work, the work to which his religious institute is dedicated. Now this scope is always of great import. It is as in an army: the humbler guard cooperates in the war effort and the victorious outcome sometimes depends on him. If it is a matter of an evil undertaking, as for example betrayal of the country, is not a man severely punished, even if the part he knowingly played in the betrayal is a very insignificant one? Contrariwise, he who cooperates toward a good, shares in the merit of the entire work.

ANOTHER VERY PRECIOUS advantage of the vow of obedience is that it gives value to all our most trifling actions, since the merit of an action does not depend so much on the importance of the thing done, as on the purpose or spirit behind it. Now he who has made the vow of obedience and acts according to the spirit of this virtue, looks for nothing else in all he does but the will of God, as set forth by his superior. And thus, for him every action becomes an act of love of God. Now just as without the love of God, that is, without charity, even the offering of one's life would be nothing—"If I do not have charity, I am nothing" (1 Cor. 13:2)—so with charity everything becomes meritorious, even a glass of cold water given to a poor person.

OBEDIENCE IS THE MOST secure means of enjoying peace of conscience, an abundance of blessings and the assurance of success and merit. It brings peace of heart because one is sure of doing God's will. If we make up our own minds to do some particular task and then are not successful, with reason we become upset because we fear we are to blame; instead, if we have obeyed, we can be at peace.

Obedience also brings an abundance of blessings and help because we are on the right track: the will of God. And even should God be pleased not to let us meet with success, we shall still have the merit of our labors, since "each will receive his own reward according to his labor" (1 Cor. 3:8).

THE ROUTE TO
THE HIGHEST PERFECTION
St. Alphonsus de Liguori

HIS OWN WILL is what man finds hardest to give up but it is the most valuable gift we can give God and the one he asks for most: "Son, give me your heart and let your eyes keep to my ways" (Prov. 23:26).

It is for this reason that the Lord accepts obedience with more pleasure than all the other sacrifices we might offer. "Obedience is better than sacrifices" (1 Kings 15:22).

One in the world does indeed earn merit by fastings, scourgings, prayers, etc., but since he does all these in accord with his own will, he merits much less than the religious, who does all that he does in obedience. The latter, therefore, earns much more and earns it continually, because all that is done in community is done through obedience. Not only does he merit when he prays or fasts, not only when he disciplines himself, but also when he studies, when he goes out, when he is at table, at recreation or when he takes rest.

For this reason, many spiritually-minded souls who were already leading a holy life still wanted to enter on a life of obedience by joining some religious community. They understood the difference there is between the merit gained by acting on our own and that gained by doing things from pure obedience.

A strong temptation is proposed by the devil to some. He makes them think that they could have done more good to their neighbor if they had remained in the world. "You," he tempts, "entered this community, where there are so many other people already laboring and helping souls. It would have been much better to have stayed out and helped the people of your home town. There is a great need there and the laborers are few."

One thus tempted should consider, first of all, that the greatest good we can do is what God asks of us. God does not need anyone; if he wishes to give more help to your home town, he will provide for it through others. So, my brother, since the Lord has called you to his house, the good he expects from you is that you obey your rule and your superiors. And even if obedience calls you to a place where you feel useless, or to be the dish-washer, or the housekeeper, this is the greatest good you can do.

And besides, what good do you think a person can do in his home town? Jesus Christ himself, when exhorted to preach and do good in his own home town, replied: "No prophet is acceptable in his own country" (Luke 4:24).

Moreover, whoever remains in the world will often be uncertain and bewildered, not knowing whether God wants one work or another from him. But one in religion is certain that when he obeys his superiors, everything he does is what God wants. Thus, only religious have the happiness of being able to say: "Blessed are we, O Israel, for what pleases God is known to us" (Bar. 4:4).

NOTHING IS MORE harmful to religious, who have consecrated their will to Jesus Christ, than to be led by the dictates of their own will and inclinations. Therefore, to guard against self-will, this enemy of the spirit, the vow of obedience is prescribed in every religious order.

ONLY SELF-WILL can separate us from God.

IT IS CHIEFLY by self-will that satan strives to bring about the ruin of religious.

THE HIGHEST PERFECTION which the actions of religious can reach is to be the consequence of obedience.

THE RELIGIOUS WHO does not take care to deny self-will cannot be called a religious. Rather he is a sacrilegious violator of his profession. What is more sacrilegious than to take back the will that has already been consecrated to God?

TO BE THE RESULT of obedience is an infallible sign that an action is pleasing to God.

IF YOU WANT TO BECOME a saint and to enjoy peace continually, try to conquer your own will as much as possible; adopt the rule of religious who love perfection: do everything to please God, never for self-satisfaction.

PERFECT RELIGIOUS are distinguished from the imperfect by their obedience and by their lack of self-will. The imperfect do nothing cheerfully except what pleases their self-love and self-will. In other words, they want to become saints, but only in accord with their own will and with the dictates of self-love. On the other hand, religious who love perfection do not act thus. They never omit whatever obedience commands, and they desire only that which obedience prescribes.

STRIVE TO PERFORM all your actions for reasons of obedience, and you will always move securely to salvation.

KEEP ALWAYS IN MIND the fact that the obedience which you render to your superiors is offered to God Himself. Now, if Jesus Christ Himself descended from heaven, and laid any duty upon you, or gave you any particular charge, would you try to refuse it? Or would you dare to disobey His commands? So, then, if you receive a command from one who holds God's place, you ought to observe it just as diligently as if it came from God Himself.

For our greater merit, the Lord desires to lead us to salvation through faith, and for this reason, he does not speak to us Himself; rather He manifests His will through the commands of superiors. . . . Thus, it is more meritorious to obey man out of love of God, than to obey God Himself.

YOU DO NOT GAIN thereby if superiors are resisted and thwarted. But if they receive support and consolation in their government of the community, good order and your spiritual progress will be promoted.

THE PERFECT RELIGIOUS does not need to be consulted about the office he desires: should the superior ask him what charge he would find most agreeable, he replies that it is not for him to say what occupation he desires, for it belongs to the superior to tell him what he will have him do.

THE ONLY WAY a religious can become a saint and be saved is by observing his rule. For him no other way leads to salvation.

IN ORDER TO BE PERFECT in obedience, a religious must obey promptly, exactly, cheerfully, and simply. These are the degrees of perfect obedience.

NOTHING DOES GREATER harm to the Church of God than the opposition of disciples to the opinion of their teachers; nothing is more ruinous to a religious community than the disregard of religious for the judgment of their superiors.

IT IS OBEDIENCE that brings all saints to glory.

SPEAKING TO St. Catherine of Siena, Christ said, "Religious will not have to give an account to me of what they do out of obedience; for this, I will demand an account from the superiors."

IF YOU ARE OBEDIENT, when Jesus Christ asks you after death why you did not do greater penance, why you did not practice mental prayer more, or why you have done such-and-such an action, you can confidently answer that in all this you only carried out His commands through obedience to your superiors, whom He commanded you to obey as you would Him; and that if you did wrong, the blame is to be laid to your superiors, whose authority you obeyed.

IF YOU WANT TO FULFILL your obligations with true joy, you must do so out of the pure intention of pleasing God. If you comply with them to win the superior's friendship, to induce him to satisfy your desires, to avoid his displeasure, or the accusation of disobedience, or through any other self-interested motive, you may succeed in satisfying the superior, but you will not please God, and as a result, you will suffer all the fatigue and hardships of obedience without enjoying the serenity of an obedient religious. In addition, if God's pleasure be the only end of your obedience, you will obey cheerfully, not only when the superior's tone and ways are sweet and agreeable, but also when his directives are given in severe and authoritarian language: in this lies the merit.

LOVED BY THE LORD is the man who does with cheerfulness whatever he does for God's love.

WITH REGARD to the offices of religious life, observe St. Francis de Sales' excellent rule: "Never seek and never refuse any." Prefer the least honorable always, and whatever is least suited to your convenience. Few religious merit the full reward of obedience in carrying out the duties of their office, because few accept them and carry them out in the true spirit of obedience, and with a pure intention of pleasing God. Imperfect religious have an eye only to the advantages and disadvantages of office. Perfect religious instead are concerned only about the will of God, and therefore they do not look for comfort or convenience, but cheerfully embrace sufferings and labors. Strive to belong to the number of the perfect. Do not think that the refusal of an office, out of fear of committing faults in the fulfillment of its duties, will be excusable in the eyes of God. Be convinced, rather, that by becoming a religious you committed yourself to serve the convent. If the fear of committing faults justified you in declining a responsibility, the same fear would exempt all religious from the obligation to accept offices. And if they were to yield to such fears, who would serve the monastery or support the community? Have a pure intention of pleasing God, and fear not —He will assist you.

IN THE SPIRIT OF OBEDIENCE, accept the office entrusted to you. And in accepting it, do not think of the power of domination; do not be concerned about self-comfort or self-esteem. Look solely to the obligations of obedience. Accept it with holy trust and do not listen to the devil, who may suggest that the duties of such an office are more than you can handle. If you are obedient, the Lord will give you the strength which you do not have. Do not think that because the duties of your office are of the distracting type they will destroy your spirit of fervor and recollection. Be certain that if you comply with your duties, God will give you more graces in a quarter of an hour spent in prayer than you would receive in a ten-day retreat without performing them. In the fulfillment of your office, strive as much as possible to set aside some time to recollect yourself in prayer. Do not declare that your office demands every moment of your time. Perfect religious who have an affection for prayer can find more than enough time for the fulfillment of their duties and for recollection.

OBEDIENCE IN THE
SPLENDOR OF THE CATHOLIC VISION *
Henri de Lubac, S.J.

The Meaning of Catholic Obedience

THE MAN OF THE CHURCH does not stop short at mere obedience; he loves obedience in itself, and will never be satisfied with obeying "of necessity and without love." [1] For the fact is that all action which deserves the description 'Christian' necessarily unfolds itself over a basis of passivity. The Spirit from whom it derives is a Spirit received from God. It is God Himself, giving Himself to us in the first place so that we may give ourselves to Him; insofar as we welcome Him into ourselves we are already not our own. [2] This law is verified in the order of faith more than anywhere else. The truth which God pours into our minds is not just any truth, made to our humble human measure; the life which He gives us to drink is not a natural life which would find in us the wherewithal to maintain itself. This living truth and this true life only find foothold in us by dispossessing us of ourselves; if we are to live in them we must die to ourselves, and that dispossession and death are not only the initial conditions of our salvation; they are

* From *The Splendor of the Church,* by Henri de Lubac, S.J. Copyright by Sheed and Ward, Inc., New York 1956.
    1. Footnotes begin on page 141.

a permanent aspect of our life as renewed in God. And this essential condition is brought about, *par excellence,* by the effect of Catholic obedience. In that obedience there is nothing of this world and nothing servile; it submits our thoughts and desires, not to the caprices of men, but to 'the obedience of Christ.'[3] Fénelon says justly: "It is Catholicism alone which teaches, fundamentally, this evangelical poverty; it is within the bosom of the Church that we learn to die to ourselves in order to live in dependence."[4] An apprenticeship of this sort never comes to an end; it is hard on nature, and those very men who think themselves most enlightened are the ones who have most need of it (which is why it is particularly healthy for them), so that they may be stripped of their false wealth, "to humble their spirits under a visible authority."[5]

This is perhaps the most secret point in the mystery of faith, and that which is hardest of access to a mind which has not been converted by the Spirit of God. So that it is scarcely surprising that many men consider the exercise of authority in the Church[6] as an intolerable tyranny. Moreover, whether the unbeliever condemns it or admires it, he cannot help but form a very misleading idea of it, for "if the Church were only a human society, even though the most venerable and experienced ever known," her demands would not be justified.[7] For his part, the Catholic knows that the Church commands only because she obeys God.[8] He wants to be a free man, but he is wary of being one of those men who make liberty 'a cloak for malice.' He knows, too, that obedience is the price of freedom, just as it is the condition of unity: "He who is not bound by this chain is a slave." [9] He will be careful to distinguish it from its counterfeits and caricatures—unfortunately all too freely current—and his aim will be to please not men but God. [10]

History and his own experience combine to show him both the desire for the knowledge of divine things which stirs the human spirit, and the weakness which lays that spirit open to falling into every kind of error. In consequence he appreciates the benefit of a divine magisterium, to which he freely submits. He thanks God for having given him that magisterium in the Church, and experiences a foretaste of the peace of eternity in placing himself under the eternal law by the obedience of faith. [11] He will make the appropriate evaluation of the scope of each one of the acts of the hierarchy—numerous and varied as they are—without splitting them up one from another or setting them in mutual opposition; he will accept them all as obedience demands and understand them as obedience understands them, never adopting an argumentative attitude where obedience is concerned, as if there were some question of defending at all costs a threatened autonomy. He will not countenance any contest with those who represent God [12] any more than he would with God Himself.

Even in the grimmest cases—in such cases most of all, in fact,—he will find a certain harmony of what seems to be imposed from outside and what is inspired from within; for the Spirit of God does not abandon him, any more than the Spirit of God ever abandons the Church as a whole, and what He does in the Church as a whole is also what He does in each Christian soul. [13] The baptismal instinct of the child responds with a leaping joy to the demands made upon it by its Mother: [14] "Wherever the Spirit of the Lord is, there also is freedom." [15]

Even when doctrine is in no sense involved—in the day-to-day sphere of exterior activity where the question is one of decisions whose object is in itself a matter for discussion—the man who has the real spirit of obedience will not spend any longer than he can help over considerations at the human level which, however shrewd and sensible, cannot in the long run help but obscure the light of faith. Even though he can neither obscure them nor always hold all of them as of no account—a supernaturalized attitude is not something built up on the ruins of common sense—he will, for all that, rise above the contingencies which are in danger of coming between him and pure divine will. He will have confidence in his superiors and make it his business to see their point of view from the inside. Whether or not there be a bond of natural sympathy between him and them, he will owe them a sincere affection and try to make less onerous for them a responsibility from which his own soul benefits: [16] bearing in mind the axiom *discernere personam est tollere oboedientiam,* [17] he will see in them Christ

Himself. Granted, the aid given to the Church by the Holy Spirit is no guarantee that he will never have any orders to carry out save those arising from the wisest possible choices—the history of the Church is not that kind of idyll, and there would be something rather absurd about it if it were. Yet it does not matter whether the man who gives him a command in the name of God be right or wrong, obtuse or clearsighted, pure or mixed in his motives, determined (in his heart of hearts) to act justly, or not—as long as that man is invested with legitimate authority and does not command him to do evil, it is certain that it will be wrong to disobey. And the man of the Church knows that though obedience "can never oblige us to do anything evil" it can "cause us to interrupt or omit the good which we were doing or wanted to do." [18] That is something which he knows in advance, and with a conviction of faith which nothing can shake; and history confirms the fact with a whole series of examples both good and bad. Even if this truth is in certain cases a hard one, it is, as far as he is concerned, first and foremost a 'wonderful truth.' [19] Certainly, as long as the order is not final he will not abandon the responsibilities with which he has been invested by his office or circumstances. He will, if it should be necessary, do all that he can to enlighten authority; that is something which is not merely a right but also a duty, the discharge of which will sometimes oblige him to heroism. But the last word does not rest with him. The Church, who is his home, is a 'house of obedience.' [20] If then he finds himself prevented from realizing some apparent good, he will remember that even if his action be justified, it is not that action which matters. The work of redemption, to collaboration in which he has been called by God, is not subject to the same laws as human undertakings. And ultimately all he has to do is to take his place in the divine plan by which God leads him, through His representatives; thus, he cannot fail to have a share in 'the infallible security of Providence.' [21] In the last analysis no man can ever betray a cause, or break faith with another man, himself, or God, when he simply obeys. There will be no sophism, no appearance of good or persuasion of justification which can cut off from the man of the Church the light of St. Paul's words when he proposes for our imitation Christ *factus obediens*. He can never forget that the salvation of mankind was accomplished by an act of total self-abandonment, and that the Author of that salvation, "whereas he was indeed the Son of God . . . learned obedience by the things which he suffered," [22] and that it is through Him alone, with Him alone and in Him alone that we can be "at one and the same time the saved and those who save." [23] The mere recalling of this fact carries more weight with him than any amount of theory and discussion; it will always be a safeguard against his reducing Christian obedience—which is conformity with the obedient Christ—to a virtue which is primarily of social importance. For to see nothing more in it than that particular aspect—which is, of course, most certainly there—will be, in his eyes, a misunderstanding of its most valuable element. [24]

A true son of the Church will not, of course, be preoccupied to excess with these extreme cases (which must nonetheless be taken into account if the principle of Catholic obedience is to be isolated in its pure state). Even where he has a duty to act, and in consequence a duty to judge, he will on principle maintain a certain distrust with regard to his own judgment; he will take good care to have himself in hand, and if it so happens that he incurs disapproval he will, far from becoming obstinate, if necessary accept the fact that he cannot clearly grasp the reasons for it. He will apply to himself on such occasions this homely truth—that even with the best of intentions we can still grossly deceive ourselves (or perhaps simply fail to take everything into account), and that it is a healthy thing to be warned of the fact. And finally he will under all circumstances be very aware that he cannot be an active member of this Body if he is not, first and foremost, a submissive member, quick and easy in response to the direction of the head. Even if he is submissive to all that is obligatory, he will not be content to carry on his work in the odd corners of his community, as it were. He will not grant himself the right to call himself a son of the Church unless he is, first of all and always, a child of the Church, and that in all sincerity.

Here we come again upon the fundamental distinction which was made earlier. [25] The Church is a community, but in order to be that community she is first a hierarchy. The Church which we call our Mother is not some ideal and unreal Church but this hierarchial Church herself; not the Church as we might dream her but the Church as she exists in fact, here and now. Thus the obedience which we pledge her in the persons of those who rule her cannot be anything else but a filial obedience. She has not brought us to birth only to abandon us and let us take our chance on our own; rather, she guards us and keeps us together in a maternal heart. [26] We continually live by her spirit, "as children in the wombs of their mothers live on the substance of their mothers." [27] And every true Catholic will have a feeling of tender piety towards her. He will love to call her "mother"—the title that sprang from the hearts of her first children, as the texts of Christian antiquity bear witness on so many occasions. [28] He will say with St. Cyprian [29] and St. Augustine: [30] "He who has not the Church for mother cannot have God for Father."

When a Catholic wants to expound the claims which the Church has on his obedience, he feels a certain embarrassment, or rather a certain melancholy. It is not that her titledeeds are inadequate. But when taken in the dryness of the mere letter the claims do not do justice to something which is, as far as he is concerned, essential. He can comment on the illuminating complex of Scripture texts,

point to the facts of history, develop the arguments
that are suitable to the occasion. But when he has
done all this, all he has done is to establish the fact
that we ought to submit, as a matter of justice and
our own good; he has not been able to convey the
spontaneous leap of his own heart to obedience,
nor the joy which he feels in his submission. [31] He
has established an obligation, but he has not communicated an enthusiasm. He may have justified
the Church, but he hasn't been able to make her
true character understood from within. If he is to
do that he must achieve much more. If he is to overcome the revulsion of the 'natural man,' he will have
to turn his argument into a channel for the living
witness of his own faith; he will have to show the
splendor of the Catholic vision. The Church who is
the bringer of the good news and the bearer of life
must not be presented as a domineering power or
a pitiless draftsman of rules. He must not be content with giving a precise explanation of how the
Church's authority is in principle neither arbitrary
nor extrinsic; [32] he must go on to give some idea at
least of how, through the exercising of that power,
each one of the faithful is effectively sustained in
his self-giving to Christ; how the fabric it weaves
links each man effectively to his brethren; how all
still hear today the voice of their Lord through the
human voice which teaches and commands. [33] And
finally he must explain—or rather communicate
some sense of—the spiritual fruitfulness of sacrifice.
He must display some of the great miracles of Cath-

olic sanctity—miracles which spring up under the shadow of obedience in the seedbed of humiliation.

The Roman Church is the object *par excellence* of accusations of tyranny; she is even sometimes—absurdly—put on a parallel with the various systems of political absolutism. And she is also the primary object of the objections of many Christians, who nevertheless recognize the necessity of a visible authority. Conversely, it is primarily of her that the Catholic thinks when he calls the Church his mother. In common with tradition, he considers her as "root and mother of the Catholic Church," [34] as "the mother and mistress of all the Churches," as "mother and mistress of all the faithful of Christ." [35] He considers her head as "the head of the episcopate" and "the father of the Christian people," [36] "the master of the whole household of Christ" as St. Ignatius Loyola puts it. For him, the See of Rome is the "Holy See," the "Apostolic See" *par excellence*. [37] He knows that Peter was given the charge of not only the lambs but the sheep as well; that Christ Himself prayed that the faith of Peter might not fail, and that He gave Peter the keys of the Kingdom of Heaven and the command to confirm his brethren. [38] He realizes that Peter personifies the whole Church, [39] and that just as each bishop is the bridegroom of his own particular Church, so Peter, the Bishop of Rome, may be said to be the bridegroom of the Universal Church, [40] the whole of which has in him its visible foundation. [41] As against a frequently lodged objection (based on a misunderstanding), it will, of course, be equally clear that this visible foundation in no way prejudices that unique Foundation which is Christ, any more than the visible chief shepherd puts into eclipse the Good Shepherd, [42] since here there is no question of duplication, the very name 'Peter' having been chosen by Christ to express this identity of submission, which is in itself the fruit of faith. [43] Believing as he does that the Church has received the promise of perpetuity and victory over death, and holding that it was she who was in Christ's mind in that scene on the road to Caesarea, he will naturally grasp the consequence that as long as the Church goes on building herself up and subsisting in her visible state—that is to say, as long as this world lasts [44]—she cannot be without a visible foundation for her building. Peter was not given his office simply in order to relinquish it almost at once; he was given it to hand on after him. [45] "In his successors—the bishops of the See of Rome, which was founded by him and consecrated by his blood—he lives, presides and judges perpetually." [46]

Finally the Catholic will not be content merely to grant and grasp that in the last analysis the Church is, so to speak, concentrated whole in Peter; the seeing of the fact will be an occasion of joy to him. He will not be worried by those who try to persuade him that he has "lost the sense of the totality of the Church," and that in submitting himself to the power of the Pope he has resigned himself to a belief which is, as it were, merely belief at the word of command—as if "in Romanism properly understood" the whole doctrine and life of the Church resided only in the single person of its head. [47] For we do not deny the existence of a circle when we know that it must have a center; and it is no abolishment of the body when we say that it has a head. To superficial explainings-away of this kind, which are the result of what one might describe as an optical illusion, he will oppose the evidence of faith and reply, in the words of one of his bishops:

"When the pope makes an act of doctrinal authority, this is no exterior yoke which a particular man imposes on a religious society in the name of his own intelligence, even though it might be that of a genius. He is defining the faith of the Church. He is in no way subject to her consent; yet the truth which he translates into our language and renders precise is the truth by which she lives; the belief whose meaning he confirms is our belief—he analyzes its content, counters its potential weakenings and maintains its vigor. Thus, when we say to the Church, in the words which the Apostle used to Christ, who founded her: 'To whom shall we go? Thou hast the words of eternal life,' this is not in virtue of some fatigue of spirit which seeks to place itself under an authority to escape the effort of thought and the labor of living; rather it is, as Newman put it, in virtue of a sense of coming to rest in the Catholic plenitude." [48]

He can also appeal in this matter to the declarations of the popes themselves who, when they are preparing to define some point of the faith, far from considering themselves as having to "pronounce an oracle," [49] weigh up not only Scripture but "time-honored tradition, the perpetual belief of the body of the Church, and the agreement of the bishops and the faithful." [50] In this way the meaning of papal infallibility becomes clear—as well as the reason for it; it is an infallibility which is not something separate from that of the whole Church any more than it is derived from an infallibility of the bishops or other members; it is an infallibility which is in reality that of the Church herself, although, in the case of the man who gives it sovereign interpretation in order to bring all controversy to a close, it is personal and absolute. [51]

That is why, in short, the Catholic recognizes Peter as he who has charge of the Universal Church, without any of the petty reservations of Gallicanism. [52] That is why he holds that he is—to quote the expression given authoritative status by the Vatican Council—"the supreme judge of the faithful" and him who holds the fullness of power in the Church, [53] that is why he makes his own the words of St. Ambrose: "Where Peter is, there the Church is." [54] He will always see in Peter both the unshakeable rock upon which his own firmness is based, [55] and "the center of Catholic truth and unity," [56] the one and only visible center of all the children of God. [57] In the authority of Peter he sees the support

of his faith and the guarantee of his communion. [58]
And thus his fidelity to the Christian faith finds
concrete expression in his love for Peter, [59] to whom
he is bound, despite all exterior vicissitudes, by
every fiber of his soul.

That picture of the Catholic in whom the con-
sciousness of churchmanship is lively is, of course,
altogether too meager and abstract an affair, besides being—obviously—over-idealized. Here, as in
all things, there is normally a big gap between the
sincerest faith and the most loving disposition, on
the one hand, and effective practice, on the other;
for man is always an inconsequential creature. But
the important thing to take note of is not the tribute
we all pay, more or less heavily, to human weakness, but rather the nature and scope of our desires.
The mystery of the Church and the good things she
brings are always beyond what we manage to experience in reality. We never draw upon more than
a meager part of the wealth which our Mother has
at her disposal. Yet every Catholic who is not an
ingrate will have in his heart that hymn of gratitude which has been given words by a great contemporary poet: "Louée soit à jamais cette grande
Mère majestueuse, aux genoux de qui j'ai tout
appris!" [60]

It is she who daily teaches us the law of Christ,
giving us His Gospel and helping us to understand
its meaning. It is hard to imagine where the Gospel
would have got to or in what state it would have
reached us if, *per impossible,* it had not been com-

posed, preserved and commented on within the great Catholic community [61]—hard to picture the deformation and mutilation it would have suffered both as to text and as to interpretation. . . . But there is, after all, no need to have recourse to these hypotheses; history speaks forcefully enough. There is no counting the number of aberrations which have been based upon an appeal to the Gospel, or the number of those who have, in consequence of them, toppled over into "atheistic and impious doctrines, or stupid and ridiculous beliefs." Origen had already noticed this, and that great biblical thinker did not hesitate to point a warning finger at "the temptation hidden in the reading of the sacred books," [62] when they are not read *in the Church*. And our own day adds its own lessons to those of the past. "The meaning of the written mystery can belong only to the social unity which carries within itself the revelation of that mystery;" [63] and although we may say, with St. Francis de Sales, that "Scripture is entirely adequate to teach us all things" in a certain sense, we should also add, as he did, that "it is in us that there lies the inadequacy since, without tradition and the magisterium of the Church, we should not be able to determine the meaning which it ought to have." [64] Thus, when we consult tradition and listen to the magisterium "it is not that we prefer the Church to the Scriptures, but rather the explanation of the Scriptures given by the whole Church to our own explanation." [65] We believe that the Word of God is "addressed to the Church," and that is precisely why we listen to it and read it *in the Church*. We do not, however, praise the Church—as has been done on several occasions—for having surrounded the Gospel with a protective covering so as to render it 'harmless,' or for having purged it of its 'impurities.' For praise of that kind would be the worst of blasphemies. The Church has neither glossed over the paradoxes of the Gospel nor changed its vividness nor sentimentalized its power [66] nor betrayed its spirit. The Church is always the paradise in the midst of which the Gospel wells up like a spring [67] and spreads out into four rivers to make the whole earth fruitful. Thanks to the Church, the Gospel is proposed to all, both the great and the small of the world, from generation to generation, and if it does not produce in us its fruition of life, the fault is ours.

We owe our praise, therefore, to this great Mother of ours for the divine mystery which she communicates to us through the twofold and ever-open door of her doctrine and her liturgy; for the centers of religious life which she brings into being, protects and maintains; for the interior universe which she discovers to us, and in the exploration of which she gives us her hand as guide; [68] for the desire and the hope which she sustains in us, [69] and for her purifying of our worship by unmasking and dispersing the illusions which deceive us. This chaste Mother pours into us and sustains a faith which is always whole and which neither human decadence nor spiritual lassitude can touch, however deep they may go. This fruitful Mother continually presents us with new brothers; this universal Mother cares equally for all, little and great alike—the ignorant and the wise, the common-or-garden parishioner and the picked body of consecrated souls. This venerable Mother makes sure for us the inheritance of the ages and brings forth for us from her treasure things new and old. This patient Mother is always making a fresh start, untiringly, in her slow work of education, and gathering together again, one by one, the threads of unity which her children are always tearing apart. This careful Mother protects us against the enemy who prowls around us seeking his prey; this loving Mother does not hold us back for herself, but urges us on to the encounter with God, who is all love. Whatever the shadows which the adversary casts, this clear-sighted Mother cannot help but recognize one day for her own the children whom she has borne, and she will have the power to rejoice in their love while they in their turn will find security in her arms. This zealous Mother sets in the hearts of her best children a zeal which carries them all over the world as the messengers of Christ; this wise Mother steers us clear of sectarian excesses and the deceptive enthusiasm which is always followed by revulsion; she teaches us to love all that is good, all that is true, all that is just, and to reject nothing without first having tested it. [70] This sorrowful Mother with the sword-pierced heart re-lives from age to age the passion of her Bridegroom; [71] this strong Mother exhorts us to fight and bear witness to Christ, [72] and she does not hesitate to make us pass through death—from the first death, which is baptism, onwards—in order to bear us into a higher life. For all these benefits we owe her our praise; but we owe it to her above all for those deaths which she brings us—the deaths which man himself is incapable of, and without which he would be condemned to stay himself indefinitely, going round and round in the miserable circle of his own finitude.

The Church is the Mother of love at its most lovely, of healthy fear, of divine knowledge and holy hope. Without her our thought is diffuse and hazy; but she gathers it together into a firm unity. [73] She scatters the darkness in which men either slumber or despair or—pitifully—"shape as they please their fantasies of the infinite." [74] Without discouraging us from any task she protects us from the deceptive myths of the Churches made by the hand of man, and spares us from the aberrations and the revulsions that follow them. She saves us from destruction in the presence of God; she is the living ark, the gate of the east. She is the unflawed mirror of the activity of the Most High; as the beloved of the Lord of the Universe she is initiated into His secrets and teaches us whatever pleases Him. Her supernatural splendor never fades, even in the darkest hours, [75] and it is thanks to her that our darkness is bathed in light; through her, the priest goes up every day to the altar of the God who gives joy to our youth. The Glory of Libanus is in her,[76] under the obscurity of her earthly covering; each day she gives us Him who is the Way and the Truth, and it is through her that we have hope of life in Him. [77] The memory of her is sweeter than honey, and he who hears her shall never be put to confusion. [78] For she is the holy Mother, the unique Mother, the immaculate Mother, the great Mother, the holy Church, the true Eve, sole true Mother of all the living. [79]

[1] *The Imitation of Christ*, bk. i, ch. ix.

[2] 1 Cor. 19; cf. St. Augustine, *De Trinitate*, bk. xii, ch. iii: "Subhaeremus" (PL, 42, 999).

[3] 2 Cor. x. 5; cf. Rom. i. 5.

[4] Fénelon, *Entretien avec le Chevalier de Ramsay*, in A. de Campigny and others, *Les Entretiens de Cambrai*, 1929, p. 136: "Up to this point you have desired to possess the truth; now the truth must possess you, make you captive and strip you of all the false wealth of the intellect . . .": *Lettres sur l'Autorité de l'Eglise*, I (*Oeuvres*, vol. i, p. 202); cf. the Pseudo-Augustine, *Sermo de Obedientia*: "O sancta obedientia! Tu humilitatem nutris, tu patientiam probas, tu mansuetudinem examinas . . ." (PL, 40, 1249).

[5] Fénelon, *Lettres sur l'Autorité de l'Eglise*, 2 (op. cit., pp. 202–3). However, Fénelon is only showing one of the two aspects of the truth when he adds: "The mysteries are proposed to us in order to subdue our reason and sacrifice it to the supreme reason of God." Quesnel wrote

maliciously of him (May 12, 1704): "He is as outlandish about the authority of the Church as he is about the love of God."

6 On the practice of obedience the reader should consult the article by Fr. Mersch, "La Raison d'Etre de l'Obéissance Religieuse", NRT, 1927, and Henri Mogenet, S.J., *La Vocation Religieuse dans l'Eglise,* 1952, pp. 101–8, the principles of which work hold good for all varieties of Catholic obedience.

7 Yves de Montcheuil, *Mélanges Théologiques,* pp. 121–2: "That is why those among the unbelievers who have exalted the conception of authority and discipline in the Church while reducing her to a merely human institution have only been able to do so by underestimating the value of the person; hence their doctrine of obedience, far from being in true conformity with the Catholic faith, is an immoral one."

8 Cf. St. Cyril of Alexandria, *Fragmenta in Cantica* (PG, 69, 1292a): Rom. i. 5: St. Peter Damian, *Sermo XLV* (PL, 144, 743b).

9 St. Augustine, *Sermo CCLXVIII,* no. 2 (PL, 38, 235); cf. Pope St. Gregory the Great, *Moralia in Job,* bk. xxxv, ch. xiv, no. 28: ". . . Sola namque virtus est oboedientia quae virtutes caeteras menti inserit, insertasque custodit . . . Tanto igitur quisque Deum citius placat, quanto ante ejus oculos, repressa arbitrii sui superbia, gladio praecepti se immolat . . . Vir quippe obediens victorias loquitur, quia dum alienae voci humiliter subdimur, nosmetipsos in corde superamus" (PL, 76, 765b and c): Carl Feckes, *Das Mysterium der heiligen Kirche,* p. 211.

10 Cf. Gal. i. 10: Pope St. Gregory the Great, *In Evangelia,* hom. vi, no. 2: ". . . Et quid per arundinem, nisi carnalis animus designatur? Qui mox ut favore vel detractione tangitur, statim in partem quamlibet inclinatur?" (PL, 76, 1096c).

11 St. Augustine, *De Civitate Dei,* bk. xix, ch. xiv (PL, 41, 642); cf. Ps. 12 45: "And I walked at large; because I have sought after thy commandments."

91 Cf. Massillon, *Sermon sur la Parole de Dieu* (*Oeuvres,* ed. Lefèbvre, 1838, vol. i, p. 165): Fénelon, *Lettres sur l'Autorité de l'Eglise,* 1: "A man may reason with another man; but with God he can only pray, humble himself, listen, be silent and follow blindly."

13 On this principle, which we have already met with earlier on, which guarantees the life of the person by saving it from individualism and is equally important for ecclesiology and the spiritual life alike, see my *Histoire et Esprit,* ch. iv.

14 Cf. H. Clérissac, O.P., *Le Mystère de l'Eglise,* 1918, p. 121: St. Augustine, *In Epist. Joannis,* tract. iii, no. 13 (PL, 35, 2004).

15 2 Cor. iii. 17; cf. Ps. cxviii. 45: "And I walked at large; because I have sought after thy commandments": St. Augustine, *De Spiritu et Littera,* ch. xvi., no. 28 (PL, 44, 218): Pope Gregory the Great, *Moralia in Job,* bk. xxxv, ch. xiv, no. 32: "Ipsa obedientia, non servili metu, sed caritatis affectu servanda est" (PL, 76, 768a).

16 Cf. Heb. xiii. 17.

17 A. Gagliardi, *De Plena Cognitione Instituti S.J.* (1841 ed.), p. 67.

18 Pope St. Gregory the Great, *Moralia in Job,* bk. xxxv, ch. xiv, no. 29: "Sciendum vero est, quod numquam per obedientiam malum fieri, aliquando autem debet per obedientiam bonum quod agitur, intermitti" (PL, 76, 766b): Leo XIII, Encyclical *Diuturnum Illud:* "Whenever

there were question of infringing either the natural law or the will of God both command and execution thereof would be equally criminal": St. Ignatius Loyola, *Letter on Obedience,* no. 16 (he is quoting St. Bernard): "Ubi tamen Deo contraria non praecipuit homo."

[19] Cf. R. Grosche, *Pilgernde Kirche,* pp. 210–25, "Newman and die kirchliche Autorität": Pope St. Gregory the Great, *In Evangelia,* hom. xxvi, no. 6: ". . . Sed utrum juste an injuste obliget pastor, pastoris tamen sententia gregi timenda est, ne is qui subest, et cum injuste forsitan ligatur, ipsam obligationem suae, sententiae ex alia culpa mereatur . . . Is autem qui sub manu pastoris est, ligari timeat vel injuste; nec pastoris sui judicium temere reprehendat, ne etsi injuste ligatus est, ex ipsa tumidae reprehensionis superbia, culpa quae non erat, fiat" (PL, 76, 1201b): St. Thomas, *Suppl.,* q. 21, a. 4.

[20] Origen, *In Matt. Series,* lxxvii: "Oportebat autem haec in Bethania fieri, quae interpretatur domus obedientiae . . . Domum autem obedientiae Ecclesiam intelligi oportere dubitat nemo" (The phrase was, of course, taken over by St. Ignatius in his *Letter on Obedience*).

[21] François Charmot, S.J., *La Doctrine Spirituelle des Hommes d'Action,* 1938, p. 315: "I do not maintain that superiors are infallible— that is to say, that if we consider their views and their reasons we shall not be able to find error in them. What I do maintain is that Providence is infallible—as the Vatican Council affirms—and that in conforming our conduct to its plans we do participate in that Wisdom, in practice."

[22] Heb. v. 8; cf. x. 5–13; Philip. ii. 8; Preface for Feasts of the Holy Cross.

[23] His Holiness Pope Pius XII, Encyclical *Mystici Corporis Christi,* following Clement of Alexandria, *Stromata,* bk. vii, ch. ii.

[24] It is for this reason that I consider inadequate Fr. Deman's explanation in his *Pour une Vie Spirituelle Objective.* Everything not comprised under the term "object"—understood in Fr. Deman's sense—is not necessarily the pernicious and inconsistent "subjective" element which I deplore as much as he does; cf. Louis Lallemant, S.J., *La Doctrine Spirituelle,* Sixth Principle, s. 3, ch. v (pp. 400–3 in the new edition of 1908).

[25] In Chapter III.

[26] St. Cyprian, *De Catholicae Ecclesiae Unitate,* ch. xxiii: ". . . ut consentientis populi corpus unum gremio suo gaudens Mater includat" (vol. i, p. 230 in Hartel's edition) and again: "Quicquid a matrice discesserit, seorsum vivere et spirare non poterit, substantiam salutis amittit" (ibid., p. 231): *Epist. XL,* no. 3 (ibid., p. 607). Some other texts are given in my *Catholicism.*

[27] Bérulle, *Discourse de l'Etat et des Grandeurs de Jésus,* 10.

[28] Cf. Joseph Plumpe's excellent monograph, *Mater Ecclesia: An Inquiry into the Concept of the Church as Mother in Early Christianity,* Washington, 1934, and Christine Mohrmann in *Vigilae Christianae,* ii, 1.

[29] *De Catholicae Ecclesiae Unitate,* ch. vi (p. 214 in Hartel's edition): *Epist. LXXIV,* no. 7: "Ut habere quis possit Deum Patrem, habeat antea Ecclesiam matrem" (ibid., p. 804): *De Lapsis,* ch. ix (ibid., p. 243): Tertullian, *De Oratione,* ch. ii (PL, 1, 1154).

[30] *In Psalm.,* lxxxviii, sermo ii, no. 14: "Amemus Dominum Deum

nostrum, amemus Ecclesiam ejus, illum sicut patrem, istam sicut matrem . . . Tenete ergo, carissimi, tenete omnes unanimiter Deum patrem et matrem Ecclesiam" (PL, 38, 1140–1): *Sermo de Alleluia*: "Neque poterit quispiam habere Deum patrem, qui Ecclesiam contempserit matrem" (pp. 332–3 in Morin's edition): *Contra Litteras Petiliani*, bk. iii, ch. ix, no. 10 (PL, 43, 353): *Sermo CCXVI*, no. 8: "Pater Deus est, mater Ecclesia" (PL, 38, 1081): *De Symbolo ad Catechumenos* (PL, 40, 668): *Epist. LXXX*, ch. ii (PL, 33, 188): *Epist. XCVIII*, ch. v (ibid., 362), etc. Cf. Origen, *In Levit.*, hom. ii, no. 3 (p. 452 in Baehrens' edition).

[31] The point has been noted by Fr. Pierre Charles, "Vicarius Christi", NRT, 1929, p. 450.

[32] In particular, the supreme decisions of the magisterium interpret the tradition of the whole Church and assume the collaboration of the faithful themselves, as being a declaration of their faith. See, for example, J. V. Bainvel in his introduction to Bellamy's *Théologie Catholique au XIXe Siècle*, p. xiv.

[33] The Church, said Moehler, is "Jesus Christ renewing Himself without ceasing" (*Symbolik*, ch. v, no. 36).

[34] St. Cyprian, *Epist. XLVIII*, ch. iii; cf. *Epist. LIX*, ch. xiv.

[35] Fourth Council of the Lateran, ch. v: Eugenius of Carthage, in Victor de Vita's *Historia Persecutionis Africanae Provinciae*, bk. ii, ch. xli (p. 40 in Petschenic's edition): Paschasinus, at the Council of Chalcedon (Mansi, vol. vi, 580): Council of Sardica: Hadrian, Letter to the Patriarch Tarasius (Mansi, vol. xii, 1081): Innocent III: ". . . totius Christianitatis caput et magistra" (PL, 214, 59a, 21d, 215, 710), etc.

[36] St. Augustine, *Epist. XLIII*, ch. v, no. 16: "Patrem christianae plebis" (PL, 33, 167): Pope St. Leo the Great, *Sermo IV*, ch. ii: "Unus Petrus elegitur, qui . . . omnibus apostolis cunctisque Ecclesiae patribus praeponatur ut, quamvis, in populo Dei multi sacerdotes sint multique pastores, omnes tamen proprie regat Petrus, quos principaliter regit et Christus" (PL, 54, 149–50): St. Paschasius Radbert, *Expositio in Mattheum*, bk. vii, ch. xv: "In ipso [Petro] est forma omnium in quo unitas Ecclesiae commendatur" (PL, 120, 528a); cf. P. Batiffol, *Cathedra Petri*, 1938, pp. 169–95, 95–104: ". . . petrus initium episcopatus".

[37] For the history of this title cf. Batiffol, op. cit., pp. 151–68: St. Augustine, *Epist. XLIII*, ch. iii, no. 7: ". . . Romanae Ecclesiae, in qua semper apostolicae cathedrae viguit principatus" (PL, 33, 162).

[38] Matt. xvi. 18–19: For the exegesis of this text see Léon Vaganay, "Pierre Chef et Docteur", *Tu es Petrus*, 1934, pp. 3–26: F. M. Braun, O.P., *Aspects Nouveaux du Problème de l'Eglise*, 1942, pp. 81–98: J. C. Didier, "D'une Interprétation Récente de l'Expression Lier-Délier", *Mélanges de Science Religieuse*, 1952, pp. 55–62. With regard to the fundamental text in Matt. xvi, it may be noted that while Loisy accepted its application to Peter as head of the Church but denied its historicity and authenticity (*Evangiles Synoptiques*, pp. 7-8), today Herr Oscar Cullmann accepts the historicity of it but would restrict all legitimate application to Peter as an historical individual, i.e., to the exclusion of his successors.

[39] St. Augustine, *Epist. LIII*, ch. i, no. 2: ". . . [Petrus] cui totius

Ecclesiae figuram gerenti Dominus ait: super hanc petram . . ." (PL, 33, 196): *In Joannem*, tract. cxxiv, no. 5 (PL, 35, 1973): *Sermo CCXCV*, no. 2 (PL, 38, 1349). On the significance of the Papacy in the Church cf. G. Dejaife, S.J., "Sobornost ou Papauté", NRT, 1952.

40 Cf. Pius VI, *Caritas Illa*, 16 June 1777.

41 Cf. the anti-Modernist oath of 1910: "Ecclesiam . . . super Petrum apostolicae hierarchiae principem . . . aedificatam": Origen, *In Exod.*, hom. v, no. 4: ". . . magno illi Ecclesiae fundamento et petrae solidissimae": *In Rom.*, bk. v, no. 10 (PG, 14, 1035): St. Augustine, *Epist. LVII*, ch. ix, no. 21: "Petrus etiam, Apostolorum caput, caeli anitor, et Ecclesiae fundamentum" (PL, 33, 145); these phrases are drawn from a text of Roman provenance sent to Augustine by the priest Casulanus, but Augustine does not query them when he quotes them: cf. *Liber Mozarabicus Sacramentorum*, ed. M. Ferotin, col. 140.

42 John x. 1–18 and xxi. 15–19: St. Thomas, *In Sent. IV*, d. 17, q. 3, a. 1, sol. 5: the *potestas excellentiae* pertains to Christ alone "qui est Ecclesiae fundamentum"; cf. Berengard, *In Apoc.*: "Non enim aliud fundamentum est Petrus, et aliud Christus Jesus, quia Petrus membrum est Christi Jesu" (PL, 17, 849c–d): see *supra*, p. 84, n. 6.

43 St. Augustine, *Sermo de Amore Petri*: ". . . in Petro Ecclesiam cognoscendam. Aedificavit enim Christus Ecclesiam non super hominem, sed super Petri confessionem. Quae est confessio Petri? *Tu es Christus Filius Dei vivi*. Ecce petra, ecce fundamentum, ecce ubi est Ecclesia aedificata, quam portae inferorum non vincunt . . . Ergo iste discipulus a Petra Petrus, quomodo a Christo christianus est" (ed. C. Lambot in *Revue Bénédictine*, 1937, vol. xlix, p. 253): *Sermo LXXVI*, no. 1 (PL, 38, 479): cf. *Retract.*, bk. 1, ch. xxi, no. 1 (p. 400 in Bardy's edition) and the commentary thereupon given by Rozaven, *L'Eglise Catholique Justifiée*, pp. 161–2: Rupert of Deutz, *In Matthaeum*, bk. iii: "Super petram fidei, quam confessus est Petrus, Ecclesiam suam aedificat . . ." (PL, 168, 1385a); Gilbert Foliot, *Exposito in Cantica*, iii, 1: "Tu es Petrus, id est, in fide mei tanquam petra firmus, et sic Petrus a me tanquam petra nominatur. Et super hanc petram quam me esse intelligo et in te esse constituo, aedificabo tam firmiter, quod portae inferi non praevalebunt adversus eum" (PL, 202, 1244d).

44 Vatican Council, Constitution *Pastor Aeternus*, 18 July 1870: Pope St. Leo the Great, *Sermo III*, ch. iii: "Manet ergo dispositio veritatis, et beatus Petrus in accepta fortitudine petrae perseverans, suscepta Ecclesiae gubernacula non reliquit" (PL, 54, 146b); ch. ii: "Soliditas illius fidei quae in apostolorum principe est laudata, perpetua est; et sicut permanet quod in Christo Petrus credidi, ita permanet quod in Petro Christus instituit" (ibid., 145–6): St. Thomas, *Contra Gentiles*, bk. iv, ch. lxxiv: "Tamdiu igitur oportet hanc potestatem perpetuari, quamdiu necesse est post mortem discipulorum Christi usque ad saeculi finem": cf. Geoffrey of St. Victor, *Microcosmus*, ch. ciii (p. 115 in Delhaye's edition of 1951).

45 Cf. Cerfaux, "Saint Pierre et sa Succession", RSR, 1953, pp. 188–202: G. Dejaife, S.J., "M. Cullmann et la Question de Pierre", NRT, 1953, pp. 365–79: ". . . the interpretation of the *logion* which attributes to Christ the will to build an enduring Church on a fragile foundation which was destined to disappear does scant justice either to the coherence of the image or the wisdom of its author".

46 The Roman legate Philip, at the Council of Ephesus (Mansi, vol. iv. col. 1296).

47 Cf. A. S. Khomiakov, *L'Eglise Latine et le Protestantisme au Point de vue de l'Eglise d'Orient*, 1872, pp. 104, 142, 160, 301.

48 Mgr. Blanchet, at the Institut Catholique inaugural Mass, Nov. 1950.

49 A. S. Khomiakov, op. cit., pp. 107–10.

50 Pius IX, Bull *Ineffabilis*, 1854: ". . . quam divina eloquia, veneranda traditio, perpetuus Ecclesiae sensus, singularis catholicorum Antistitum se fidelium conspiratio et insignia Praedecessorum Nostrorum acta, constitutiones mirifice illustrant atque declarant . . ."

51 Controversy has often misunderstood the phrase "Ex sese, non ex consensu Ecclesiae" used by the Vatican Council, as if it meant a separate infallibility.

52 Cf. Pope St. Leo's phrases—"Totius ecclesiae princeps", "curam Ecclesiae universalis habens", etc.—and P. Batiffol, *Le Siège Apostolique*, 1924, pp. 613—14.

53 Constitution *Pastor Aeternus*, ch. iii: "Judicem supremum fidelium . . . totam plenitudinem hujus supremae potestatis."

54 *In Psalm.*, xl, no. 30 (PL, 14, 1082a). While others, whose view stops short at detail on the human and earthly level, seem to be perpetually afraid of some campaign to dominate, such a man as this will have a spontaneous confidence in the explanation given by St. Ambrose in the name of the heads of the Church: "Nec quaedam nos angit de domestico studio et ambitione contentio, sed communio soluta et dissociata perturbat." There is a commentary on these words in Batiffol's *Cathedra Petri*, pp. 78–9.

55 Pope St. Leo the Great, *Epist. X*, ch. i: ". . . Qui ausus fuisset a Petri soliditate recedere" (PL, 55, 629a): *Sermo III*, ch. ii (PL, 54, 145–6): *Sermo V*, ch. iv (ibid, 155a): *Sermo LI*, ch. i (ibid, 309b): Hormisdas, *Epist. Inter Ea* (A.D. 517): "Sedes apostolica . . . in qua est integra et verax christianae religionis et perfecta soliditas": Pope St. Gregory the Great, *Epist. ad Theodolindam* (A.D. 594): "In vera fide persistite et vitam vestram in petra Ecclesiae, id est in confessione beati Petri, solidate" (PL, 77, 712–13).

56 Pius IX, Bull *Ineffabilis Deus*.

57 Cf. Fénelon, Letter to Alamanni of July 15, 1710: "By the grace of God, I am bound to the Holy See by the most lively and tender affection. One cannot love religion without loving that Holy Mother who has given us birth in Jesus Christ and who still feeds us with the spirit of life. One cannot love unity save inasmuch as one desires that all Christians should be reunited in this one and only centre of the children of God" (quoted in Guérin, pp. 394–5).

58 It is worth reading Bossuet's extremely shrewd reflection in his *Exposition de la doctrine de l'Eglise Catholique* (ch. xix), on the subject of dissidents: "Moreover, if our adversaries consult their conscience, they will find that the name of the Church has more authority over them than they dare to admit in controversy; and I do not believe that there is amongst them one single man of good sense who, if he saw himself to be alone in holding some particular view, would not be horrified at such singularity, however evident the point seemed to him in itself;

so true is it that in these matters men have need to be supported in their attitudes by the authority of some society which thinks the same as they. That is why God, who has made us, and who knows what is fitting for us, willed, for our own good, that all particular matters should be subject to the authority of His Church, which is without doubt the best established of all authorities . . ." (vol. i, col. 1165, in Migne's edition).

[59] Cf. the wonderful *Spiritual Testament* of Cardinal Faulhaber, reprinted in *Documentation Catholique*, Oct. 19, 1952, cols. 1505–10.

[60] Paul Claudel, "Ma Conversion", in *Contacts et Circonstances*, also *Pages de Prose*, chosen and presented by André Blanchet, p. 279.

[61] Cf. Jacques Guillet, S.J., "La Naissance de l'Evangile dans l'Eglise", LV, Oct. 1952.

[62] *De Oratione*, ch. xxix, no. 10: St. Irenaeus, *Adversus Haereses*, bk. iv, ch. xxvi, no. 5 (he is talking about bishops): "Scripturas sine periculo nobis exponunt" (PG, 7, 1056a–b); ch. xxxiii, no. 8: among the bishops is to be found . . . "sine fictione Scripturarum tractatio . . . secundum Scripturas expositio legitima, et diligens, et sine periculo, et sine blasphemia" (ibid., 1077b–c).

[63] Cf. A. S. Khomiakov, *L'Eglise Latine et le Protestantisme*, p. 279.

[64] Letter to a Jesuit Father, 17 Aug. 1609 (*Oeuvres*, vol. xiv, p. 191).

[65] Fénelon, *De l'Education des Filles*, ch. vii; cf. *Deuxième Lettre sur l'Autorité de l'Eglise*: "A visible authority [is necessary] which speaks and decides, so that all minds may be submitted, united and fixed in one and the same explanation of the Holy Scriptures": "It is necessary that there should be an authority which lives, speaks, decides and explains the sacred text" (*Oeuvres*, vol. i, pp. 223–4): Moehler, *Die Einheit in der Kirche*," Appx. 7: cf. Luther, *Appelatio Fr. Martini Luther* (to Frederick of Saxony against Leo X, 17 Nov. 1520): ". . . quod sacram Scripturam sibi subjiciat [Papa]" (*Opera Omnia*, ed. of 1600, p. 258).

[66] Harnack himself had to recognize the fact, in the very course of a lecture in which his anti-Catholic prejudice comes out, *Das Wesen des Christentums*: "In the Church the temporal has not diminished the power of the Gospel; in spite of the weight which threatens to crush it, it continually frees and renews itself. It works as a leaven." Cf. St. Irenaeus' phrase, ". . . potestatem Evangelii . . ." (*Adversus Haereses*, bk. iii, preface).

[67] Cf. ch. ix. St. Irenaeus, *Adversus Haereses*, bk. v, ch. xx, no. 2 (PG, 7, 1178a–b): St. Cyprian, *Epist. LXXIII*, ch. x (p. 785 in Hartel's edition): St. Paulinus of Nola, *Epist. XXXII*, no. 10 (PL, 61, 336):

Petram superstat ipsa Petra Ecclesiae
De qua sonori quatuor fontes meant
Evangelistae viva Christi flumina.

See also the descriptions by Lucien de Bruyne of the early baptisteries of Naples, Milan, Oued Ramel (Tunisia), in his "La Décoration des Baptistères Paléochrétiens", *Miscellanea Liturgica in Honorem L. Cuniberti Mohlberg*, 1948, vol. i, pp. 200–4: St. Peter Damian, *Sermo XIV* (PL, 144, 572c).

[68] Cf. Pierre van der Meer van Walcheren, *Journal d'un Converti*, p. 240: "I—being still outside the Church, in a state of expectancy—sense in advance, and with an ever-increasing joy, an infinite world into which the spirit may go exploring and in which the soul may find God—

abyssus abyssum invocat—and in comparison with which the visible world must be a negligible thing, almost non-existent. What a magnificent, unimaginable universe must be hidden within the Church!" A presentiment, of course, not to be proved false.

[69] Cf. Apoc. xxii. 17 and 20: "And the spirit and the bride say: "Come . . . Surely I come quickly: Amen. Come, Lord Jesus!" It is through her that we remain "immovable from the hope of the gospel" (Col. i. 23).

[70] Cf. 1 Thess. v. 21; 1 John iv. 1, etc.

[71] Cf. Luke ii. 35: St. Augustine, *Sermo LXII*, ch. iii, no. 5: "Quod tunc corpus ipsius in turba patiebatur, hoc patitur Ecclesia ipsius" (PL, 38, 416): Ambrose Autpert, *Sermo in Purificatione* B. M., no. 13: "Ipsam beatam Virginem, cujus animam gladius transfodisse, perhibetur, typum Ecclesiae praetendisse reperimus . . ."; cf. Charles Journet, *Les Sept Paroles du Christ en Croix*, 1952, p. 130.

[72] St. Augustine, *Sermo CCCI*, no. 1, on the mother of the Machabees: "Una mulier, una mater, quomodo nobis ante oculos posuit unam matrem sanctam Ecclesiam, ubique exhortantem filios suos pro illius nomine mori, de quo eos concepit et peperit?" (PL, 38, 1380).

[73] Pope St. Gregory the Great, *Moralia in Job*, bk. ii, ch. lii, no. 82: "Exhortatione sanctae Ecclesiae cunctae in auditorum mentibus diffusae cogitationes ligantur . . ." (p. 240 in the edition of De Gaudemaris).

[74] Renan, discourse given at Quimper, 17 Aug. 1885.

[75] Cf. Wisd. vii. 26; viii. 4; ix. 9 and 18; vi. 12; cf. vii. 10–11: "For her light cannot be put out. Now all good things come to me together with her . . ."

[76] Isa. lx. 13; cf. xlv. 14.

[77] St. Irenaeus, *Adversus Haereses*, bk. iii, ch. iv, no. 1: "Haec est unum Vitae introitus" (PG, 7, 855b).

[78] Cf. Ecclus. xxiv. 17–31; Judith xiii. 25.

[79] Tertullian, *De Anima, ch. xliii*: "Vera mater viventium . . . Ecclesia" (p. 372 in the Reifferscheid-Wissowa edition): *Adversus Marcionem*, bk. ii, ch. iv (p. 338 in Kroymann's edition): St. Ambrose, *In Lucam*, bk. ii, ch. lxxxvi: "Haec est Eva mater omnium viventium . . . Mater ergo viventium Ecclesia est" (PL, 15, 1585a), etc. On the motherly care of the Church, see St. Augustine, *De Moribus Ecclesiae Catholicae*, bk. i. ch. xxx (PL, 32, 1336): *De Nuptiis*, bk. ii. ch. iv, no. 12: "Nam in hoc, quod appellata est vita materque viventium, magnum est Ecclesiae sacramentum" (PL, 44, 443): *De Genesi Contra Manichaeos*, bk. ii, ch. xxiv, no. 37 (PL, 34, 216), etc.: Ambrosian Rite, Preface for the Dedication of a Church (Paredi, 1937, p. 201): Guerricus, *In Assumpt.*, s. 1, no. 2 (PL, 185, 188b–c).

AUTHORITY, CONSCIENCE AND LOVE *
Bernard Häring, C.SS.R.

Education to Freedom

GENUINE FORMATION in obedience is without doubt also education in the law (in the established norm of good), but it is even more initiation into liberty which goes beyond the universal law, into that liberty which is born of the insight into the good and of love for the good and for that which is always more perfect. Freedom unfolds its capacity as it exercises itself in obedience, but it must be obedience of the spirit. And this is impossible without the true spirit of independence and self-mastery. The spirit of true independence (virtue of freedom) reigns when the Christian acts even without bidding, when he possesses the disposition and will to obey even though there may be no mandate or precept. The spirit of obedience is marked by free initiative and acceptance of responsibility even without command.

* From *The Law of Christ*, 2 vols., by Bernard Häring, C.SS.R. Used by permission of the Newman Press.

Mutual Interplay of Conscience and Authority

CONSCIENCE IS NOT an oracle which can draw the truth from its own obscure depths or even create it. It is the proper task of conscience to move the will in accordance with the truth of which it is aware and to search for the truth prior to its decision. Accordingly, conscience and objective truth, and ultimately also conscience and the authority of God teaching us, essentially belong together. By its very nature conscience seeks illumination and guidance, which it finds naturally in the order and harmony of creation, in the supernatural order with wonderful fullness in Christ, and through Christ and the Holy Spirit in the teaching Church.

But on its part genuine authority—such is its nature—also postulates conscience. Without conscience it would not have the character of moral authority, nor be able to exercise authority over human persons. We can have moral authority over men, guiding, directing them only if authority appeals to conscience. For each individual man his own conscience is the norm of moral conduct. We call it the ultimate subjective norm, but it is always dependent, a norm which must conform to a higher norm, an objective norm! This it must always seek in the objective world of truth in order to be correct and valid.

God, the ultimate norm, the truth to which every conscience must conform, is free to determine in what way and to what degree He will teach the human conscience. But He always instructs conscience in accordance with its nature: the natural conscience through the order of nature, the conscience endowed with the supernatural grace of faith through the supernatural revelation. Just as it is not alien to natural conscience to draw from the natural revelation expressed in creation and to learn from the natural communities which correspond to it, so it is also "according to nature" for the believing conscience elevated by grace and steeped in humility to harken to the word of revelation communicated to us in the Church, even though, of course, the "old man" shrinks from the ordeal of obscurity and obedience demanded of him by faith.

Conscience: *Obedience and Freedom*

THERE CAN BE no absolute freedom of conscience for the simple reason that conscience does not free one from the law. On the contrary, it is conscience alone which actually binds one to the law of the good. Everyone, of course, must ultimately follow his conscience; this means he must do right as he sees the right with sincere desire and effort to find and to do what is good. But there are certain moral principles which no one can fail to recognize. No one may set himself above these fundamental principles and invoke the right of conscience as justification of his act. In instances of inculpable ignorance or error, one has the right and duty to follow one's conscience, although it may be necessary occasionally for society to intervene and interfere with certain acts in order to prevent evil consequences. Tragic conflicts can readily arise in such instances.

But when conscience is in error culpably, the right of a free conscience may not be invoked. In such instances it is within the province of higher authority to correct the error and safeguard the community from the ravages of pernicious principles. It is one of the greatest evils of our day that so few generally recognized moral principles still prevail among the masses of men. Consequently and consistently men will give an entirely free rein to the erroneous conscience, culpably lax or actually malicious. To cite an example, the state does not uphold a correct conception of conscience when it appeals to freedom of conscience in permitting and legally safeguarding the spread and sale of vile literature, means of contraception, and even abortion. The state has the duty to guarantee the liberty of sane and sound conscience, but not the license of evil and perverted conscience. Failure to do so can have only one result, the inevitable violent dominance of the evil over the good.

Human Law and the Following of Christ

WHEN SAINT JAMES says, "There is one lawgiver" (Jas. 4:12), he does not thereby reject human law as superfluous, but on the contrary indicates its supreme source, the source of all right and law,

God. Similarly our moral life in the domain of right must not be reduced to human subjection and human law, but must always in its inmost depths remain centered in the following of Christ. But if Christ directs us to the Church and her law and, in the secular sphere, to the civil laws, it follows that obedience to them is obedience to Christ Himself. The following of Christ, however, must also furnish us with the measure and the limits of our obedience to human laws.

Christ Himself in His own life gives us the example of obedience to the norms of law and the cultal precepts of His own people, as also of the perfect fulfillment of the moral law as such. He pays the tax for Himself and Peter; He makes the pilgrimage to the temple at the prescribed liturgical times. He observes the Sabbath (though, of course, not according to the barren formalism of the pharisaical interpretation). He lives in the midst of a human family, choosing to practice obedience. He carries obedience to secular authority to the extreme of unresisting submission to its iniquitous verdict of death, victim of the most heinous legal murder ever perpetrated in human history. It is true that He did pronounce a stern condemnation of this injustice against Pilate and even more against the Sanhedrin. More than once he castigated the narrow legalistic and even sinful interpretation of law enunciated by the Pharisees. And still He did not withdraw from the oppressive obedience to human authority whenever obedience was not contrary to the will of the Heavenly Father.

Jesus "himself knew what was in man" (John 2:25). Through painful experience He knew the deficiencies of the secular and religious authority and the craven weakness of His own apostles, and yet He placed them and their successors over His Church with legislative authority. "He who hears you, hears me" (Luke 10:16). "As the Father has sent me, I also send you" (John 20:21; compare Matt. 16:19; 18:18).

Only too frequently secular authority proves sinful and unbelieving. Obedience to such authority, and for that matter even obedience to ecclesiastical authority established by Christ, cannot be practiced for long without painful realization of the frailty and imperfection of the bearers of that authority. It also must be borne in mind that the laws imposed by men do not possess either the clarity or the certainty of the divine laws regarding the absolute good. But since man has a social nature, he is simply under the necessity of human law. He stands in need of authority and its law for his moral development. But most of all it is the community which has need of law in order to create the climate for the individual person to move within a realm of order in the service of the community, and to enrich the soil for moral growth and development of community itself. Doubly necessary because of original sin is the penal regulation through law. Were there no legal restraints checking the abuse of freedom by evil men, the enticement and violence on the part of the evil would rob the good of their freedom to act virtuously. The law with its sanctions is an indispensable means of education for men in their frailty and a shield against human malice (Rom. 13:3ff).

The imperfection of human laws and the consequent burdens often weighing so heavily upon men are a part of the cross of Christ which we must share with Him. The cross which He Himself bore He cannot lift from the shoulders of His disciples. In the cross of Christ the problem and crisis of human authority was revealed in all its poignancy and horror. By patiently suffering a death inflicted in the name of the law, legal murder through mockery of justice, Christ redeemed our subjection to human legislation, which often imposes an almost intolerable burden upon us. Bearing the weight of the woeful inadequacy of human laws has become far more than a mere matter of expediency. Now there lies before us the sanctified way of obedience to the will of God our Father, consecrated by the footprints of Christ who followed this way obediently to the death of the cross (Phil. 2:8).

But human law is not merely a cross; in its inner sense it is the way to justice, a support of weakness, a fulfillment of the order of the divine wisdom, a work of love through community and for community. Above all, we must note that even the laws of the Church are clothed in the vesture of earthly imperfection and therefore cannot escape the problem and crisis of all that is human.

But in their inner depth there is a heavenly security. Does the Church not possess in her task of guidance through law the assistance of the Holy Spirit, so that she cannot command anything sinful and, at least in essentials, anything false? Likewise through the Church the burden of the problem of civil law is greatly lightened, since she as the infallible guardian of the morality of her children can caution them against morally dangerous and sinful laws.

The persistent problem of submission to imperfect human laws has not merely a negative phase. There is also a positive phase. Obedience to law constantly directs our attention, with ever increasing emphasis, to what lies beyond the legally regulated, to the actual basic sources of the good, though human law can do little more than give us a hint of it. Precisely through the painful experience of the limits of human legislation the Christian is constrained to look into the mirror of the perfect law of love, to adhere to the spirit of Christ.

There is a certain advantage in this very imperfection of legislative enactment. It serves to remind us that law and fulfillment of law are only a portion of the moral perfection. "Even though no society can live without law, neither the family, nor the state, still they do not live through law, but in the law. Marriage, family live through love" (St. Thomas). This is singularly true of the Mystical Body of Christ, of the Church, and of our relation to her. She too lives in the law; that is, she has a legal domain which is essential to her life, but she does not live through law. Law is not the source of her life, for she lives through the love of Christ and the grace of the Holy Spirit and through the fulness of grace and love of her members, which, of course, also implies obedience to her laws. The legislative activity belongs to the pastoral care of the Church, which is a function of love.

Subjection to legislative authority of men produces the spirit of humility in man. Submission is a constant reminder of our created nature. Man is not a god. In prayer indeed, we can directly approach God and speak to Him. However, only if we join in community and obey its laws to the best of our ability, only if we do the works of love in the reign of law will our obedience and our love be acceptable to God.

The constant necessity of applying to human law the test of the eternal law of God and the law of the imitation of Christ through divine grace does not in the slightest diminish the value of obedience to men. The value is in fact enhanced, since obedience is anchored more firmly than ever in its foundation of eternal values. These basic principles enable the Christian to act wisely despite the imperfections of human law.

Obligation To Observe Human Law

THE OBLIGATION IN CONSCIENCE to observe the laws of the Church is clear from the establishment of ecclesiastical authority by Christ. Obligation in conscience to obey civil law can be shown through natural reasoning from the social nature of man. Sacred Scripture clearly teaches that human authority is derived from the divine: "By me kings reign, and lawgivers decree just things" (Prov. 8:15). "Admonish them to be subject to princes and authorities, obeying commands, ready for every good work" (Titus 3:1). "Let every one be subject to the higher authorities, for there exists no authority except from God, and those who exist have been appointed by God. Therefore he who resists the authority resists the ordinance of God.... For it is God's minister to thee for good.... Wherefore you must needs be subject, not only because of the wrath, but also for conscience' sake.... Render to all men whatever is their due; tribute to whom tribute is due; taxes to whom taxes are due; fear to whom fear is due; honor to whom honor is due" (Rom. 13:1-7). Very terse is the evangelist's rendering of the injunction of Jesus: "Render, therefore, to Caesar the things that are Caesar's" (Matt. 22:21; compare I Pet. 2:13ff).

Discipline of Will and Spiritual Formation

IN HIS WORK on the training of the will, Lindworsky pointed out the danger of overestimating the pure technique of exercising oneself in will power. Such discipline without deeper motivation is not much more than mere 'training.' Even though he overshot his mark, this noted psychologist directed our attention to the need for a more profound cultivation of motive. Man as a body-soul unity absolutely stands in need of the technique which comes from training and exercise. Exercise is essential for mastery over stubbornness and native resistance to good; it imparts a certain external proficiency. But it does not have the value of virtue except through the virtuous motive which animates it. One must concede the point to Lindworsky that in times of spiritual crisis it is not the external exercises and the habitual repetition of acts which enable the soul to stand firm. This is possible only through motivation profoundly rooted in conscience, although motivation is much more easily sustained if the action has become familiar through exercise than if it is new and untried.

A single act flowing from an intense and vital experience of love for God (that is, a profoundly motivated act) can lead to greater progress on the way of virtue than a thousand merely formal acts of the presence of God. A solitary sublime act of sacrificial renunciation arising from the inmost love for one's neighbor leads one more deeply into the realm of the virtue of fraternal charity than a thousand external exercises or gestures without vital realization and experience of the real value of service to others, that is, of the real value of one's neighbor whom one must serve.

Usually one single act does not open the way to the depth of value. Precisely planned coordination and tenacious effort make it possible for man to penetrate ever more deeply into a moral motive. Not merely meditation on motive leads us into the inner realm of virtue, but motive pondered and likewise put into action (for we are not pure spirits). Moreover, precisely the zeal manifested in this exercise is usually evidence of the high esteem for virtue. It shows that we are taken up with the motive of virtue.

One of Lindworsky's insights must absolutely be accepted as genuine: in education of self and of others it is not sufficient to insist merely on the performance of the external act. The motive must ever be kept in mind and presented with all its vital significance. Only in this way can we really arrive at virtue, not merely through exercise or 'training.' Perhaps secular lawmakers may be altogether satisfied if they constrain men to a mere external or mechanical compliance with their laws. But the educator must place everything in the light of the value of virtue, always indeed in the light of the highest loving value which is God. Similarly, as far as the practice of virtue is concerned, we must ever be on the alert against the danger of pursuing a futile course, a course of mere mechanical acts of virtue. The danger can be met and overcome only through constant revitalization of our motive, the very point Lindworsky wishes to stress and which makes very plain that the importance of the role played by meditation in the spiritual life can scarcely be exaggerated.

Love of God, Supreme and Fundamental Motive in Religious-Moral Life

OVER AND ABOVE the motive proper to each particular virtue there must be operative in all our activity, if it is to be perfectly good and supernaturally meritorious, the comprehensive motive of love embracing all the others. But it does not follow at all that the motive must explicitly intervene in every single action, but that it must be vitally operative. Of course, it does mean that the motive of divine love must be renewed with sufficient frequency so that it is in some degree effective, influencing and animating the individual act. But we cannot at all fix a minimum period of universal validity, after which the motive would cease to be effective without further explicit or implicit renewal. But it is clear that as long as divine love remains in the heart of man and his motives are still virtuous, it must follow that the motive in some way exerts its ennobling influence, no matter how faintly. Evidently, however, Christian perfection demands that the Christian see to it that this divine and basic motive impel and animate all his activity, not merely in some fainthearted manner, but with all possible force and interior penetration.

The central motive of Christian morality is love, love in so far as it is obedient. Man's relation to God is the relation of filial love, with its call to eternal participation in God's own love. Still, His love amidst the trials of our earthly pilgrimage is not the love of an equal whom God loves as His like, but the love which is to be proved, the love of a creature for his Lord and Creator. It must manifest itself in acts of religion in which love always adores and in acts of the moral virtues where love is stamped with obedience, where love always obeys (cf. Heb. 10:5-9). Accordingly we may also look upon obedience through love as the fundamental motive. Or if we turn to the basic objective value and basic motive of obedience, we can say: the basic motive must be the will of God. loving and loved.

And since the love of God and His paternal will were revealed to us and given to us to share in Christ, the fundamental motive must ultimately be God's loving will for us in Christ, who brings to us the love and message of His Father. Ultimately the fundamental motive of the Christian merges into the ideal of the following of Christ. The pilot light, the fundamental motive, the ideal of life for the Christian must in some form or another be reducible to obedience and love, as God has taught them to us through Christ and through Him demanded them of us, and as we offer them in return to God in Christ and through Christ.

The Law of Christ, Vol. 1

Love and Obedience: Love and Law

IN EVERY CHAPTER of moral theology, if we conceive of it as the doctrine on the imitation of Christ, it is apparent that love and obedience taken together constitute the essential attitude of the disciple of Christ. We enjoy real friendship with Christ; and in Christ true friendship with the Father. We are united with Him in an ineffable bond of love. But humility, which attests to the truth and authenticity of this love, demands that we remain ever aware of the infinite chasm between our love and that of God, ever conscious of our essential dependence on the all-loving God. Our love for Christ is genuine only if it is reverential adoring love (according to the essence of Christianity as religion) and obedient love (according to the essence of Christian morality). Christ attested His love for the Father and for us through His divine condescension by obediently abasing Himself to the the death of the cross. Through His obedient love He reestablished between man and God the communion of love which was disrupted by the sin of disobedience of our first parents. Our supernatural capacity for love derives from the act of obedience of the new Head of the human race. As with the race as a whole, so it is with the individual. Each individual Christian must prove and preserve his love through obedience. He must merit the eternal communion of love with God through loving obedience on earth. Our life has its supreme purpose and its profoundest meaning in love. Its highest mission is to prove our love in the test of obedience. On the most exalted level love and obedience are one.

In our friendship with Christ our love is always the love of the disciple of Christ. The disciple is always anxious to learn; he seeks to be a truly submissive disciple and never to fail to manifest his appreciation of the Master's authority through his obedience. Obviously the perfection of the disciple's obedience is found only in his love. The world must be made to recognize in our manifestation of obedience to Christ the evidence of our love as Christ attested His love for the Father through His obedience. "But he comes that the world may know that I love the Father, and that I do as the Father has commanded me" (John 14:31).

As love implies obedience, so it implies law, and love and law are essentially and mutually interchangeable. Obedience of love is surely more comprehensive than mere legal obedience, for mere observance of law is the lowest degree of obedience. Mere legal obedience is not yet in the shadow of love. External laws are no more than universal regulations and therefore basically only minimum requirements. Universal rules cannot in fact even prescribe what is highest and best, since the best is not universal and cannot be demanded from men universally. On the contrary, love by its very nature strives for the highest and best and seeks the most perfect manifestation of its ideals in actions.

How can anyone who does not fulfill the minimum requirements of the law progress toward that which is higher and better? Since the minimum requirements are basic for the fulfillment of the law of love, love may never violate or ignore the law. At the same time one who truly loves may not remain at the lowest level of obedience and be satisfied with the bare legal minimum.

In order to avoid confusion in this important matter we must clarify the term *law* as used here. If we understand by law the lowest limits of the least requirement (prescriptive laws), then indeed one must demand of love that in fulfilling the law (which it may never violate) it refuse to rest content with mere observance, but seek constantly to surpass the law. However, if by law (in its total meaning) we understand the directive toward ever loftier heights (laws directed to ends and ideals rather than merely to the prescription or prohibition of acts), then love and only love fulfills the law entirely. "Love ... is the fulfillment of the law" (Rom. 13:10). "For the whole law is fulfilled in one word: Thou shalt love thy neighbor as thyself" (Gal. 5:14). "Now the purpose of this charge is charity" (1 Tim. 1:5).

The new law which embraces everything is the love of Christ (John 13:34ff.; Matt. 22:36ff). Each individual law or command, each individual precept is intended as an expression and a directive or application of the great commandment of love. Hence one can fulfill the individual laws according to their profoundest significance, only if one obeys them in the spirit of love, for only love divines and carries out the deepest purposes of every law.

As much as the virtue of love and the law are intimately correlated, so much do the spirit of love and the spirit of sheer legalism stand in irreconcilable opposition to each other. Love is entirely personal. It regards the person of the lawgiver, it has insight into his mind and purpose and the intention of the law. One possessed of this personal love feels called in person by the lawgiver, summoned to respond with all his powers and according to all the circumstances of the situation. One who is motivated by sheer legalism faces the impersonal law (even though it may not be the mere letter of the law) and asks only: what is the minimum requirement of the law, in order that I may avoid violation of law?

If love demands only this: what must be exactly done or avoided to shun loss of grace and the fall from love, it is very imperfect. But if the fulfillment of the law is still realized through such effort to avoid the total loss of love, the concern is not to be characterized as sheer legalism. Though such love is far from perfect, it is not without real value and genuinely fulfills the law.

Genuine charity, the great-hearted and magnanimous love of the disciple for the Master, is not satisfied with the minimum requirement of the law as ultimate norm, but looks to the loftiest ideals as its ultimate goal. But of course the disciple must be prudent! True charity will prompt him to ask humbly and modestly: In my own present situation, with the capacities now at my disposal (perhaps these are not very prepossessing), what is the better course for me, what is most pleasing to God for me?

The man whose love is truly penetrated with the spirit of humility will never be convinced that he can dispense with the norms laid down by universal law as long as he continues to come into contact with its sternest restrictions. The external law is essential for the discernment of spirits. One whose love is mingled with fear will not be altogether free from concern regarding his steadfastness and perseverance in doing good (although there can be no greater assurance of steadfastness in good than charity, according to the thought of St. Augustine: "Love and do what you will: *Ama et fac quod vis!*"). Humility will assure this steadfastness in good by creating in the loving disciple of the Master an unfailing instinct for the will of God; for humble love gives proof of its steadfastness in good and preserves the disciple in the good, precisely through the constant contacts with the law of God and above all through the living example of Christ. The clear path of love is learnt from the humble insight into God's law and the example of the Master, not for the purpose of discovering merely how to avoid sin but to find what must be done at any time to be able to progress to the higher levels of love.

The spirit of sheer legalism deadens, blinds, depersonalizes. On the contrary, love ceaselessly seeks the divine good pleasure and aims at the most perfect realization of the holy will of God. It sheds the clearest light on the individual commandment or precept of God and bids us harken to the call of the Master in each concrete situation. Love looks upon every command as an invitation of love and responds with love in obedience.

THROUGH THE THREE vows in religion the three great obstacles to holiness are attacked in their very roots: the lust of the eyes through the vow of poverty, the lust of the flesh through the vow of perfect chastity, the pride of life through the vow of obedience.

St. Jerome, St. Bernard, St. Thomas, and others speak of religious profession as a 'second baptism' which deletes all guilt and all punishment for past sins. This view derives its plausibility from the very nature of the religious profession. The day of profession is a great occasion of grace, on which one can most readily rise to the heights of perfect submission to God. The very act of profession through the holy vows is a most direct and immediate effort to give one's self entirely to God. On this occasion the grace of baptism and the baptismal vow, by virtue of the cultal power of the baptized, are uniquely renewed. Hence it is altogether probable that one is freed from all guilt and penalty of sin on this holy occasion.

The vows, most particularly the vows of religious profession, have a great value for the ecclesial community. They assure the Church of the necessary stability, promptness of submission, and readiness of engagement in service on the part of her religious communities, societies, and priests. They safeguard the thoroughness and permanence of the work of the Church; here too the tree and its fruits are assured for the divine service.

The Law of Christ, Vol. 2

THE GRANDEUR OF OBEDIENCE *
R. Garrigou-Lagrange, O.P.

OBEDIENCE IS THE HIGHEST of the three evangelical counsels, just as the pride of life is in itself a graver disorder than the concupiscence of the flesh and that of the eyes. Pride, which was the sin of the rebellious angel and of the first man, is the source of all deviations because it turns us away from God to put our trust in ourselves. In this sense it is a more serious sin than other more shameful sins which incline us toward vile things, but which turn us less directly away from God (St. Thomas). Cold, hard pride, which leads man to refuse to adhere to the word of God or to obey Him, is a more serious sin than inordinate attachment to the pleasures of the senses or to earthly goods. For this reason Christ said to the Pharisees who were led astray by their pride: "Amen I say to you, that the publicans and the harlots shall go into the kingdom of God before you. For John came to you in the way of justice, and you did not believe him. But the publicans and the harlots believed him: but you, seeing it, did not even afterwards repent, that you might believe him" (Matt. 21:31).

* From *The Three Ages of the Interior Life,* by R. Garrigou-Lagrange, O.P. Used by permission of B. Herder Book Co.

We know these things theoretically, but in practice we forget them. We think more readily of the manifest disorders which arise from the concupiscence of the flesh or from that of the eyes, and we do not adequately recognize that the great sin is the sin of him who said: "*Non serviam,* I will not serve." This is the principal sin of the world that calls itself 'modern', while claiming to separate itself from the Church. It still desires indeed to repress gross instincts, to struggle against avarice, to labor for the amelioration of the lot of the working class, but it intends to do all this by itself, without the help of God, of our Lord, and of the Church. Only too often it wishes to obey only its own reason, its own judgment, its own will, and this rationalism leads it to disobey reason rather than to obey God. Its own reason leads it, like the prodigal son, into dishonorable, debasing servitude, occasionally into real tyranny, that of rebellious popular passions and that of criminal, unjust laws, put into effect in spite of the protests of conscience, in the interest of the party in power. Obedience to the commandments of God and of the Church would free society from these servitudes which oppress the best and lead society into disorder, confusion, and ruin. Such an evil can be cured only by a holy reaction in the direction of profound, humble, Christian obedience. Yet the grandeur of obedience, even in relatively good circles, is too often misunderstood.

A contemplative religious wrote to us recently as follows:

"In our days people have often lost sight of the intrinsic value of religious profession. They no longer see how the great vows chiefly uplift intrinsically the whole of religious life. This profound and superior idea is exiled; it no longer finds a milieu to understand it. Very frequently people think only superficially and extrinsically about this fundamental idea. The influence of the great theology of the Middle Ages has lost its dominion. For this great error, casuists, who have materialized the concept of religious life, are responsible. Under the pretext of avoiding sin, they have considered everything from a negative point of view. Religious obedience has lost its profound meaning. The vows of poverty and chastity, which are more frequently transgressed, and often mortally, have in fact come to the foreground in several manuals; whereas obedience, which is the foundation of the whole edifice, has been placed in the background, because it is rare that disobedience is a mortal sin.

"They have thus actually reversed supernatural values. In many centers this condition of affairs has become a general state of mind. The positive and profound value of religious immolation by the vows, the complete domination of the religious life and of its activity by the virtues of religion and obedience, which render the existence of a religious something 'sacred,' has been lost sight of. As a consequence, they no longer see the intrinsic value of the religious life, and some have remarked that this deficiency often works on vocations like a 'fatal corrosive.' For many, obedience is no longer anything but a 'discipline,' an 'exterior religious observance,' a professional practice which one can personally sublimate if one is noble-hearted, as a soldier or a clerk can sublimate the practices of his profession or his position."

The better to see the value of this virtue, we shall consider first of all from what servitude it delivers us and what are its spiritual fruits with regard to union with God.

The Type of Servitude from which Obedience Delivers Us

OBEDIENCE DELIVERS US from a two-fold slavery: that of self-will and that of our own judgment.

Obedience to God, to His spiritual and temporal representatives, daily assures the conformity of our will with the divine will. It thus delivers us from self-will, that is from a will which is not conformed to that of God, and which through pride goes astray, acting contrary to the current of grace and refusing to act in the true direction.

Self-will thus defined is the source of every sin. For this reason St. Bernard says: "Take away self-will, and there will no longer be any hell." Self-will is particularly dangerous because it can corrupt everything. Even what is best in man becomes evil when self-will enters in, for it takes itself as its end instead of subordinating itself to God. If the Lord sees that it inspires a fast, a penance, a sacrifice, He rejects them as pharisaical works accomplished through pride in order to make oneself esteemed. Without going that far, we must admit that we cling greatly to our own will. Occasionally we hold to our way of doing good more than to the good itself; we wish it to be done, but by ourselves and in our way. When this egoism becomes collective, it may be called a corruption of family spirit; it is the source of a great many unpleasantnesses, partialities, defamations. Sometimes a certain group wishes to promote a good work, or it hinders one from being developed. It is like wishing to smother a child who seems to be one too many, when as a matter of fact it may become the honor of the family. Evidently such a course of action can only displease the Lord.

In religion, the vow of obedience assures the mortification of this dangerous self-will which turns the soul away from salvation. That it may control self-will, the vow must be practiced with a spirit of faith, seeing in the orders of superiors, in spite of their imperfections or defects, orders given by God, from whom all power comes. Religious obedience should be prompt and universal: that is, it should extend alike to little and great things; it should obey all legitimate superiors, whether they be amiable or not, particularly prudent or less enlightened, holy or less perfect, because it is always God who speaks, as long as the order given is not contrary to a higher law and does not exceed the limits of the constitutions which the religious promised to observe. Such obedience is a deliverance, for it assures from day to day the conformity of man's will with God's will, and by that very fact it greatly fortifies the will while rectifying it.

Obedience delivers us also from the servitude of our own judgment, that is, from an excessively subjective judgment not sufficiently founded on truth, not conformed to the judgment of God. Our own personal judgment is in this sense the source of singularity in conduct and stubbornness which leads to nothing and impedes the good which others wish to do. It is a hasty judgment springing from our prejudices, our evil dispositions, our self-love, our pride. Occasionally the enemy of our soul is the one who suggests it to us or confirms it when we ourselves have already formed it. Following Aristotle, St. Thomas often says: "According as we are well or ill disposed in our will and sensible faculties, a given end seems good or evil to us." The proud man judges that what flatters his pride is excellent, whereas the humble man judges that humiliation is good for him.

Our own judgment often leads to rash judgment, contrary to justice and charity. In it there is servitude, slavery; we are the slaves of our egoistic prejudices, and they lead us away from salvation and union with God.

Obedience delivers us from this slavery by assuring the conformity of our practical judgment with that of the representative of God, who has the right to give us an order in His name.

Obedience demands the conformity of the practical judgment (which immediately directs voluntary choice) to the order given. The thing commanded, materially considered in itself, may be at times imprudent, inopportune; obedience does not then demand its approval as such by a speculative judgment (another superior in a few months will perhaps see the thing in a different light). In this case, let us leave the thing commanded for what it is materially in itself, and consider only that it is formally commanded to us, here and now, and commanded by God, in spite of the imperfection of His messenger. At this moment, it is what we should do, and even if the superior is mistaken, we are not mistaken practically in obeying him. It may be that this representative of God is mistaken on some point or another; he is not infallible like the pope speaking *ex cathedra*, but as long as the order given is not manifestly contrary to a higher law and does not exceed the powers of the one who commands, we are obliged to obey, and our practical judgment is not deceived in obeying. Sometimes the messenger of Providence may limp, but he is still God's messenger; he brings us a letter or an order of divine origin.

The effective practice of the counsel of obedience is found especially in the religious life; it is a much surer road for reaching perfection more rapidly by progressive conformity to the will of God even in the depths of our will and the details of daily life.

But we must at least have the spirit of the counsel actually to reach Christian perfection, that is, the spirit of detachment from self-will to which we cling. As a child should obey his father, his mother, and the teachers who train him, every Christian should obey all who are for him the spiritual or temporal representatives of God. There is the obedience of the wife to her husband, that of the soldier to his leaders, of the servant to his master, of every subordinate to his superiors, of every Christian to the Church and to the constituted authorities in the Church. If this obedience is practiced, not merely in a servile, mechanical, exterior manner, but in the spirit of faith, it greatly forms the will, renders it flexible, and fortifies it while subordinating it daily a little better to the will of God, of the living God who vivifies us. It is well to recall often that "there is no power but from God" (Rom. 13:1), that one cannot obey an equal, but only a superior, and that, in short, it is God who is obeyed.

Similarly we must obey events so far as they are signs of the divine will. Theology teaches that the divine will is manifested to us not only by the precepts and the counsels, but also by events willed or at least permitted by God. Nothing, in fact, happens unless God has willed it (if it is a good), or permitted it (if it is an evil). To be perfect our obedience should take into consideration these signs of the will of God. For example, legitimate success in an examination gives us a position that makes possible for us the accomplishment of a more extended good; let us not compromise this good by imprudent or cowardly acts. On the contrary, we are humiliated by a failure, or by an illness, which sometimes shows us that the way we are engaged in is not what God wishes for us.

There are particularly significant events which, from the temporal point of view, change the situation of a family or the organization of society. We must know how to draw the greatest spiritual profit from them and not wish at any cost to revert to an order of things which was useful in the past and which probably is no longer willed by God in the period in which we are living. One does not go back up the course of life or that of history; the old man does not return to adolescence; and our century cannot return to what existed in the thirteenth, though it should seek to profit by all the good handed down by past ages in order to prepare a future in which God truly reigns.

In all these forms of obedience to all that manifests the will of God, in obedience to the duty of the present moment from minute to minute, the Christian ought always to have before his eyes as his model the Savior, who was "obedient unto death, even to the death of the cross" (Phil. 2:8). Thus the martyrs and all the saints obeyed, finding their joy in dying to self-will that they might feed on that of God according to the Savior's words: "My food is to do the will of Him who sent Me" (John 4:34).

The Fruits of Obedience

To COMPREHEND the grandeur and the fruits of obedience, we should remember that it is more perfect to offer God one's will and judgment than to offer Him exterior goods through voluntary poverty, or one's body and heart though chastity. It is also more perfect to offer Him one's will than to sacrifice to Him exteriorly a lamb or a dove, as was done in the sacrifices of the Old Testament. With this meaning, Scripture says: "Obedience is better than sacrifices: and to hearken rather than to offer the fat of rams" (1 Kings 15:22).

The fruits of obedience are chiefly the following: it gives a great rectitude of judgment, great strength of will, the highest liberty of spirit.

The greatest rectitude of judgment comes from the fact that obedience makes us participate in the very wisdom of God; it renders us more wise than the wisest, more prudent than the ancients. In the most difficult and the most complicated situations, it brings us the solution that is practically true for us here and now. Practically, we do not make a mistake in obeying, even if the superior is mistaken. By humble obedience a simple lay brother, St. Martin de Porres of Peru, did more for his country than statesmen who do not think of praying to obtain light.

As a reward for fidelity, perfect obedience obtains from the Holy Spirit, even here on earth, the inspirations of the gift of counsel that direct us in the most hidden things of the spirit which a director or a superior could not state precisely and which our prudence could not succeed in settling properly. The gift of counsel is particularly necessary for those whose duty it is to command, that they may do so supernaturally; for this reason if a man does not begin by obeying well, he will never know how to command. God gives His lights to the obedient.

Obedience also gives great strength of will. Naturalism declares at times that obedience weakens the will; on the contrary, it strengthens the will tenfold. When, in fact, there is no reason to doubt that an order comes from God through the intermediary of a legitimate superior, it is also certain that by divine grace the fulfillment of this order is possible. As St. Augustine says: "God, in fact, never commands the impossible; but He tells us to do what we are able and to ask Him for the grace to accomplish what we cannot do of ourselves." Therefore St. Augustine used to pray: "Lord, give me the strength to accomplish what you command, and command what you wish."

Because God never commands the impossible, when in certain circumstances martyrdom is of precept, in the sense that it must be undergone rather than deny the faith, God gives the strength to obey, to be faithful to Him in the midst of torture; and He gives this strength even to children, to young virgins, like St. Agnes, or to old men weakened by age.

Without going as far as martyrdom, obedience works prodigies. We need only cite the example of the first sixteen sons of St. Dominic. Strong in the pope's blessing, the holy founder sent them from Toulouse into various parts of Europe to found convents and to carry on the apostolate. Having no money to give them, the saint said to them: "You shall beg your food; I will pray for you three times a day. I promise you that, in spite of the distress of poverty, you will never lack what is necessary." The sixteen religious, trusting in the words of their Father, obeyed; they left joyfully like the first apostles, and were not slow in multiplying in Italy, Spain, England, even in faraway Poland, and among the infidels of the Orient whom they went to evangelize. This example and many others confirm the grandeur of obedience. When an order is given, and there is no doubt but that it comes from God, the grace which makes its fulfillment possible is most certainly bestowed. If a person prays to be faithful to this grace and not to resist it, he accomplishes the command not without difficulties sometimes, but he accomplishes it.

Finally, obedience, far from being a servitude, bestows the highest liberty, that of the children of God, as voluntary poverty gives true spiritual riches, as perfect chastity obtains the intimacy of the love of God. Of this obedience St. Paul speaks when he reminds us that we should desire to be "delivered from its slavery to corruption into the freedom of the glory of the sons of God" (Rom. 8:21): "Where the Spirit of the Lord is, there is freedom" (2 Cor. 3:17), that is to say, deliverance, for divine truth delivers the soul from error. Injecting truth into life, obedience sets man free from the prejudices of the world, from its maxims, modes, and infatuations. It frees him from excessive preoccupation about the judgment of men, from concern about what people will say, instead of doing good and letting them talk. Obedience delivers him from his doubts, hesitations, and anxieties. It simplifies life while elevating it. With it liberty grows, for in man liberty comes from the intellect, and the more enlightened his intellect is, the more free he is. The more man understands that God is the sovereign Good, the freer he is not to respond to the attraction of earthly goods, and the stronger he is against the threats of the impious. Who was freer than the martyrs? Through love and obedience they freely gave their blood in witness of divine truth, and neither iron nor fire could force an abjuration from them. They obeyed in a spirit of faith and for love of God, like the Savior, who was obedient "unto death, even to death of the cross."

The grandeur of obedience is expressed in this frequently quoted, holy expression: "To serve God is to reign," that is, to reign over one's passions, over the spirit of the world, over the enemy of souls and his suggestions; it is to reign in the very kingdom of God and, so to speak, to share in His independence toward all created things. It is to place oneself like a docile instrument in His hands for all that He wishes, following out St. Augustine's words which we have already quoted: "Lord, give me the strength to accomplish what you command, and command what you wish."

Of a certainty obedience thus understood prepares for the contemplation of divine things; it prepares us to see the will of God or His permission in all pleasurable or painful events, and it helps us to understand "That to them that love God [and persevere in His love], all things work together unto good."

IN DIFFICULT CIRCUMSTANCES, zeal should beg the Holy Spirit for the light of the gift of counsel, not that it should propose to do extraordinary things, but to accomplish as perfectly as possible the ordinary duties fixed by the wisdom of the Church and obedience: to say Mass well or to unite oneself intimately to it, to be faithful to prayer under its different forms, and to one's duties of state. Sometimes heroic obedience may be demanded; should it be lacking, the greatest qualities of mind and heart would not suffice to compensate for its absence. Some servants of God, who were manifestly called to sanctity, seem not to have reached it because they lacked this heroic virtue.

The Harmonizing of Docility to the Holy Spirit with Obedience and Prudence

THE INSPIRATION of the Holy Spirit, far from destroying the obedience due to superiors, aids and facilitates its practice. Inspiration should be understood with the implied condition that obedience enjoins nothing contrary to it.

In the words of Father Lallemant, S.J.: "The only thing to be feared is that superiors may sometimes follow human prudence excessively, and that for want of discernment they may condemn the lights and inspirations of the Holy Spirit, treating them as illusions and reveries, and prescribe for those to whom God communicates Himself by such favors as if they were invalids. In this case, a person should still obey, but God will one day correct the error of these rash spirits and teach them to their cost not to condemn His graces without understanding them and without being qualified to pass judgment on them."

Father Lallemant adds: "What renders them incapable of judging rightly of these things, is that they are entirely exterior souls, completely engrossed in external activity and with only a meager spiritual life, never having risen above the lowest degrees of mental prayer. And what leads them to judge these things is that they do not wish to appear ignorant in these matters of which, nevertheless, they have neither experience nor knowledge" (*La Doctrine Spirituelle*).

Neither should it be said that docility to the Holy Spirit renders useless the deliberations of prudence or the counsel of experienced people. The interior Master tells us, on the contrary, to be attentive to what we can see for ourselves; He also invites us to consult enlightened persons, but adds that we should at the same time have recourse to Him. As St. Augustine says: "God orders us to do what we can, and to ask for the grace to accomplish what we cannot do by ourselves." The Holy Spirit sent even St. Paul to Ananias to learn from him what he was to do. This docility then harmonizes perfectly with obedience, prudence, and humility; it even greatly perfects these virtues.

The Firmness of Faith

THE FIRMNESS of faith manifests itself more and more by love for the word of God contained in Holy Scripture, by the cult of tradition preserved in the writings of the fathers, by perfect adherence to even the most minute details of the doctrine proposed by the Church, by docility to the directions of the supreme shepherd, the vicar of Jesus Christ. This firmness of faith appears especially in the martyrs, and also, during great conflicts of opinion, in those who, far from vacillating, are capable of sacrificing their self-love in order to keep immutably to the right road.

In the practical order, this firmness of perfect faith is also evident when the servants of God, faced with the most painful and unforeseen events, are not astonished at the unsearchable ways of Providence, disconcerting to reason. Of this firm faith Abraham gave evidence when he prepared to sacrifice his son Isaac, in spite of the fact that God

Himself had promised him that from this son was to spring his posterity, the multitude of believers. In the Epistle to the Hebrews, St. Paul says: "By faith Abraham, when he was tried, offered Isaac: and he that had received the promises, offered up his only begotten son.... Accounting that God is able to raise up even from the dead. Whereupon also he received him" (Heb 11:17, 19). This was a remote figure of the sacrifice of Christ.

This heroic obedience emanated from heroic faith. In the practical affairs of daily life as well as in the mysteries which we must believe, the obscurity of certain ways of God comes from a light too strong for our weak eyes. So in the life of Christ, His passion was at one and the same time the darkest hour, considered from a worldly point of view, and the most luminous from a spiritual point of view. This is what made St. Philip Neri say with admirable firmness of faith: "I thank thee, Lord God, with all my heart, that things are not going as I wish, but as thou dost." In Isaias the Lord says: "For my thoughts are not your thoughts, nor are your ways my ways" (Isa. 55:8).

OUR OBEDIENCE AND
OUR UNION WITH CHRIST OUR SAVIOR *
Bernard Leeming, S.J.

OUR LORD greatly commends obedience to us. "For whoever does the will of my Father in heaven, he is my brother, and sister and mother" (Matt. 12:50). Even his own dear mother was dear to him most of all because she "heard the word of God" and kept it (Luke 9:28). "He who has my commandments and keeps them, he it is who loves me. But he who loves me will be loved by my Father, and I will love him and manifest myself to him." Our Lord could not make us a greater promise than to be loved of His Father, to be loved by Him, and to receive a manifestation, a revelation of Our Lord Himself.

ONE CANNOT BE UNITED to God in will without somehow coming to be aware of that fusion of wills and thus coming into almost direct contact with God Himself. St. Catherine of Siena was told that "the truly obedient man always retains the desire of submission, and that this desire is like an inward refrain of music" (quoted by Marmion from the

* From *The Mysticism of Obedience*, by Rev. Bernard Leeming, S.J. Copyright by the Daughters of St. Paul, 1964.

187

"Dialogue on Obedience": *Christ the Ideal of the Monk*, p. 262). In this way, obedience is really a form of contemplation, simple, easy, and effective; and not wearisome to the head. "This is what I am ordered to do. It is God's will for me. I do it. That is God. That is all."

Nor is this hindered if our obedience is very active, and if in obedience we use initiative and ingenuity and resource. It is then that the very powers of the mind are given to God, what intelligence we may have, what force of character, what gift of imagination, even what magnetism we may have to attract others. These are given to God, through the hands of human beings who represent Him, and used gladly as we are directed, because there is great security in using all our gifts as the mind of God, represented by a human superior, directs. Nothing could be more mistaken than to take the comparisons often used by the saints, of a dead body, or an old man's staff, and apply them beyond their real application. They are not used to indicate complete passivity, but to indicate that we make no resistance to being moved from this house to another, from this post to the other, or, even, that we are content if obedience makes no use of our talents at all.

WHAT IS CALLED 'blind' obedience certainly does not mean unintelligent obedience; it only means an obedience that is 'blind' to considerations merely human and selfish. The more intelligent people are, the more obedient they can be, since they must use their intelligence to obey well.

All this granted, there still remains the case of a command or a direction, the reasonableness or wisdom of which is difficult or even impossible to accept. It is here that both natural and supernatural motives can help the understanding. Naturally, one can appreciate that a superior may not be able to disclose all the information he or she may have. A superior is bound, in a variety of cases, by the obligation of keeping confidences. Moreover, a superior, in concrete situations, may be faced by what amounts to a choice, if not of evils, at least of one good as against another.

There is a mental attitude that can be built up which gives antecedent inclination towards cooperation and happy acquiescence in the direction or the orders from superiors. There can, of course, be no assent contrary to the known truth; but often the truth about the wisdom of a course of action, or of policy, comes to be perceived differently according to the way one allows the mind to act. Obedience,— even granted all the obligation of making representations to higher authorities,—requires faith and the object of faith is obscure: we see now in a glass darkly, and only after this life shall we see clearly, face to face. Yet faith does give understanding, and the vision it gives can perceive the action of God and His over-riding providence, beneath the deficiencies of the human agent, and can perceive God's will in what naturally may only appear as prejudice, favoritism or vanity.

In the Church today, as the Council shows, there is need of adaptation to modern conditions; and what is true of the Church may be true, too, of religious orders and congregations. But the exact nature of the adaptations needed gives rise to different judgments. Some think that changes are not, in fact, needed in this or that body; others may think that suggested modifications of rule or custom may be too small or too great. But whatever may be decided, the connection between faith and obedience remains unchanged; it is that faith which can give serenity and glad cooperation even amid discussions of adaptations, and in any decisions ultimately made.

Obedience in faith can and does take the long view, and not the narrow and restricted view. God's providence works oddly. St. Paul confessed that God's ways are unsearchably mysterious. Christians know that God never permits evil save for the ultimate purpose of drawing good from His permission of evil. But *how* God draws good from His permission of evil, what particular good He secures by the permission of a particular evil,—this the human mind cannot fathom. No man can see the whole of the course of God's providence; only a small part of it falls within our observation and our awareness. Our human perspective is necessarily restricted and only through union with God can the perspective be enlarged to embrace, even though only obscurely, the whole plan and purposes of God.

PERHAPS GOD SOMETIMES wishes a poor superior, an incompetent superior, in order to use them as a lesson for subjects, or perhaps one special subject, a lesson to teach them what to do, and what not to do, when they themselves are superiors! And to oppose that superior, to magnify his defects, to allow feelings to become ruffled, or depression to take possession of the spirit—this is clearly to oppose God Himself, contrary to what we have promised Him. Perhaps God wants a certain work to fail, and to fail precisely through our most obedient efforts and strivings, in order to obtain some greater good of which we cannot be aware. In this sense, it is perfectly true that obedience, although its proper fruit may seem to be to perfect the will, nevertheless also perfects the understanding: it gives the understanding length and breadth and depth, conforming it to the infinite wisdom and knowledge of God. Often only in retrospect are we able to see that it was not only virtuous to obey, but was very wise, also.

"Because you are conscious within yourselves," says St. Ignatius of Loyola, "that you have undergone this yoke of obedience for the love of God, to the end that you might, in following the superior's will, more assuredly follow the divine will; doubt not, but that the most faithful charity of Our Lord continually directs you and leads you in the right way by the hands of those whom He gives you for superiors."

THE YOKE OF OBEDIENCE: it can indeed bear heavily, it can chafe and sometimes cut, and force us to go on and on dragging a wearisome burden. Christ Himself felt the burden and even prayed that it might be lifted from Him. And yet to Him, His Father's charity was faithful, most faithful; and even through the hands of Annas and Caiphas, of Judas and of Pilate, that faithful charity of His Father led Christ in that right way that led to our salvation. Christ obeyed for me. Christ trusted His Father for me. Christ loved me and delivered Himself for me, delivered Himself for me not only that my sins might be forgiven, that grace might come to me, but also that to me might come the honor of sharing His obedience with Him, of offering the noblest part of me to His Father with His offering, even of making myself one with His self-giving for the redemption of mankind.

NOTHING SO UNITES US to Christ as obedience; for perfect obedience gives to Him our liberty, our memory, our very understanding. What more have we that we can give? And this giving is the most perfect charity: if you love me, keep my commandments. Yet we give them in such simple, often almost commonplace, ways: doing what we are told, be it great or small, be it important or unimportant, be it hard or easy. Nevertheless, if we do give our whole selves to Him in this simplicity of obedience, be sure that His most faithful charity does stay with us. Gradually He takes us all: our remnants of self-contentment, our rags of pride, our pettiness of devious self-seeking; of all these and suchlike His faithful charity gradually strips us: a pain at once and yet a joy. He is meek and humble of heart, even in His purifying of us to make us more fit to share with Him in His unutterably pure sacrifice to God. He fills us with His own love of His Father. He gives us sometimes to feel something of that joy with which He went to His Father. He allows us sometimes to see that His saving work goes on, even through me; but yet not through me, only through Him, and I spoil it, and yet He does not let me spoil it quite, because it is truly He who obeys in me, and His obeying is of infinite love, even God's own love.

The mystery of obedience: it is the mystery of Christ; the mystery of the Blessed Trinity, in whom all is one, even to the blessedness of giving of the Whole and yet receiving of the Whole. And yet, it is quite simple: if you love me, keep my commandments.

Consequently, let us pray for opportunities of obedience: that we may do each task because God commands it, that we may find our love and our life in doing His will. If the commands are simple, thank God; if they are difficult—perhaps removal from an office, perhaps subordination to an uncongenial superior—thank God more, for what else are we for but to obey?

Our Share in the Life of God

OBEDIENCE IS LIKE FAITH. Often, though we know it is fully reasonable to believe, the obscurity of faith comes home to us: *how* can it be that Christ is present beneath the appearances of a wafer? *How* can a good God permit so many evils? Nevertheless, this obscurity does not shake our faith, though it may afflict the imagination and the power of reasoning. We know that He is King of kings and Lord of lords, and that His dwelling is in unapproachable light; no human eye has ever seen Him or can ever see Him (Tim. 6:16). We know that "my thoughts are not your thoughts, nor your ways my ways; for as the heavens are exalted above the earth, so are my ways exalted above your ways and my thoughts above your thoughts" (Isaias 4:8, 9). Nothing could shake our faith, because it is God whom we believe.

Now similarly, our obedience like our faith involves obscurity. How *could* God be represented by one so narrow, prejudiced, and unlikable? How could God ratify so inept a policy, one based on complete failure to appreciate the conditions? How can God permit this situation to continue, when His own interests are at stake? Such obscurities may indeed trouble our imaginations and even our powers of reasoning; nevertheless they cannot shake the deep conviction that in obeying *this* superior, in *this* policy, in *this* manner of proceeding, I am obeying

God Himself; I am doing *His* will, and not the ignorant, stupid, or prejudiced will of any creature. My obedience rests on the faith that believes God does act through creatures, that He is immanent to creatures and not afar off. St. Margaret Mary had revelations from Our Lord, revelations approved by the Church afterwards; and yet Our Lord said to her that she should prefer the will of her superiors to any command of His. We look with eyes of faith, not upon a weak creature, but upon the infinitely holy and infinitely wise God of all consolation, who acts in and through the creature.

Blessed Claude de la Colombiere once wrote: "A superior may govern badly, but it is impossible that God should not govern you well by means of him. My dear Sister, let that be your deep conviction. For if you do not base yourself firmly on this principle, you are losing your time in religion; for your whole life is nothing but obedience, and this obedience is meritless unless offered to God in the person whom He has put in place of Himself. And we certainly do not turn our gaze on God when we undertake to judge, examine—and above all condemn what is commanded us. When it is the Holy Ghost who possesses us, He inspires us with the simplicity of a child who finds everything good and everything reasonable; or, if you prefer, with a divine prudence which discovers God in everything, and recognizes Him in all those who represent Him, even in those who are poorest in virtue and in natural and supernatural qualities" (Oeuvres).

How IS IT POSSIBLE to be united in mind with a superior who is narrow, unwise, and imprudent in his commands? Christ could obey His Father absolutely because His Father was absolute truth, absolute wisdom; but how can we conform our minds to one who is by no means absolute truth or wisdom?

The answer is that when the superior commands, we unite our wills and minds with his in so far as he commands, not necessarily in so far as his command is designed to attain a particular purpose. The purpose of the command is not part of the command. For instance, a provincial superior may order a local superior to be indulgent, or to be severe, with a particular subject. The local superior may on natural grounds be convinced that indulgence, or severity, is injurious to the subject, that the provincial superior is mistaken in his estimate of the method required. It is here, partly, that the mystery enters; for the theory of obedience holds that the judgment about success or failure is irrelevant: who can tell what, in God's eyes, is success or failure? The order must be obeyed, and in the spirit, with trust in God's over-riding providence; He will bless the obedience, although we cannot see how. For me, I see Christ in the command and that is enough. What does it matter, in the last analysis, about the 'success' or 'failure' of the policy? God must look to that; and I can leave it to Him, doing so the more trustfully the less I see how He can draw good out of it.

How do we progress in obedience? Very generally at the beginning of our religious life obedience on the whole is not difficult; there may be strange customs, repugnances to be overcome in accommodating ourselves to different points of the rule. But on the whole, obedience is likely to be taken more or less for granted as part of the religious regime. Nevertheless, sooner or later trials are likely to arise. A superior may not understand us, or may disapprove of us; and then obedience can be a very arid affair indeed. There is small comfort in it; and if one takes literally the superior for God, one is inclined to imagine that a superior's disapproval means God's disapproval. This is not, of course, strictly true; for a superior is not judge of our spiritual state, but takes the place of God in telling us what to do. Nevertheless, a superior's disapproval may be a searing trial, especially for some characters; and it is then that one must walk by blind faith, hoping against hope, as it were, that God will bring all right, possessing our soul in patience and bending our minds and wills as best we can. This may be only a purifying trial: to wean us from our purely natural obedience, to prevent us thinking obedience is within our own natural power. Then we can only be faithful, be patient, and trust God: believing still that He is acting in the superior.

But, if we are faithful, the light will surely break through: there can come a certain sense of reverence for God, even in this superior; a sense that we are really held captive by God, and so a cer-.

tain peace in obeying which is not upset by surges of feeling, whether of depression or of irritation or of rebellion. God is there in spite of everything; and somehow fears begin to vanish: in sickness or in health, in success or failure: "For I know whom I have believed, and I am certain that he is able to guard the trust committed to me against that day" (2 Tim. 1:12). Our transformation into Christ proceeds; and His obedience begins to seem a reality to us, and self-will, self-settlement, self-judgment begin to fade away. The memory, the imagination, and even the reasoning powers may play tricks; but the calm conviction remains that it is good for me to cleave to the Lord, and that at the head of my book it is written that I should do thy Will, O God.

St. Ignatius of Loyola puts three degrees of obedience: the first, when we actually do what we are commanded; the second, when we do it willingly; and the third, when we submit our understanding to the superior's and come to have the same judgment as his. Now these are not necessarily stages through which we have to pass; though indeed they may be kinds of stages through which we pass; but they clearly indicate divisions into which obedience may fall. It is possible to do what we are ordered but to rebel interiorly, or even to grumble and complain and yet carry out the order. It is possible also to cajole a superior into an agreement with what we want. This is indeed a certain kind of obedience. Then there is willingness in obedience:

to do the thing promptly, perseveringly, and putting our best efforts into it to make it succeed. But the highest degree is had when we agree with the superior's mind and have the same view and outlook on the thing as he has.

It is clear that this last most closely approaches to the obedience of Christ to His Father: His doctrine was not His own, but His Father's. He judges with the Father; He does not speak of Himself, but as the Father gives Him to speak; and He is the very word of the Father, the expression of the Father, the very mind of the Father: He and His Father are one. If the superior represents God for us, then no lower standard than Our Lord's obedience to His Father can content us.

REFLECTIONS ON OBEDIENCE *
A Basic Ignatian Concept
Karl Rahner, S.J.

Jesuit obedience is something that is poorly understood; some people even call it the obedience of a corpse. But although Ignatius emphasized the importance of this virtue for the members of his Society—understandably enough, for an order engaged in the active care of souls—Jesuit obedience does not differ in fact from that of the other religious orders of the Catholic Church.

Our subject is far from being neglected: in the last ten years, just in Western Europe, at least fifty books and articles have been devoted to this theme. One has the disturbing sense that perhaps one is only writing in order to be listed in the bibliography of this subject. In a short article, one can hardly expect to say anything at all comprehensive or conclusive, and the following pages are offered as nothing more than marginal notes on a vast topic.

Misconceptions

In its essence, obedience in religious life has nothing to do with the obedience which children owe their parents and others in authority, who are

---

* Used by permission of *Cross Currents,* a quarterly review.

supposedly equipped to watch over their upbringing. The reason is that this latter type of obedience aims directly at its own eventual transcendence. By means of this training in obedience, the obedience of childhood later becomes unnecessary; the adult, liberated from the domination of blind instinctive drives, is able to command himself. On the other hand, in the case of obedience in religious life, we assume that the subject is already an adult. Also, we do not assume that the person who commands is necessarily more intelligent, more foresighted or morally more mature than the one who obeys. If this were so, the relationship of superior to subject would be an educational relationship. The one obeying would be a child or a man of infantile character, who is not yet responsible for his own behavior. Human nature being what it is, there are such people even in religion. Their percentage, however, should not be greater than that found in other walks of life. And I suppose that, generally speaking, it is not. After all, if people are childish and unfit for life, they have many places to hide; religion would hardly be their only refuge.

One conclusion can be drawn from these rather obvious considerations: Superiors should not act as if by nature or by reason of their office they are more intelligent, more clever, more morally steadfast, or more provident and wise in the ways of the world. This may be true in individual cases, for the world is not so constructed that only the more stupid become superiors. But it should be soberly stated (for subjects, lest they demand too much of superiors, something which would be unjust and show a lack of charity; for superiors, lest they delude themselves): the higher the office, the smaller the possibility, humanly speaking, of filling it. For we may reasonably presume that the degrees of variation in mental and moral gifts among men are less than the degrees of difficulty found in the management of various social enterprises. As a rule, therefore, more important duties will unavoidably be more poorly performed than lesser ones. No judgment is passed here on any particular case. As a matter of fact, sometimes people do grow in stature in performing more difficult tasks. But for the most part, the opposite takes place. Along with the assumption of a more important responsibility comes the painful realization, felt both by the superior and those about him, that the man is far from being equipped for his task. The defective fulfillment of higher obligations cruelly lays bare the shortcomings of a man's capacities which previously escaped our attention.

Let us repeat once more: obedience in religious life is not the obedience of children. Therefore, the religious superior should not play the role of an Olympian papa. In the life of the cloister (even in orders of women) there are still to be found age-old rituals governing the etiquette of superiors, involving demands of respect from subjects, secretiveness, manifestations of superiority, appeals of superiors to a higher wisdom, displays of condescension, etc. All this should gradually be permitted to wither away. Superiors should cast a long and quiet glance at the world around them: those who are truly powerful and influential, who receive a great deal of unquestioning obedience, place no value on ceremonial of this sort. They find no need of concealing their weakness, anxiety, and insecurity behind a pompous front. Superiors should quietly admit that in certain circumstances their subjects know more than they do about the matter at hand. Given the specialization of modern life with its need for countless types of ability to cover its many areas, present-day superiors can no longer act as if they can understand any and every matter that falls under their authority. In the good old days a superior could do everything that he commanded his subject to do. He had previously done the very thing himself. He had distinguished himself (otherwise he normally would not have been made superior) and so had given proof that he understood at least as much as his subject. At least this was the rule in the past, though naturally there were exceptions to it even then. Today it is quite inevitable that what formerly was the exception should become the rule. Every religious superior has many subjects who necessarily possess a knowledge of science, of pastoral functioning, of current affairs, which the superior (who can be a specialist himself only in a single, limited field) cannot possess. He finds himself or ought to find himself, in the same position with regard to the knowledge of others as the President does with respect to the mysteries about which his atomic experts advise him. The superior, therefore, is dependent upon the information of counselors to an extent not required in the past. The advisors, usually provided for superiors by the constitutions of an order, today in many ways possess an utterly new and more urgent function than in former times when they were in practice only a democratic check on an excessively authoritarian and uncontrolled government of one individual.

It would be well, therefore, if superiors would always seek the information they need in a spirit of objectivity and concreteness, for they must give commands for objective and concrete situations, no matter what be the value of obedience to an objectively erroneous command. This is not always done. A secret-cabinet policy may often be a well-intentioned means of acquiring such objective counsel, but it is not always effective. In religious life, on final analysis, there can be no real democratization of obedience, as will later be shown. But there can be objective and clearly determined methods of procedure for achieving the counsel and information needed for decision. Unfortunately this is not always the case. Again I insist, mostly for the benefit of the hostile critic of religious obedience: those in religious life realize that religious obedience is not the obedience of children. It does not presuppose children, but mature adults. And only in the measure that it can legitimately presuppose this can it be at all true to it own proper nature.

Again, religious obedience is no mere "regulation of traffic." Certainly where men live together in a community there must be order. That there be order, the power to command must be present. Not everyone can do as he pleases, and moreover, not everyone can discover for himself just what is required by the total whole. Command, however, implies obedience. When obedience is conceived merely as a rational or rationally prescribed function of order for the life of a community and for the coordination of its organs and activities toward a common goal, then perhaps the pattern has been discovered which can intelligently explain civic and national obedience.

In this concept, however, the peculiar nature of religious obedience has not been grasped, even though it cannot be denied that in religious life this aspect of obedience is also present, and necessarily so. Religious obedience is no rational and inevitable regulation of traffic, by which every sensible person submits himself to the traffic policeman, and in which a coordinating agency takes care that everything moves without friction toward the common good. At times attempts have been made to explain religious obedience in this merely rational fashion. But this explanation is too easy and cannot reach the real roots and depths of religious obedience. And yet the obedience entailed in the rational regulation of traffic and of the sensible coordination of work in a common effort is part of religious obedience, though it is not the most characteristic nor the most profound element of the evangelical counsel. For the daily functioning of obedience in religious life it ought to be noted that this element of obedience is present; yes, that it is almost identical with the superficial tasks of quotidian obedience. For day-to-day life, therefore, a certain de-mystification of obedience should quietly take place, perhaps to a greater extent than is now permitted in some parts. In the many small details of daily life, obedience is in reality nothing else than a rational method by which rational beings live together.

Therefore, the superior should not try to give the impression that he stands under the immediate inspiration of the Holy Ghost, but should be courageous enough to seek approval for his commands by giving reasons for them. It is incomprehensible how such an approach to mature and much-loved brothers or sisters in the Lord should be a threat to the authority of the superior, who, according to the command of Christ, should see in the authority of his office only the greater obligation to serve. This does not mean that there should be long debates and discussions over every small decree of a superior. That was the folly of the Parliaments in the past. This would be irrational and childish (although unfortunately it does occur). The problem can be met and overcome by an appeal to higher ascetical motives. Without irritating himself or others, the subject should calmly and maturely consider the many unavoidable regulations of daily life in a religious community for what they really are:

inevitable burdens of earthly life which weigh upon people in the world just as much as they do on people in religious life. Much irritation among religious persons caused by details of common life flows solely from immaturity which does not comprehend that a person does not prove his independence and personal integrity by rebelling against communal rules and regulations. And yet it still remains true: religious obedience, according to its own proper nature, is more than a merely rational regulation of traffic.

There is a third consideration which must guard religious obedience from misconception and excess. It is not true, even in religious communities, that all initiative should take its rise from superiors. Nor should we be too quick to consider this statement a mere platitude. To comprehend it really, we must make use of metaphysics, a metaphysics which consists in pondering with wonder on the commonplace and the obvious and then drawing some conclusions. Human authority (even when exercised in God's name) must not be conceived as adequately and exclusively competent to monopolize all initiative, all effort and all personal decision. Nor does it imply that subjects are called to initiative and decision only when authority gives the signal.

One frequently gets the impression, both in religious orders and in the Church in general, that initiative, action, militancy, and the like, are indeed considered necessary and desirable in subjects, but only on condition that the go-ahead is given "from above," and only in the direction which has already been unequivocally and authoritatively determined by superiors. Unconsciously and spontaneously a tendency is vigorously at work to make the subject feel that he is so built into his order or the Church that only the total structure through its hierarchy is capable of initiative; that opinion or enterprise find their legitimacy only in express, or at least tacit, approval from authority.

Unless we wish to absolutize the community, the principle of subsidarity has application not only between smaller and larger societies, but also between individuals and their communities as well. Yet there can be no subordination of the individual to a community and to the authority representing it, if it tries to make the individual an exclusively dependent function of the community and its authority. We need only put the question in all simplicity: may one propose a wish to a superior, or, with due modesty, propose an alternative policy? Everyone will answer: "Obviously, yes." Hence it is unnecessary first to ask the superior whether he wants the request to be presented or the alternative proposed. Yet this request, this alternative suggestion is also initiative, in which one must take the responsibility of deciding whether it is to be presented or not. For even when with all obedience and modesty the decision is left to the superior, the suggestion alters the situation of the superior in making his decision. It broadens or narrows the field of choice. Indeed even when the subject shows the greatest discretion, the superior is "influenced," whether he likes it or not, whether or not he would have followed the suggestion on his own.

There is no autarchic human authority which is pure activity and in no way passivity. To command absolutely is proper only to the Creator, who is not faced with opposing structures and unavoidable initiatives, because He Himself in the strict sense makes everything out of nothing. All other authority, even in the Church and in religious orders, is not the only determining initiative but is one force in an immense network of forces, active and passive, receiving and giving. Authority has and should have the function of directing, coordinating, overseeing, and planning the whole interplay of human initiatives. It is not, to speak strictly, even in the ideal order, so representative of God that it alone is the autarchic planner and designer of all human activity. This would be the hybrid of a totalitarian system which cannot exist, and, more significantly, should not exist.

Even in religious orders, therefore, in practice authority needs, calls for, and puts to use the initiative of subjects. Even in the abstract, there can be no *absolute* ruler and director of it. Independently of authority there exists initial sparkings of forces which cannot be controlled by authority. Because this is so and cannot be otherwise, it also *should* be so. That is to say, in no community or society, not even the Church or religious orders, *may* authority act as if all good initiatives originated from it, so that every execution of plan, command, and wish originated in authority alone. Even the most laudable initiatives of the Holy See often are only the reaction to an action which originated elsewhere, and this is important. The same is true in the case of authorities of religious orders. Subjects are not mere receivers of commands, because that is simply impossible. The aim of obedience is not to make merely passive subjects. This is not even an "asymptotic" ideal, but a chimera and the usurpation of the creative power reserved to God alone, which He can delegate to no one. Only God has "all the threads in His hand," and He has empowered no one to act in His fashion.

Consequently the superior cannot be a god in the fulfillment of his office. Not to prevent his subjects from assuming initiative is not enough for a superior. He must positively count on it, invite it; he must not be irked by it. He must, to a certain degree, recognize himself also as only *one* of the wheels in a heavenly mechanism whose ultimate and comprehensive significance is directed by one only, by God and no one else. The superior always remains something moved. In an ultimate sense, he does not know exactly to what end evolution is moving. In spite of all the authority given him, and in spite of all the supervision he is charged with, he acts in trust and ventures into the unknown. He too never knows exactly what he is doing or starting when he commands or refrains from doing so.

He must remember that authority is one, but not the only, source for heavenly impulse, direction, and stimulation. He must realize that God never took on the obligation first to advise the authorities selected and authorized by Himself about God's own activity in the Church for the salvation of souls and the progress of history. The superior has no exclusive vision of the divine will with the mission to pass it on to his subjects. There is no God-given warrant for such a process of communication. Rather the superior must also be an obedient man, a hearer. The formal correctness and juridical validity of his commands does not guarantee that they are likewise ontologically guaranteed. If the subject must obey in order not to be disobedient before God, this fact is no proof that the command given was the command which, according to God's antecedent will, should have been given. It can be the product of a permitted fault in the superior. It can proceed from dead traditionalism, from human limitations, from routine, from a shortsighted system of uniformism, from a lack of imagination, and from many other factors.

There is in the world a plurality of forces which can in no way be hierarchically subject to authority—though such forces cannot contradict authority as far as the latter succeeds in bringing them within the field of direction and command. This latter task, as has been said, can and should be only partially achieved. Hence the subject in religious life has no right simply to take refuge behind obedience, as if he could thus be free from a responsibility which he himself must bear, the responsible direction of his own personal initiative. We often hear apologies of obedience which praise this supposed advantage. It does not exist. At least not in the sense that the religious can thereby escape from the burden of personal responsibility. He himself chooses obedience; otherwise he would not be in religious life. He must then answer for the consequences of his choice.

The received command is a synthesis of elements. One is the superior's personal and original activity, the other is the external condition for that activity. This condition is constituted by the subject himself: his mode of being and action, his capacities and incapacities (perhaps culpable), his approach and attitude to the superior. The conditioning is prior to the command and makes the subject coresponsible for the command itself. Certainly the religious can often say to his own consolation that the superior has to answer for this or that decision and not the subject. But the extent of this consolation is not great. Taken as a whole, the religious cannot escape the responsibility for his own life, down to its last details. He simply hears in the command the echo of his own character and activity. There does not exist in this world a controlcenter of action from whose uninfluenced motion all else in existence originates. A human being cannot relinquish his personality to a representative, not even in religious life. That is in no way the purpose of obedience.

True Obedience

To PROVIDE A POSITIVE definition of religious obedience is by no means a simple matter. We could immediately and without further examination maintain that religious obedience is an abidingly vibrant obedience to God and the fulfillment of the Divine Will. But if we were to do that, we would have to determine how it is possible to know in what sense it can be said that that which is commanded is the will of God. For the fact remains that there can be commands which the subject must obey, provided that the things commanded be not sinful, but which in the objective order, are wrong, and which, in given circumstances, have been commanded with real culpability on the part of the superior. In cases of this kind it is no simple task to say why and in what sense the fulfillment of such a command could be the will of God. Nor should we over-simplify the matter by praising without qualification the "holocaust" and "renunciation" which obedience entails. For it is obvious that pure subjection to the will of another who is not God has no value as such in the realm of morality. In itself, pure dependence of self on the will of another is amoral, not to say even immoral, unless some further element be added to it.

We might add that if religious obedience is subordination of one's own will and decisions to those of another who holds the place of God and is the interpreter of the Divine Will, we must at least determine how we are to know how this other person received the divine commission to be the expositor of the will of God. This question is a difficult one; even more so than that of poverty and of the evangelical counsel to renounce the blessings of conjugal love. For these two evangelical counsels are recommended directly in the words of Holy Scripture and by Our Lord Himself. As far as these two counsels are concerned, it is always possible to fall back on this recommendation, even when we do not succeed in achieving a crystal-clear understanding of their inner meaning. In this matter it can be said that the religious is walking in the way of the Gospel. And to him who has set out on this path in unquestioning surrender, the meaning of these counsels will be more and more fully revealed. He can always say that he is imitating Christ. And hence he needs no further argument over and above the fact that the disciple does not wish to be above his master, and that love understands what it recognizes as a fundamental characteristic in the beloved Lord.

Concerning obedience, however, the problem is not as simple as all that. As a matter of fact, we see that in the days of the early Church, in which a continuous procession of ascetics and virgins was already a fact, there was as yet no mention of religious obedience. Nor can any direct affirmation of this concept be found in the pages of the Gospels.

The early ascetics lived the life of solitaries, and so there was no stimulus to the evocation of a notion of obedience. And even for a long time afterwards, obedience was not praised as a third vow. The religious accepted a celibate or monastic life in any form, and obliged himself to remain in a definite community which lived such a mode of life. It is clear that we will have to proceed carefully if we are to specify the content and arguments for religious obedience.

Before we proceed in the question of the meaning of obedience precisely as it exists in a religious community, we must be clearly warned against another simplification which superficially gives a quick and easy solution to these questions. We cannot simply refer to the example of Christ. Beyond a doubt He was obedient. Obedience to His Father, according to His explanation, was the form, the driving power and the content of His life. We must by all means imitate Christ. But this is precisely the question: how do we know that in subordination of self to human authority we exercise the deepest obedience to God? Christ did not do it. Certainly the Apostle knows that there are human authorities which in some fashion take the place of God as far as we are concerned, and whose decrees ought to appear to us as the will of God. But Paul is speaking of the authorities which are not freely chosen nor created by us, but exist prior to us and prior to our will, namely parents, masters, and the civil governors. Can we extend and complete this Divine

Will imposed on us by subordinating ourselves to new régimes of our making? If we answer that religious superiors have ecclesiastical authority because they are appointed by the Church, this reply alone does not lead us to any clear-cut doctrine. Subordination to the authority of religious superiors is not imposed on men by the Church without their own free and deliberate consent as implied by the vows. Hence the question remains: why is it meritorious to submit to the authority of another, when it has not been imposed on us by God Himself? Should we not safeguard the freedom that God has entrusted to us as much as our function of personal responsibility, since, as we have already said, an absolute surrender of innate responsible freedom is in no way possible or reasonable?

Hence the argument from the Gospel in favor of religious obedience is not so simple, nor can it be proved immediately or without further examination. Our problem could be expressed succinctly in the following question: is religious obedience a concrete prolongation of obedience to the will of God, either in general, as it finds expression in the commandments of God, or in particular as it is manifested in God's direction, inspiration and providential disposition of the lives of men?

Religious obedience should by no means be considered primarily as obedience to individual commands, nor is it even the abstract notion of a general readiness to fulfill such commands. Primarily it is the permanent binding of oneself to a definite mode of life—to life with God within the framework of the Church. It involves the exclusive dedication of one's energies to those things which are the concern of the Lord and to what is pleasing to Him. We accept as a form of life the expectation of God's coming Kingdom of grace from on high. Obedience is concerned with the sacrifice and renunciation of the world's most precious goods; the renunciation of the right to erect a little world of our own as a field of freedom through the acquisition of wealth; the renunciation of the right to one's own hearth and the felt security to be found in the intimate love of another person through the conjugal bond. It is concerned with prayer, and with the testimony to God's grace which is to be found in what is commonly known as the care of souls and the apostolate. Here we need make no further description or argument for this life based on the evangelical counsels. Obedience is a permanent life-form giving man a God-ward orientation. Such orientation is ecclesiological because by it the religious reveals the peculiar essence of the Church.

It is the manifestation of God's other-worldly grace beyond the reach of earthly merit, to be accepted by faith alone in spite of all human impotence. In this manifestation the Church achieves her existential visibility and becomes historically tangible through doctrine and sacrament. This is the life to which the religious immediately and primarily pledges himself. His obedience, with reference to the individual commands which a superior may enjoin, is specified by this life-form giving it its definite religious significance. Otherwise there would be no sense to vowed obedience. It would not be a religious matter at all. It would rather be perversity to praise this kind of obedience in any other field of life; for instance, if one were to vow obedience for the better functioning of a center of chemical research in which one is employed as a research collaborator. If we suppose that a permanent vowed obligation to a religious life is of positive value in the moral order (and this is presupposed here), and if we further assume that it is proper and reasonable, though not necessary, to lead such a life in a community, then it follows that obedience to the directors of this community is justified and meaningful in the concrete pursuit of this permanent way of life.

Hence we are not trying to canonize an abstract notion of obedience as the execution of another's will as such. Such abstract obedience is due to God alone permitting no transfer to another. Beyond this case we cannot obey purely for the sake of obeying or of not doing our own will and determination. Something like this, considered abstractly in itself, would have no positive significance in the realm of morality. It would be downright absurd and perverse. The fact that this sort of thing would be "difficult" and "a perfect holocaust," hard and troublesome for him who is obedient at all times and in all things, can scarcely be itself an argument for the meaningfulness of obedience. The implied presupposition of this argument, namely that the more difficult and repugnant thing is always better and more pleasing to God, just because it is a renunciation difficult for man, cannot be the legitimate starting point of discussion.

Our concept of obedience also explains why religious obedience has its place exclusively in a religious society approved and sanctioned by the Church. The content of obedience must be guaranteed, if such obedience is to possess moral value. It is not enough that commands be morally indifferent. They must be morally good in their total context. The totality must represent for the Church and to the world the content of the evangelical counsels. One can vow only that which is better. Thus one cannot vow directly and as an end in itself to do something which under certain circumstances (even if not sinful) is less prudent, less good, less significant. Whence it immediately follows that the proper and essential object of religious obedience is an abiding way of life according to the evangelical counsels. For in accord with the teaching of the Church this is certainly the better thing, but in what this superiority consists will not be further explained here. Obedience is not at all to be conceived as the "heroic" (or almost foolhardy) concession of a *carte blanche* to a superior, so that the religious simply does not do his own will, either because this is always pleasing and hence its renunciation especially difficult, or because it is fraught with danger and hence to be avoided. Thus it is that obedience is always specified with reference to the constitutions of the given order, and the superior can only command within the framework determined by the constitutions.

The real essence of obedience is missed if it is only the particular command of the superior that is considered, and then only in terms of the abstract formula: I declare myself ready to execute the command of another, if this command be not evidently immoral. This is not the case. Obedience is the acceptance of a common mode of religious life in imitation of Christ according to a constitution, which the Church has acknowledged to be a true and practical expression of a divinely oriented existence. By virtue of this acceptance and obligation the vow explicitly or implicitly includes the carrying out of the just commands of the authority necessary in any society, when they are directed to the concrete realization of the life-form of religious commitments "according to the constitutions." Such realizations cannot be determined *a priori* once and for all.

Whoever, therefore, is critical of the notion of religious obedience, is really attacking the wisdom of the life of the counsels in the Church. He is attacking, moreover, the wisdom of a life that is not primarily concerned with the tangible realizations of worldly objectives, but which through faith makes the expectation of hidden grace the ground of existence, and translates this faith into act. Without such an act, faith itself would be meaningless.

This act is representative of the Church and bears the Church's witness to the world. If this mode of existence is to have meaning, then it must inspire a willingness to carry out in any given instance the concrete actions, undertakings and renunciations, which in the judgment of competent authority are deemed necessary for the concrete realization of this way of life.

This is why obedience is connected with the teaching and example of Christ who was obedient even to the death of the cross. Whoever enters into a religious community, whoever perpetually and irrevocably makes this way of life his own, chooses for himself an unforeseeable destiny. For the consequences of such an election and dedication to the community and its rationale of action cannot be foreseen in detail. And these consequences can be difficult and painful. But this gamble (considered in its formal structure) is involved in every human obligation, whereby another person with his own proper will becomes an inseparable part of one's own life. We find it in marriage, acceptance of the duties of citizenship, the responsibility of office, and so forth. Hence if the religious community and its basic ideals are justified and meaningful (which in our case we legitimately assume to be true), so too is the obligation toward all its consequences which cannot be seen in advance. A human mode of life which consists in the free subordination to something higher than itself cannot exist without this element of risk. And without such a surrender the individual will remain in his own egotism behind the defenses of his own existential anxiety, which is the surest way to destruction. But the man who gives himself to what is higher and nobler, who takes the gamble, knows that he is only doing what Christ Himself did in His obedience.

Under this aspect, that which in a given instance is irrational and indefensible but actually unavoidable really becomes the will of the Father. In this way the cross of Christ, "had" to be; it was the will of the Father who had planned it, even though it came about only as the result of the short-sightedness and guilt of men. The permanent dedication to the ideal of the counsels in imitation of Christ, who was poor and self-denying, the crucified legate of God, consecrated to prayer and atonement, is lived all but exclusively in a community professing the same ideal. Hence the obedience which it entails must be regarded as the will of God, even if a particular command appears to be senseless (just as death, failure and the other tragic circumstances of human existence appear), provided of course that what is commanded is not immoral in itself. Religious obedience is thus a real participation in the cross of Christ. Nor should one protest that the irrationality of a mistaken command frees the subject from his contract, and cannot be considered as a share in Christ's mission. We must realize that religious obedience is more than a rationally accepted agreement governing "traffic-arrange-ments" in a common enterprise. This, of course, is included, for life in any community demands obedience, though in our case community life is directed to God.

In any other society, in the event of an unwise command, obedience would be justified only by the rational insight that such unavoidable eventualities must also be reckoned with in the original bargain. Otherwise, obedience, which is always to some degree necessary, would end, for it would be left to the discretion of the subject to obey. But in religion the imitation of Christ is practiced. There the cross of Christ is considered not merely as something inevitable, or as the misfortune of life, by and large to be evaded, but rather as the embodiment of grace and its acceptance through faith, as something which "must" be, "so that the scriptures might be fulfilled," since only "thus" can one enter into one's glory. There the command, judged unwise according to its immediate historical context, will be seen as something which in the framework of religious life is worthwhile, even desirable. This of course does not justify the superior in issuing such a command. Yet such an order can be understood in the same way as the saints in their imitation of Christ understood failure, shame, the shattering of cherished plans, martyrdom, and thousands of other unjustifiable contingencies. They secretly longed for them as the embodiment of their faith in God's grace now reaching its perfection.

It might here be in place to recognize that morality and spontaneous moral judgment have a greater function than is ordinarily supposed. The command of a superior may be objectively sinful, and if recognized as such by the inferior it should not be put into execution. Everyone will agree that a superior, even with the best intentions, can issue an order which is objectively wrong. If one does not consider as sins only those things which are expressly labeled as such in confessional manuals, then it will be hard to deny that that which is materially false can also very often be objectively immoral. What is more, it is not easy to explain why this is not generally so.

Perhaps a fictitious example may be of help. A higher superior instructs the principal of a boarding school that he must under all circumstances make the boys go to confession once a week. Let us suppose that the subordinate, in this case the principal, clearly realizes what the superior in his idealistic remoteness cannot comprehend, that such a demand will eventually prove very harmful to the spiritual life of his charges. Question: have we here merely an inept pedagogical practice, which must be "carried out" because commanded, or have we in fact an innocent but unjustified demand which, since it is actually a serious threat to the genuine spiritual development of these youths, should not be carried out by the subordinate? The very ineptness of the practice offends against moral principles. Must the subject now declare that he cannot square it with his conscience, and ask to be relieved of his office? Reading the older moralists one gets the impression that they were more concerned with such cases than we are today. Have we today become more moral, or has the principle "an order is an order" gained foothold even in such holy quarters as religious communities? Do we avoid talking about such possibilities out of fear of evils produced by the conscientious objector, and so act as if something of this kind practically never occurs? But is not the consequent evil caused to conscience greater than the utility of a frictionless functioning of external government requiring of subjects a literal obedience to commands? Even the subject has the duty in conscience of examining the moral admissibility of what has been commanded. The just "presumption" that the command of a superior is not only subjectively but also objectively morally unobjectionable does not constitute a simple dispensation from the essential obligation of every man to attain to moral certitude respecting the moral liceity of a free action before it is undertaken. This action is no less his own, and no less one for which he will be responsible, simply because it is commanded.

As a religious grows older he asks himself with a deep and secret anxiety whether he has done anything in his life which can stand judgment in God's sight. Nothing of course can so stand, except what He has given out of pure mercy. What is worthy of God comes from God's grace alone. For this very reason what one does is not indifferent. There is an absolute difference between man's potentialities when God's grace is accepted and when it is rejected. God has told us, and He is greater than the human heart, that there are deeds of selfless devotion, obedience to God's holy will and self-forgetting dedication. Yet we always discover in ourselves, if we are not stupid, naive or conceited, things which always make us afraid that there is nothing in us but open or disguised egotism. Are we sure that God's grace was ever operative in us? Such an event should have been life-transforming. Yet was there ever a moment when we did not seek ourselves, when success was not the fruit of egotism, when our love of God was not anxiety, when patient prudence was not really faintheartedness? The divine achievement of miraculous cleansing takes place in different ways, giving us the right to hope that not everything in our life was open or covert self-seeking. Nor need painful anxiety about it be another manifestation of self-seeking or secret self-justification before God. Whoever is so concerned has made his life essentially simple and easy. We act on our own but the last and most important deed will be effected in us by God Himself operating through the bitterness of life itself. The individual can always do one thing at least. He can give himself over to something greater than himself. He can also see to it that this greater Reality be more than an ideal or a theory, which on final analysis is under his own control. The individual can strive to make this nobler Reality actual. This Reality must make demands on us, when we do not desire to be constrained; must act even when we do not wish it; must cause us suffering when we ourselves would rather avoid it. This happens when the greater Reality to which we dedicate ourselves becomes a tangible force of incomprehensible greatness, whose word of command is directed towards us—and we obey. This means to obey silently, and in the true sense, unquestioningly; to submit to a demand we have not ourselves invented.

When this happens we have too little time and too little interest to defend or develop our personal integrity. We might even be so fortunate as to become a true person, who exists insofar as he forgets and sacrifices self, insofar as he obeys. But we must remember that life's good fortune is God's grace. In order to become obedient, and in transcendence lose ourselves—the only way of ever really finding ourselves—we must perhaps see nothing at all extraordinary in obedience, hardly ever think of it directly. We should rather think of the Reality which we serve as a matter of course. That Being is worthy of all love and service, because ultimately it is no mere cause, but *The Person*: God. Perhaps the truly obedient man is simply the lover, for whom the sacrifice of self-surrender is sweet and a blessed delight. Perhaps we should not speak so much of obedience, for it is already threatened when we praise or defend it. Either tactic is only meaningful as an encouragement for the young in order to strengthen their wills to embrace in silence a matter-of-course service of God in the Church through a life of prayer and witness. They must learn that this is meaningful even though the heart shudders and the wisdom of this world panics at the thought of losing self in the loss of freedom.

As for the ultimate obedience, which demands and silently takes everything, it will be exacted by God alone. It is the command to die the death which overshadows every minute of our life, and more and more detaches us from ourselves. This command, to move on and to leave all, to allow ourselves in faith to be absorbed in the great silence of God, no longer to resist the all-embracing nameless destiny which rules over us—this command comes to all men. The question, whether man obediently accepts it, is decisive for time and eternity. The whole of religious life grounded in obedience is nothing more than a rehearsal, a practical anticipation of this situation, which more and more envelopes human existence. For the religious it is the participation in the death of Christ and the life concealed in Him.

THE VIRTUE OF OBSERVANCE *

Antonio Royo, O.P. AND *Jordan Aumann, O.P.*

OBEDIENCE IS A MORAL VIRTUE which makes one's will prompt to carry out the commands of a superior (*Summa Theol.*). The word 'commands' signifies, not only a precept which would oblige an individual in conscience, but also the simple will of the superior as manifested externally, either explicitly or tacitly. The obedience will be the more perfect as the individual is more prompt to execute the will of the superior even before an express command is given. Moreover, one should not think that only religious are bound to practice obedience. All subjects of all legitimate superiors are obliged to obey authority, whether that authority be one's parents, the civil officials, the pastor in a parish, the teacher in a classroom, a military officer, one's employer, etc.

The basis of obedience is the authority of the superior, received directly or indirectly from God. Actually, it is God whom one obeys in the person of the lawful superior because, as St. Paul says, (Cf. Rom. 13:1) all power comes from God. For that

* From *The Theology of Christian Perfection,* by Antonio Royo, O.P. and Jordan Aumann, O.P. Used by permission of The Priory Press.

reason St. Paul adds that he who resists authority resists God. If one externally performs the act which has been commanded by a superior, but does so with internal rebellion, the obedience is purely material and is not a virtue in the strict sense of the word. Nevertheless, even material obedience suffices to avoid breaking the vow of obedience in case the subject is bound by vow. But when one obeys both internally and externally precisely because something has been commanded by a superior, the obedience is then called formal obedience and is an excellent act of virtue.

It follows from this that there are many acts which seem to be acts of obedience but actually are not so in the sight of God. Whenever a person performs the external act which has been commanded, but at the same time complains or criticizes or rebels, the action has lost its essence as an act of the virtue of obedience. The same thing is true if one obeys *exclusively* out of an attachment or affection for the superior as a particular person, or because the command seems reasonable to us or suits our particular taste and liking, etc. In all of these cases the formal motive of obedience—the authority of the superior as representing God—is lacking, and for that reason, as the Angelic Doctor points out, there is no act of the supernatural virtue of obedience (*Summa Theol.*). St Thomas teaches that not even martyrdom would have any value if it were not directed to the fulfillment of the divine will.

As a virtue, obedience is inferior to the theological virtues. By reason of its object it is also inferior to some of the moral virtues (e.g., religion). But by reason of that which is sacrificed or offered to God, it is the most excellent of all the moral virtues, because through the other virtues one sacrifices external goods (poverty), corporal goods (virginity), or certain goods of the soul which are inferior to the human will, which is sacrificed in the virtue of obedience. For this reason St. Thomas does not hesitate to affirm that the religious life, primarily because of the vow of obedience, is a true holocaust offered to God.

The classical division of the grades or degrees of obedience is as follows: a) mere external execution; b) internal submission of the will; c) submission of the internal judgment. St. Ignatius Loyola explains these grades in an inspiring letter to the fathers and brothers of the Society in Portugal. The following outline gives the basic points of doctrine contained in the letter.

1) St. Ignatius desires that obedience should be the characteristic virtue of the Society because of the blessings produced by this virtue, because it is highly praised in Sacred Scripture, and because it is the compendium of all the other virtues. He states as the fundamental principle of obedience that one should see Christ in the superior, without thinking of the goodness or evil of the superior as an individual person.

2) Listing the grades of obedience, he states that the first is obedience of execution, which is of little value; the second grade is obedience of the will, which possesses the intrinsic value of the sacrifice of obedience, so that it is of great merit and it perfects man's free will; the third degree is obedience of the intellect. As regards obedience of the intellect, St. Ignatius states that it is *possible* because the will can control the intellect; it is *just* because it is reasonable to control one's judgment and to conform one's will to God's; it is *necessary* for the attainment of perfect subordination, for safeguarding oneself against the illusions of self-love, for preserving one's tranquillity in obedience, and for preserving union with God; and it is *perfect* obedience, because in this grade of obedience a man immolates that which is most excellent, which implies a marvellous victory over self.

3) Then the saint lists the general and particular means for achieving the third grade of obedience. The general means are humility and meekness. The particular means are to see God in one's superiors, to seek reasons in favor of the command that is given, and to accept the command blindly, that is, without any further inquiry, but with a docility similar to that which one should have in regard to matters of faith. This does not mean, however, that it would be opposed to the perfection of obedience if one were to state reasons to the superior for desisting from that which has been commanded, as long as due conditions are observed. However, if a

subject should make such a representation to his superior, he should do so with complete indifference and with full freedom.

4) In his final observation, St. Ignatius remarks that obedience also extends to those who have some charge or office under lawful authority. And he says that the prosperity of religious institutes depends on obedience, because of the principle of subordination which applies to religious institutes. In his final exhortation he refers to the example of Christ in regard to obedience and the great reward that is earned through obedience.

The fundamental quality which comprises all the others is that obedience should be supernatural, that is, inspired by supernatural motives. Only then is obedience a truly Christian virtue. Obedience inspired by any purely human motive, however right and lawful in itself, cannot be supernatural. But in order that the supernatural quality of obedience may be augmented and preserved, we shall enumerate some of the more important characteristics of Christian obedience. We do not mean to imply that this list is exhaustive, but if one keeps in mind the fundamental quality which we have just mentioned, all the other characteristics of obedience will spring forth spontaneously.

1) A spirit of faith, by which the subject obeys and reveres his superior as another Christ, and looks upon the commands of the superior as coming from God himself.

2) The firm conviction that by obeying lawful commands of superiors we are fulfilling the will of God, and that, although a superior may make a mistake in commanding, the subject never makes a mistake in obeying lawful commands.

3) Obedience out of love of God and acceptance of difficult or distasteful commands in a spirit of sacrifice.

4) Promptness in fulfilling the commands that are given, realizing that we should not make Christ wait for our obedience but that we should be prompt to do His will.

5) A true devotion by which we give complete submission of our will to the superior as the representative of God.

6) Spontaneity and joy in obedience, and even the attempt to anticipate the desires of the superior, manifesting by our instant and joyful acceptance of commands that obedience makes us happy.

7) Humility and simplicity, so that we can perform the act of obedience as if it were the most natural thing in the world, without giving any attention to the heroism involved in self-immolation.

8) Magnanimity, which gives virility to our obedience and provides us with the energy of heroes and the fortitude of martyrs.

9) Universality, so that at all times and to any superior whatever, we obey all commands without exception.

10) Perseverance, so that in times of joy or sorrow, in health or in sickness, regardless of any personal condition or taste, we would obey, realizing that obedience gives power and that the obedient man shall speak of victory.

The blessings of obedience are very great, both for the intellect and the will, as well as for the heart. Obedience gives to the intellect a certitude that one knows and does the will of God. It gives the assurance of divine assistance, because God has promised that he would be with those who are obedient to his will. Obedience also gives certitude to the outcome of one's actions, because, as St. Paul says, "For those who love God all things work together unto good" (Rom. 8:28).

Obedience is also the source of true liberty for the will, because there is nothing that so enslaves a man as attachment to his own will. It is likewise the source of fortitude; to obey to the point of heroism one needs great valor. And it is the guarantee of one's perseverance in good. As regards the heart, obedience gives peace and tranquillity, which can come only from doing the will of God. It preserves right order in the life of the individual and in the community, because the best assurance of order is found in the subjection of inferiors to superiors. It is, finally, one of the greatest safeguards against scrupulosity; for that reason, one of the first demands that the spiritual director must make of a scrupulous penitent is that he give complete obedience to all commands.

Without reaching the excess of formal disobedience, there are many actions which constitute a falsification or deformation of the virtue of obedience. The following are some of the principal manifestations:

1) *Routine or mechanical obedience*—the purely external act of obedience, without any internal spirit. One acts like a machine or a robot, and may perform the external act with the greatest precision and perfection, but he lacks the proper attention and awareness of the supernatural motive for his obedience, or he may even lack the supernatural motive entirely.

2) *Legal obedience*—the obedience of the person who is constantly referring to a law or rule, in order to know how far his obedience extends, or to check lest the superior exceed his authority in commanding. Such persons are pharisaical, and very often lack the generosity of spirit which should prompt them to obey out of love.

3) *Critical obedience*—the obedience of those who recognize the superior's authority and obey him, but constantly find fault with the superior for being unsympathetic, too rigorous, too impulsive, lacking in tact, etc. Such persons obey the superior and at the same time criticize him for his personal defects, thus predisposing themselves to lose respect for the authority of the superior, and even to disobey him.

4) *Paralyzed obedience*—one does not have the occasion to practice formal obedience because the superior does not dare to give commands, or is too lax or indifferent in the discharge of his duties. This defect on the part of the superiors is more frequently noticed in communities of men than in communities of women, and it is likewise true in family life in many instances. However, it is not always due to incompetent superiors. There are some subjects who do not obey because, for one reason or another, they find reasons to excuse themselves from carrying out commands that are given, or they obtain all permissions by bending the will of the superior to their own.

5) *Pseudo-mystical obedience*—the individual who disobeys the superior under the pretext of obeying the Holy Spirit. This is pure illusion because the general norm of obedience is that we are bound to obey the lawful commands of legitimate superiors.

6) *Camouflaged disobedience*—the art of inducing the superior, by means of excuses and objections, to withdraw his commands or to modify them.

7) *Paradoxical obedience*—the pretense of giving obedience to a superior while one does his own will, or even imposes his will upon the superior. This defect is frequently noted in those communities in which the superior has special friends in the community, or is afraid to govern as he ought.

8) *Pharisaical obedience*—an obedience in which one performs the acts commanded but does not submit his will. This is a combination of cowardice and hypocrisy.

9) *The spirit of opposition*—the existence of groups or parties within a community which are opposed to the superior and are usually waging a constant war against the superior. This is a diabolical spirit, which sows the seeds of discord and division in the community.

10) *Egoistic obedience*—inspired by the desire to win the sympathy and affection of the superior and to obtain from him the duties or commands which are in accordance with one's own tastes and desires.

11) *The spirit of murmuring*—the obedience of him who accepts unwillingly the commands of his superiors and murmurs interiorly or sometimes complains to others about the superior or the task assigned.

12) *Half-hearted obedience*—the imperfect or careless execution of orders. This is sometimes malicious, as in the case of those who do not wish to obey and therefore deliberately perform their tasks badly so that the superior will change the assignment.

13) *Slothful obedience*—the neglect to fulfill commands without sufficient reason. Such persons must be commanded repeatedly before they per-

form the task, and when they finally do it, it is often done badly because they had no desire to do it in the first place.

Such are the principal falsifications and defects in the practice of the virtue of obedience. With good reason did Christ say to St. Catherine of Siena: "My dear daughter, how numerous they are who live in the practice of obedience, but how few they are who obey perfectly." But those who obey perfectly offer to God a sacrifice of praise which rises to heaven with the odor of sweetness because of the perfect immolation of their self-love.

THE VIRTUE OF OBEDIENCE *
Adolphe Tanquerey, S.S., D.D.

OBEDIENCE IS A SUPERNATURAL, moral virtue which inclines us to submit our will to that of our lawful superiors, insofar as they are the representatives of *God.*

Obedience rests upon God's sovereign domain and upon the absolute submission creatures owe Him.

First of all, it is evident that we must obey God.

We must, indeed, be entirely dependent upon the holy will of God since we were created by Him: "All things serve you" (Ps. 118:91). As rational creatures, we are all the more obliged to this submission because we have received more from Him; we have received in particular the gift of a free will, which we can best acknowledge by freely submitting it to the will of our maker.

Being *children of God,* we must obey our heavenly Father as Jesus Himself did, who having come into the world through obedience, through obedience went out from it: "He was made obedient unto death."

---

* From *The Spiritual Life,* by Very Rev. Adolphe Tanquerey, S.S., D.D. Used by permission of Desclée and Co.

Redeemed from the bondage of sin, we no longer belong to ourselves, but to Jesus Christ, who gave His blood to make us His own: "And you are not your own, for you are bought with a great price" (1 Cor. 6:20). We must, therefore, obey His laws.

For the same reason we must yield obedience to God's lawful representatives. This point must be thoroughly understood. Because man is not self-sufficient for his physical, intellectual, and moral well being, God willed that he live in society. Society, however, cannot endure without an *authority* which coordinates the efforts of its members towards the common good. Hence, it is God's will that in society there should be superiors commissioned to command, and subjects whose duty it is to obey. In order that this obedience might be more readily practiced, God has delegated His authority to legitimate superiors: "For there is no power but from *God*" (Rom. 13:1). This is so true that to render obedience to lawful superiors is to render obedience to God, and to disobey them is to provoke condemnation: "Therefore he that resisteth the power, resisteth the obedience of *God*. And they that resist, purchase to themselves *damnation*" (Rom. 13:2).

The duty of superiors lies in exercising their authority solely in the capacity of God's representatives in order to procure glory to God and to promote the general welfare of the community. Should they fail in this, they are responsible before God and their own superiors for such abuse of their authority.

The duty of subjects is to obey God's representatives, to obey them as they obey God Himself: "He that heareth you heareth me; and he that despiseth you, despiseth me" (Luke 10:16). The reason for this is evident. Without such submission, there would be but chaos and disorder in each of the different parts of society to the detriment of all.

But, *who are the lawful superiors?* The answer is, those who are placed by God at the head of the different kinds of societies.

In the *natural* order three different sorts of society may be discerned: *domestic* society or *the family,* at the head of which are parents, and especially the father; *civil* society, ruled by those who are the lawful holders of authority according to the different systems of government accepted in the different nations of the world; *professional* society, where we find employers and employees, whose respective rights and duties are determined by special, particular contracts.

In the *supernatural* order, the hierarchical superiors are: the *sovereign pontiff,* whose authority is both supreme and immediate over the whole Church; *bishops,* who have jurisdiction over their respective dioceses, and, under their authority, *pastors* and *curates,* each within the limits determined by the code of canon law.

Moreover, there are in the Church particular communities with constitutions and rules approved by the sovereign pontiff or by the bishops, and having superiors appointed in accordance with their constitutions or rules. Here, again, we find legitimate authority. Therefore, whoever joins a community binds himself to keep the rules and obey the superiors who command within the limits defined by the rule.

There are, then, limits set to the exercise of authority.

It is evident that it is neither obligatory nor permissible to obey a superior who would give a command manifestly opposed to divine or ecclesiastical laws. In this case we should have to repeat the words of St. Peter: *"We ought to obey God, rather than man"* (Acts 5:29)—words that proclaim and vindicate Christian liberty against all tyranny. The same would hold true, if what is commanded is clearly beyond our powers, for *no one is held to do the impossible.* In case of *doubt,* however, since we are prone to illusions, we must act on the principle: in doubt *the presumption is in favor of the superior.*

The Degrees of Obedience

BEGINNERS APPLY themselves, first of all, to observe faithfully the commandments of God and of the Church, and to conform to the orders of lawful superiors with diligence, punctuality, and in a supernatural spirit.

MORE ADVANCED SOULS carefully ponder the examples given by Jesus from the very first moment of His existence, when He pledged Himself to fulfill in all things the will of His Father, until the last instant of His life when He died a victim of obedience. They pray Him to come and live within them in that same spirit of obedience, and they strive to unite themselves to Him in submitting to their superiors, just as He was subject to Mary and to Joseph: "*He was subject to them.*"

They submit their *wills* even in things that entail hardship and go against their preferences. They do so whole-heartedly, without complaint, even with joy at being able to imitate more perfectly their Divine Model. They avoid especially taking any steps that would lead the superior to conform to their desires, for, as St. Bernard remarks: "You need not flatter yourself with the idea that you are truly obedient, if, when you desire something, you strive either openly or covertly to have your spiritual father command it to you. In this you only deceive yourself, for it is not you that obey the superior, but the superior that obeys you."

PERFECT SOULS go even further. They submit their *judgment* to that of their superior, without even considering the reasons for his command.

St. Ignatius gives an excellent explanation of this degree of obedience. "If, however, one wishes to make the perfect sacrifice of self, one must, after having submitted one's will to God, consecrate to Him one's *understanding* in such a way as not only to will what the superior wills, but to be of the same mind also, and to submit one's judgment to that of the superior to the extent that an already obedient will can sway the mind." Our judgment as well as our will can go astray in the things that touch us closely, and therefore, just as we conform our wills to that of the superior to prevent it, as it were, from losing its bearing: "so, lest our judgment go astray, we must likewise make it conform to that of the superior." The saint adds, however, that "should another view come to our mind differing from that of the superior, and, if after having consulted the Lord in prayer, it seems to us that the same should be made known to him, we may well tell him. Still, lest our self-love and our own opinions deceive us, it is proper to take the precaution of maintaining a perfect evenness of mind both before and after disclosing our opinions, ever ready not only to undertake or to relinquish the purpose in question, but even to approve and acknowledge as the best course the one to be determined by the superior." This is what is termed *blind* obedience. This obedience, however, if explained with the reservations of St. Ignatius and those we have noted above, is not unreasonable, since it is to God that we subordinate our will and our intellect.

The Qualities of Obedience

In order to be *perfect,* obedience must be *supernatural* in its motive, *universal* in its extent, and *entire* in its execution.

Supernatural in its motive, which means that we are to see God Himself, or Jesus Christ in the persons of our superiors, since they have no authority except from Him. Nothing can render obedience more easy, for who would refuse to obey God? This is what St. Paul recommends to servants: "Be obedient to them that are your lords according to the flesh, with fear and trembling, in the simplicity of your heart, as to Christ: *Not* serving to the eye, as it were pleasing men, but, as the servants of Christ doing the will of God from the *heart* with a good will, serving, as to the Lord, and not to men" (2 Eph. 6:5-9).

In the same tenor St. Ignatius wrote to his religious of Portugal: "It is my ardent desire that you should carefully strive in all earnestness to see Our Lord Jesus Christ in your superiors, whosoever they may be, and, in their persons, reverently offer the Divine Majesty the honor due to Him. . . . Let them not consider the person whom they obey but let them see in that person Jesus Christ, for whose sake obedience is given. As a matter of fact, we are bound to obey a superior not on account of his prudence, of his goodness or of any other personal qualities wherewith God may have endowed him, but because he is God's representative. . . . Even if he should seem to lack in prudence and wisdom, this is not reason for failing in exact obedience, since in his capacity of superior, he represents a Person, whose wisdom is infallible and who will Himself provide for all those things in which His minister falls short, be it virtue or any other quality."

Nothing could contain greater wisdom than this principle; for, if today we obey our superior because his qualities please us, what shall we do tomorrow if we have another superior who seems to us to be devoid of such qualities? Besides, do we not forfeit the merit that should be ours, by subjecting ourselves to a man whom we esteem instead of submitting to God Himself? We must not, therefore, dwell upon the defects of our superiors, a thing that would render our obedience more difficult, nor yet upon their personal qualities, a thing that would render it less meritorious, but we must consider God living and commanding in their persons.

Universal in its extent, in the sense that we are to comply with all the commands of a superior as long as he commands lawfully. St. Francis de Sales says: "Obedience lovingly undertakes to do all that is commanded it with simplicity and without ever considering whether the command is good or bad, provided that the person who orders has authority to order, and that the command serves to unite our mind to God." He adds, however, that if a superior orders what is evidently against the law of God, it is one's duty not to submit. Such obedience, St. Thomas says, would be injudicious: "Obedience in unlawful matters is injudicious."

Aside from this case, the truly obedient person does not go astray even when the superior is wrong and commands what is less good than what we ourselves would choose. Then as a matter of fact God, to whom the submission is given and who sees the heart, rewards this obedience by assuring success. In other words, a superior may err in commanding, but we make no mistake in obeying.

Entire in the execution, hence *prompt, without reservations, persevering* and *even cheerful.*

a) *Prompt;* for love, which is the prime mover of perfect obedience, makes us obey with readiness: "The obedient man loves the command, and as soon as he is aware of it, whether it be to his taste or not, embraces it, caresses it, and cherishes it tenderly."

b) *Without reservations;* for to make a choice to obey in some things and disobey in others is to forfeit the merit of obedience; it is to show that we submit in what pleases us and, therefore, that our submission is not supernatural. Let us, then, remember what Our Lord says: *"One jot, or one tittle shall not pass of the law, till all be fulfilled"* (Matt. 5:18).

Perseverance is likewise required of us. This is one of the great merits of the virtue of obedience, "for to do a thing cheerfully which we are only commanded to do once, costs nothing; but when our superior says to us: You will do that always, and all through your life, there lies the virtue and there also the difficulty" (St. Francis de Sales).

c) *Cheerful, "for God loveth a cheerful giver"* (2 Cor. 9:7). In those things that entail hardship, obedience cannot be cheerful unless it be animated by love. In fact, nothing is painful to him who loves, because he thinks not of the suffering undergone, but of the person for whose sake he suffers. Now, if we see Our Lord in the person of him who commands, how can we fail to love Him, how can we fail to offer with our whole heart the trifling sacrifice that He demands, who died a victim of obedience for our sake! This is why we must always return to the general principle we have established, that is, to see God Himself in the person of our superior.

The Excellence of Obedience

St. Thomas does not hesitate to say that, after the virtue of religion, it is the most perfect of all the moral virtues, for the reason that it unites us closer to God than any other virtue, inasmuch as obedience detaches us from our own will, which is the main obstacle to union with God. Obedience is, besides, the mother and guardian of the other virtues, and transforms our ordinary actions into so many virtuous acts.

Obedience *unites* us to God and makes us habitually *share* in His life.

a) It subordinates our will directly to that of God and thereby all our other faculties, inasmuch as they are in turn subordinated to the will. This submission is all the more *meritorious* because it is *freely* made. Inanimate creatures obey God by an innate necessity of their nature, but man obeys by the free choice of his will. In so doing, man tenders his Sovereign Master the homage of what he holds most dear; he offers Him a pleasing sacrifice: *"Through obedience our wills are sacrificed"* (St. Gregory). Thus man enters *into communion with God,* since he has no longer any other will but God's will. He can make his own the words of Christ in His agony: *"Not my will, but thine be done."* This is a most meritorious and a most sanctifying union since it unites the best that is in us, our will, to that of God, ever good and ever holy.

b) Since the will is the master-faculty in man, by uniting it to God we unite to Him all the powers of our soul. Such a sacrifice is greater than the sacrifice of external goods made by the virtue of poverty, greater than the sacrifice of bodily pleasures entailed by the practice of chastity and of mortification. Obedience is, in all truth, the highest sacrifice we can make.

c) Obedience likewise constitutes the most abiding and lasting union. Through Sacramental Communion, we effect a temporary union with God, but through habitual obedience we establish in our soul a species of spiritual communion which is permanent, which causes us to abide in God as He abides in us, since we will what He wills and nothing but what He wills. This is, as a matter of fact, the most real, the most intimate, and the most effective of all unions.

OBEDIENCE IS LOGICALLY the *mother* and the *guardian* of all the virtues, as St. Augustine beautifully expresses it: *"In a rational creature, obedience is, as it were, the mother and guardian of all virtues."*

a) Obedience really becomes one with *charity*, for, as St. Thomas teaches, love effects primarily a union of wills. And is not this the doctrine of St. John? After declaring that he who pretends to love God and keeps not His commandments is a liar, the apostle adds: "But he that keepeth his word, in him in very deed the charity of God is perfected; and by this we know that we are in him" (1 John 2:5). And this is the teaching of the Divine Master Himself. He tells us that to keep His commandments is to love Him: "If you love me, keep my commandments" (John 14:15). True obedience, therefore, is in reality a genuine act of love.

b) Obedience makes us practice the other virtues, inasmuch as they all fall under a precept or a counsel: *"All acts of virtue come under obedience, inasmuch as they are contained in a precept"* (St. Thomas).

Thus, obedience makes us practice penance and mortification, so frequently prescribed in the Gospels, as well as justice, religion, charity, and all the virtues embodied in the Decalogue. More, obedience likens us to the *martyrs*, who sacrificed their lives for God, as St. Ignatius explains: "Through it, self-will and self-sufficiency are ever being immolated and laid as victims upon an altar, in such wise that instead of man's free-will there remains but the will of Jesus Christ Our Lord, made known to us by him who commands us. Nor is it merely the desire to live that is sacrificed by obedience, as happens in the case of martyrdom, but here all our desires are sacrificed at one and the same time." The same thought was expressed by St. Pacomius to a young monk longing for martyrdom: "It is far better to live in obedience and to die daily to self by mortifying our own desires, than to suffer martyrdom in imagination. He who mortifies himself, dies a martyr's death as far as need be; it is a far greater martyrdom to persevere in obedience all through life, than to die in a moment by a stroke of the sword."

c) Obedience offers us perfect *safety*. Left to ourselves, we would be wondering which would be the more perfect course to take, whereas obedience, by determining what is our duty in every instance, points out to us the surest way of working out our sanctification. By doing what obedience prescribes, we realize to the fullest possible extent the one essential condition of perfection, that is, compliance with God's good pleasure: "*I do always the things that are pleasing to him*" (John 8:29).

From this arises a sense of profound and abiding *peace*: "*There is great peace for them that love thy law, O Lord*" (Ps. 18:165). When we are desirous of doing only the will of God as manifested through superiors, we are not preoccupied about what is to be done nor about the means to be employed. All that we must do is to receive orders from him who holds God's place in our regard and to carry them out as best we can. Providence takes care of the rest, demanding of us not success, but simply the effort to fulfill the orders given. Besides, we may rest assured of the final result. It is clear that if we do God's will, He will take care of doing ours, that is to say, of granting our requests and fostering our designs. Obedience, then, means peace on earth, and at the end of life's journey, it is obedience that opens for us the gates of heaven.

Lastly, obedience *transforms* into virtues and merits the most commonplace occupations of life: meals, recreations, work. Whatever is done in the spirit of obedience shares in the merit of that virtue, is acceptable to God, and will be rewarded by Him. On the other hand, whatever is done in opposition to the will of superiors, no matter how praiseworthy in itself, is in reality an act of disobedience.

CONFORMITY TO THE divine will *purifies* us. Already in the Old Dispensation God often said that He is ready to forgive all sins and to restore the soul to the stainless splendor of its pristine purity, if it but undergo a change of heart or will: *"Wash yourselves: be clean. Take away the evil of your devices from my eyes. Cease to do perversely. Learn to do well... If your sins be as scarlet, they shall be made white as snow."* Now, to conform our wills to that of God, is assuredly to cease to do evil, and to learn to do good.

In the New Law, Our Lord declares from the very moment of His entry into the world that it is with obedience that He will replace all the sacrifices of the Ancient Law: "Holocausts for sin did not please thee. Then said I: Behold I come . . . that I should do thy will, O God." And, in truth, it is by obedience unto immolation of self that He has redeemed us: "He was made obedient unto death, even the death of the cross." In the same way, it is through obedience and through the acceptance of God-ordained trials in union with Christ that we shall atone for our sins and cleanse our soul.

Conformity to the divine will works out our *reformation*. What has deformed us is the disordered love of pleasure, to which through *malice* or through *weakness* we have yielded. Conformity to the divine will cures this *malice* and *weakness*.

It cures our *malice*. This malice is the result of our attachment to creatures, and especially, of our attachment to our own judgment and our own will. Now, by conforming our will to that of God, we accept His judgments as the standard of ours, His commandments and His counsels as the rule of our will. Thus we wean ourselves from creatures and from self and rid ourselves from such attachments.

It cures our *weakness*, the source of so many failings. Instead of relying on our own frail selves, we make through obedience the omnipotent God our support: He gives us His own strength, enabling us to overcome even the severest temptations: *"I can do all things in him who strengtheneth me."* When we do His will, He takes His good pleasure in doing our own by granting our petitions and helping our weakness.

Thus freed from our malice and weakness, we no longer sin deliberately against God and we gradually effect the reformation of our lives.

Through this conformity, we make our wills one with Christ's. The truest, the closest, the most far-reaching union that can exist is that between two wills. Through conformity to the divine will, we *unite* our will to that of Jesus Christ, whose food was to do the will of His Father. Like Jesus and with Jesus, we desire but what He wills and that all the day long. This is the fusion of two wills. We are one with Him, we adopt His views, His sentiments, His choices: "*Let this mind be in you, which was also in Christ Jesus;*" and soon we can make our own the words of St. Paul: "*I live, now not I, but Christ liveth in me.*"

In submitting our will, we yield and unite to God all the other faculties which are under its sway; hence, we yield and unite unto Him our whole soul, which by degrees conforms itself to the will and wishes of the Master. Thereby the soul acquires one by one all the virtues of Our Lord. In the words of St. Francis de Sales: "Abandonment is the virtue of virtues. It is the cream of love, the fragrance of humility, the merit, it seems to me, of patience and the fruit of perseverance." Hence, Our Lord calls by the tender names of brother and sister and mother those who do the will of His Father: "*For whosoever shall do the will of my Father that is in heaven, he is my brother and sister and mother.*" He repeatedly declares that the true test of love is doing God's will: *"If you love me, keep my commandments . . . not every one that saith to me, Lord, Lord, shall enter into the kingdom of heaven; but he that doth the will of my Father who is in heaven, he shall enter into the kingdom of heaven."*

Conformity to the divine will, then, is one of the most effective means of sanctification. Hence, we cannot but end with these words of St. Teresa: "The sole concern of him who has but entered into the way of prayer,—keep it in mind, it is very important—must be to strive courageously to conform his will to that of God. . . . Herein lies, whole and entire, the highest perfection to which we can attain. The more perfect this accord is, the more do we receive from the Lord and the greater is our progress." She adds that she herself had wished to live in this way of conformity without being raised to rapturous transports and ecstasies, so firm was her conviction that the path of conformity was all-sufficient to the most exalted perfection.

IT REMAINS TRUE that the vow of obedience is one of those that come hardest to human nature, precisely because we are so much attached to our own will. To observe it we need humility, patience and meekness; we have to mortify that strong tendency of ours to criticize superiors, to prefer our judgment to theirs, to follow our likes and at times our whims. To overcome these tendencies, to bend our will respectfully before that of superiors and to see God in them is, without doubt, to tend to perfection, for it is to cultivate some of the most difficult virtues. Besides, since true obedience is the best proof of love, to practice it is to grow in the virtue of charity.

As TO THOSE that live in communities, the more generously they obey their rules and constitutions, the more perfect they are. These rules are means of perfection which the Church has explicitly or implicitly approved and to the observance of which a religious binds himself on entering the community. Undoubtedly, to fail through weakness in certain details of some rules does not of itself constitute a sin. However, often a more or less sinful motive enters into such willful negligences, and the violation of rules, even when not sinful, certainly deprives us of a priceless opportunity for the acquisition of merit. It ever remains true that to observe one's rule is the safest means of accomplishing God's will and of living for Him: *"He who lives by rule, lives unto God."* To fail willfully in this matter, with no good reason for it, is an abuse of grace.

Section 6

Obedience –
The Sure Way to Sanctity

ST. ALBERT THE GREAT

NOT TO DISTINGUISH between what is good and what may be better, being persuaded that what is commanded is the best—this is perfect obedience.

ST. ALPHONSUS RODRIGUEZ

WHEN THE SUPERIOR gives an order, remember that it is God speaking, not he. At that moment the superior is but the instrument through which the voice of God passes. This is the true key to obedience and the reason those who are perfect obey so promptly in everything, without making any distinction between one superior and another. They obey in the same manner both the lowest and the higher superiors, both the imperfect and the perfect, because they consider neither the person nor the qualities of the superior, but only God, who is always and everywhere the same, of unchanging dignity and authority.

ST. AMBROSE

TRUE OBEDIENCE is to be recognized in the cheerful, unreluctant performance of what is displeasing and personally disadvantageous.

WE MARVEL AT the rewards of the patriarchs: let us imitate their submissiveness. We speak of the grace they received: let us imitate their obedience. They left their home land for another; let us exchange earth for heaven. Theirs was a change in abode; let ours be a change in spirit.

AN OLD MAN, Abraham yet believed that he could beget a son; a father, he yet held that he could sacrifice him. And his fatherly love did not make him hesitate when reverence for God came to the aid of his aged hand, for he knew that his son would please God more as a sacrifice than alive and safe. Hence, he took his beloved son to be sacrificed; without delay, he offered the one whom he had begotten so late. Nor was he restrained by hearing himself called by the name of father—when his son called him "father" and he answered, "my son." Indeed, names are moving assurances of love, but the commands of God are deserving of an even greater love. And thus, though both felt compassion for each other in their hearts, there was no hesitating in resolution. A father's hand raised the knife over his own son, and so that the sentence might not fail to be executed, in his fatherly love, he was in the act of striking the blow. He feared that the stroke would miss, that his right hand would weaken. He felt as would any father, but he did not recoil from his duty to God. He was hastening to obey, when he heard God's voice. Now then, let us also place God before all those we love.

ST. AUGUSTINE *

As SEVERITY IS READY to punish the sins which it discovers, so charity does not wish to discover anything to punish. That was the reason which kept me from coming to you when you were expecting my presence, which would not have been a joy added to your peace, but an increase of your strife. For how could I have overlooked your quarrel or left it unpunished if it had burst out in my presence as violently as it did in my absence; when it was not visible to my eyes, yet assailed my ears with your clamor? Perhaps your rebellion might have been even worse in my presence which I was obliged to withhold from you, since you were demanding something that was not good for you, and that would have formed a most dangerous precedent against sound discipline; thus, I should not have found you such as I wished and you would have found me such as you did not wish.

* Letter 211—St. Augustine to the Consecrated Virgins. From The *Fathers of the Church Series,* Vol. 32, translated by Sister Wilfred Parson. Used by permission of the publisher, The Catholic University of America Press.

When the Apostle writes to the Corinthians, he says: 'I call God to witness upon my soul that to spare you I came not any more to Corinth; not because we exercise dominion over your faith but we are helpers of your joy.' (2 Cor. 1:23.) I also spared myself lest 'I have sorrow upon sorrow,' (2 Cor. 2:3; Phil. 2:27), and rather than show my face among you I chose to pour out my heart to God for you and to plead the cause of your great peril, not in words before you, but in tears before God, that He may not turn to sorrow the joy I am wont to feel on your account. Even in the midst of the great scandals which abound everywhere in this world I oftentimes comfort myself with the thought of your numerous community, your chaste love, your conversation, and the grace of God which has been given more generously to you that you might not only despise carnal marriage, but might also choose the fellowship of dwelling together in a house in unity, (Ps. 132:1), that you may have one soul and one heart, (Acts 4:32), toward God.

When I think upon these good things among you, these gifts of God, my heart is accustomed to find some kind of rest amid the many storms arising from other evils by which it is shaken. 'You did run well; who hath bewitched you? This persuasion is not from God who hath called you. A little leaven, (Gal. 5:7-9; 3:1; 1 Cor. 5:6)—I hate to repeat the rest; this, rather, I desire and pray for and urge that the same leaven may be changed for the better that the whole lump may not be changed for the worse, as had almost happened. If, then, you have put forth new growth of sound wisdom, 'Pray that ye enter not into temptation,' (Matt. 7:41; Mark 14:38; Luke 22:46), that you enter not again into 'contentions, envying, animosities, dissensions, detractions, seditions, whisperings' (2 Cor. 12:20). For we have not planted and watered (1 Cor. 3:6-8) the Lord's garden in you only to reap these thorns (Jer. 12:13) from you. But if your weakness still stirs up a storm, pray that you may be delivered from temptation (Ps. 17:30). Those among you who trouble you, whoever they may be, will incur judgment unless they amend their lives.

Think what a misfortune it is that in the midst of our rejoicing over those born of God in unity we should have to bewail internal schism in the monastery. Stand firm in your good purpose and you will not want to change your superior, who has persevered in that monastery for so many years, during which you have increased in numbers and in age, and who has born you as a mother—not in her womb, but in her heart. All of you at your entrance found her there, either serving under the holy superior, my sister, or winning approval as actual superior herself when she received you. Under her you have been trained, under her you have received the veil, under her your numbers have multiplied, yet you make all this disturbance to force us to change her for you—when you ought to grieve if we wanted to change her for you. She is the one you have known, she is the one to whom you came, she is the one you have had for so many years of your increase. You have not received any new superior except your spiritual director, and if it is because of him that you are seeking a change, through envy for him that you have thus rebelled against your mother, why have you not rather demanded that he should be changed for you? If you shrink from doing this, for I know what respect and affection you have for him in Christ, why should you not shrink even more from attacking her? For the beginnings of your director's term of authority have been thrown into such disorder that he should be the one to desert you sooner than be subject to the invidious criticism of having it said that you would not have asked for another superior if you had not begun to have him for spiritual director. May God, then, calm and pacify your minds; may the work of the devil make no headway among you, but may 'the peace of Christ rule in your hearts' (Cf. Col. 3:15). Do not rush to destruction in your acute regret, either because you are vexed at not having the accomplishment of what you want, or because you are ashamed of wanting what you ought not; rather, by repenting renew your courage, and let it not be the repentance of the traitor Judas; (Matt. 27:3-5), but the tears of the shepherd Peter. (Matt. 26:75; Mark 14:72; Luke 22:62).... As you are gathered into one community, see that you do dwell together in unity in the house and that you have 'one heart and one soul' toward God.

ST. BASIL

IF WE CHOOSE A LIFE of pleasure rather than a life of obedience to the commandments, can we expect to enjoy a life of blessedness, of fellowship with the saints, and of the bliss of the angelic company in Christ's presence?

WE SHALL BE OUTSTANDING in the love of God, which at the same time stirs us to observe the Lord's commands, and in turn, as a result, love itself will be permanently and indestructibly preserved. Our Lord gives us the proof of this by saying on one occasion: "If you love me, keep my commandments" (John 14:15), and again: "If you keep my commandments, you will abide in my love" (John 15:10), and with still greater insistence: "as I also have kept my Father's commandments and abide in his love" (John 15:10).

With these words He teaches us that in undertaking any task we are always to set before ourselves, as our goal, the will of Him who has commanded the work, and to direct our efforts toward Him, as He tells us elsewhere: "I have come down from heaven, not to do my own will, but the will of him who sent me, . . . the Father" (John 6:38-39).

IF ONE DOES NOT LIKE the idea of being governed and if his own will acts as his judge, why does he go on living under a superior? Why does he take him as the guide of his life? But, having once and for all allowed himself to be counted among the body of the community, if he has been deemed a suitable vessel for the ministry, when a command seems beyond his strength, he should leave the decision concerning this to the one who imposed the command, and should show himself obedient and submissive even to death, remembering that the Lord became "obedient to death, even to death on a cross" (Phil. 2:8). Rebellion and contradiction, on the other hand, indicate many evils: weak faith, dubious hope, and a conceited and arrogant character. His disobedience, indeed, implies contempt for the one who gave the order. On the other hand, one who trusts in God's promises and anchors his hope in them will never draw back from orders no matter how difficult to execute they may be, for he knows that the sufferings of this time are not worthy to be compared with the future glory to be revealed (Rom. 8:18). Moreover, one who is convinced that "whoever humbles himself shall be exalted" (Matt. 23:12), and keeps in mind that "our present light affliction, which is for the moment, prepares for us an eternal weight of glory that is beyond all measure" (2 Cor. 4:17), obeys more readily than he who gives the order expects.

So THAT NO ONE may readily fall into the vice of willful quarreling, to his own ruin and that of others, this rule should, generally be followed in the community: first of all, no one is to concern himself with the superior's administrative method or curiously inquire about what is being done—except for those who are close to the superior by reason of their position or wisdom. The superior, on his part, is obliged to consult the latter and to deliberate with them on community matters, thus obeying the advice of Him who said: "Do nothing without counsel" (Sirach 32:19). Without doubt, if we have entrusted our souls to the guidance of a superior, as to one who must give an account to God, it is entirely absurd for us not to trust him in matters of small consequence, and as a result be filled with improper suspicions of our brother and also give others occasion to be suspicious. That this may not occur, all should confine themselves to the task which has been given them and dedicate themselves entirely to their own affairs, not concerning themselves at all with the doings of others, after the example of the holy disciples of the Lord. Although the affair of the Samaritan woman might have aroused suspicion, yet the Gospel tells us: "No one said, 'What dost thou seek?' or, 'Why dost thou speak with her?'" (John 4:27)

ST. BERNARD

HAVE YOU NOT read in the Gospel how the Boy Jesus teaches His faithful servants the rule of obedience? He remained in Jerusalem and told His parents that He must be about matters concerning His Father's glory. But realizing that Joseph and Mary were not of the same opinion, Jesus left the temple and went down with them to Nazareth. He, the Master, did not disdain to accommodate Himself to the feelings of His disciples; He who is God obeyed man; He who is wisdom itself submitted Himself to a laborer and a humble woman. What does the Gospel say? He was subject to them. What? Divine Wisdom submitted to the will of a carpenter and a woman, preferring the weak intelligence of men to the splendor of His own divine knowledge—and you have difficulty in giving up your views for those of God, who wants to enlighten you through your superiors? Learn that the greatest strength of spirit consists in submitting ourselves to others. As sublime and as useful as the services you claim to render to God may be, they must always be submitted to obedience. The foundation upon which all religious should build perfection, according to the teaching of the Fathers, is this: To prefer obedience to every other work, no matter how noble it may be.

THE VOW OF OBEDIENCE is intended to assure us that we are doing the will of God.

THE OCCUPATION of a religious is to obey.

GOD HAS DEIGNED to make our superiors in a certain sense identified with Himself. He considers as given to Himself the contempt or honor they receive. It is He who said: "He who hears you, hears me and he who despises you, despises me." And our rule in its turn tells us: the obedience given to superiors is given to God Himself. Everything commanded by one who holds the place of God, unless it be manifestly against the will of God, absolutely must be received as the command of God Himself. What does it matter if He wants to let us know His will directly or else through His ministers, that is, through angels or men?

IF YOU BEGIN to judge your superior, to murmur in your heart, even though you outwardly fulfill what is commanded, this is not the virtue of obedience, but a cloak over your malice.

THE TRULY OBEDIENT religious knows of no hesitation; he has a horror of procrastination; he ignores delays; he anticipates orders. He is all intent on knowing the will of him who commands.

"OUR COUCH IS VERDANT; the beams of our house are cedars, our rafters, cypresses" (Cant. 1:17).... The bridegroom will never grace that bed which you have sprinkled with the poison-oak and thorns of disobedience rather than with the flowers of obedience. As a result, He will not hear your prayers. When called, He will not come, because He will not give His treasures to one who is disobedient—He who so greatly loves obedience that He preferred death rather than disobedience.

I am greatly amazed at the impudence of some among us. When they have caused all of us much trouble because of their singular ways, have provoked us by their impatience, have manifested their contempt for authority by quarrelsomeness and insubordination, they are nevertheless so bold as to invite, with all the importunity of their prayers, the Lord of all purity to the defiled bed of their conscience. But, *"when you spread out your hands,"* He says, *"I close my eyes to you; though you pray the more I will not listen"* (Isa. 1:15).

ST. CATHERINE OF SIENA
(Reporting Christ's words to her)

OBEDIENCE GIVES A LIGHT in the soul, which shows whether she is faithful to me and her order and superior, in which light of holy faith she forgets herself; for by the obedience which she has acquired through the light of faith, she shows that her will is dead to its own feeling, and seeks the advantage of others and not her own. Just as the disobedient man who examines the will of his superior, may judge it according to his own low opinion and darkened knowledge instead of judging his own perverse will which gives him death, the truly obedient man, illumined by faith, judges the will of his superior to be good, and therefore does not examine it, but inclines his head and nourishes his soul with the odor of true and holy obedience. And this virtue increases in the soul in proportion to the shining of the light of faith, with which the soul knows herself, and me, whom she loves, and humbles herself. And the more she loves me and humbles herself, the more obedient she becomes, for obedience and her sister patience prove whether the soul is in truth clothed with the nuptial garment of charity, which is necessary to enter into eternal life.

ST. FRANCIS DE SALES

THE PERFECTION OF OBEDIENCE does not consist in carrying out the will of a superior who is pleasant and kind, who commands more in a humble, pleading manner than with authority. It consists in being submissive under the yoke of one who is domineering, severe, ill-humored and apparently never satisfied.

WE ALL HAVE A natural inclination to give commands and a great dislike for obedience. Yet, it is certain that obeying is more advantageous to us than commanding.

OBEY WHEN YOU are commanded to do pleasant things, such as eating or recreating. Obey in indifferent matters, such as wearing this or that habit, or taking one road or another. Obey in difficult matters, those which are hard and burdensome. Obey willingly and without objection; promptly and without hesitation; joyfully and without sadness. And above all, obey lovingly—for the love of Him who became obedient for our sakes, even to the death of the cross.

I ADMIRE THE INFANT of Bethlehem; He is all-powerful, and yet does whatever He is told without a word.

EVERYONE, UPON ENTERING religion, should leave his will outside the door, so as to have no other will than God's.

NO RELIGIOUS EVER became a saint without obeying.

THE PREDESTINATION of religious depends upon the love they have for their own rule, and upon their prompt fulfillment of the duties of their state.

THE TRULY OBEDIENT religious will come out the conqueror in all the difficulties into which he may be led by obedience, and with honor from all the roads he has traversed, however dangerous.

REST OUT OF OBEDIENCE, and the rest you take will win more merit and please God more than voluntary labor.

OUR CENTER IS THE will of God. If God desires me to do this action now, if God wants this thing of me, what more is necessary? While doing this, I am not obliged to do anything else.

OH! IF ONLY THE HOLY WILL of God were to reign in us, how happy we would be! Never would we commit any sin or live in accord with our irregular inclinations, for that holy will is the rule of all excellence and holiness.

WHEN WE FIND anything within us that is not conformed to God's will, we should prostrate ourselves before Him, and tell Him we detest our own will and repudiate it, together with all in us that could displease Him, or that is opposed to His holy love. And we should promise Him that we will never desire anything except what is conformable to His divine pleasure.

LET US OPEN THE ARMS of our will, embrace the cross with love and yield to the most holy will of God, chanting this hymn of resignation and conformity to Him: *Thy will be done on earth as it is in heaven.*

SOMETIMES WE NOTE people who say when they come to the service of God: Lord! into your hands I commend my spirit, but on the condition that you always give me consolations, with nothing contradictory to my will, and also give me superiors after my liking, in every respect.

Alas! what are you doing? Can you not see that this is not an imitation of Our Lord's resignation of His soul into the hands of God? Do you not know that this is just one of those reservations from which all our troubles, disturbances and other imperfections usually arise? For, as soon as things happen which do not match our expectations and anticipations, desolation suddenly grips our poor souls. What can be the reason for this if not because we are not resigned, with detachment, into the hands of God? Oh, how happy we would be if we faithfully practiced this virtue! Without a doubt, we would reach the highest perfection.

Reflect that the eternal Son of God Himself came to teach us this submission and reverence owed to the supreme will. He did it by informing us with words that He had not come to do His own will, but rather that of His Father—but still more He did it by the example of His own resignation: "My Father! if it be possible, let this chalice pass from me; yet not my will, but yours be done." Our divine Master also taught us to ask daily that the will of God be done on earth as it is in heaven. Finally, He concluded the course of His life on this earth by surrendering Himself to the will of His eternal Father: "My Father! into your hands I commend my spirit."

Therefore, on every occasion, say with Our Lord: *My God, I commend my spirit,* absolutely and without reserve *into your hands.* Do you want me to be in aridity or in consolation? Do you want me to be opposed, to meet with difficulties and repugnances, to be loved or not loved? In every circumstance, *I commend my spirit into your hands.* Let those, therefore, who are occupied with the exercises of an active life not desire to exchange them for those of a contemplative, and likewise, let those who are contemplatives not leave their contemplation until God commands it. Let us be silent when it is necessary and speak when necessary. If we act thus, at the hour of our death, we shall be able to say, as did our divine Savior: *It is consummated.* My God! all is consummated. I have carried out your divine will in the various events that happened to me by your providence. What else remains for me to do now except to commend my spirit into your hands, at the closing of my life, as I gave it to you at the dawn of it, and during its course?

O my God! lead me by your will. Take me through cold, heat, light, darkness, labor, repose— though you lead me to the gates of death I shall fear nothing in your company.

O heavenly Father! may your will be done on this earth, where consolations come rarely and labors are innumerable. And you my soul, take it as a daily practice to say, in any suffering that comes your way: Not my will, but that of my God be done!

A SOUL IN LOVE with God is so transformed as to become identified with the will of God instead of being merely obedient to it.

THE FIRST INSPIRATION GOD ever sends a man is that of obeying. Was there ever a finer, more unmistakable inspiration than that of St. Paul: "Arise, and go into the city, and it will be told thee what thou must do" (Acts 9:6)? He was to obey Ananias, who was, according to St. Dorotheus, the renowned Bishop of Damascus. If a man claims to be inspired, and yet refuses to obey his superiors or to heed their advice, he is an imposter.

THE LOVING SOUL is so submissive to the will of God that God does what He pleases with it.

ST. FRANCIS OF ASSISI

THE TRULY OBEDIENT religious never asks whither he is sent; he is never concerned as to how he came here and he does not seek to be taken away. If he acquires honors, they only increase his humility, and the more praise he receives, the more unworthy does he deem himself.

ST. GREGORY NAZIANZUS

HAVING TAKEN the nature of a slave, Christ condescends to enter fully into the life of His fellow-slaves and of slaves generally; and assumes a form different from His own, bearing the whole of me and all that I am within Himself, in order that in Himself He may melt away my lower self, as fire the wax and the sun the morning mists, in order that I, through fusion with Him, may take in exchange all that is His. Hence in very deed does He honor obedience and make trial of it in suffering. For the mere intention was not enough, just as it is not enough for us, unless we carry it out in act. For the act is the proof of the intention. Nor would it be far wrong to understand that He experienced our obedience and measured all human things by His own sufferings, and did so because of His affection and love for men: so that He can estimate our experiences by His own, and reckon by suffering and weakness how much to demand of us and how much to yield to our infirmity.

ST. GREGORY THE GREAT *

SINCE A GOOD OCCASION has presented itself to speak of the virtue of obedience, we are pleased to treat of it in a more precise manner and to point out

---

* From *Moralia II*. Translated by the Daughters of St. Paul.

its merit. Indeed, it is only obedience which introduces the other virtues into the mind and protects them. Thus, the first man viewed a command to execute, and if he had chosen to submit docilely, he would have achieved eternal bliss without fatigue. Hence Samuel says: "Obedience is better than sacrifices: and to hearken rather than to offer the fat of rams. Because it is like the sin of witchcraft, to rebel; and like the crime of idolatry, to refuse to obey" (1 Kings 15:22-23). Rightly is obedience preferable to sacrifices, for with the latter one offers the flesh of other creatures, but with obedience he sacrifices his own will. For this reason, a person placates God much faster when he represses the arbitrary actions of his own pride and immolates himself with the sword of the divine command. . . .

Only obedience possesses the merit of faith, without which one is really unfaithful even if he seems faithful. . . . Hence Truth tells us in the Gospel: "Him who comes to me, I will not cast out. For I have come down from heaven, not to do my own will, but the will of him who sent me" (John 6:37-38). What does He mean? Does He mean that if He had done His own will He would have rejected those who come to Him? Yet who does not know that the Son's will never deviates from that of His Father? But since the first man chose to do his own will and so left the joy of paradise, the second, when He came to redeem man, made it clear that He was carrying out His Father's will and not His own.

Thus He taught us how to stay in paradise. In doing the will of the Father and not His own, He does not send away those who come to Him, for by His example He subjected us to obedience and thus closed the exit for us.

And He went on to say besides: "Of myself I can do nothing. As I hear, I judge, and my judgment is just because I seek not my own will, but the will of him who sent me" (John 5:30). We are asked to practice obedience until death. Now if Christ judges as He hears, He is obedient as a judge, too. So it is that obedience to the end of our present life should not seem hard to us when our Redeemer assures us that He will be obedient even when He comes to judge us. What is so marvelous about a sinful man's submitting to obedience for the short space of this life when the very Mediator between God and man will not stop obeying even when He comes to reward the obedient?

ST. IGNATIUS LOYOLA *

THE SUPERIOR is to be obeyed, not because he is prudent or good or qualified by any other of God's gifts, but because he holds God's place and authority, as Eternal Truth has said, "He who hears you, hears me; he who rejects you, rejects me"

* From *Letter on Obedience*. Reprinted with permission from the America Press.

(Luke 10:16). Nor on the contrary, even though he lack prudence, is he to be any the less obeyed in that in which he is superior, since he represents Him who is infallible Wisdom and who will supply what is lacking in His minister; nor even if he lack other desirable qualities, since after Our Lord had expressly said, "The Scribes and the Pharisees have sat on the chair of Moses," He continued, "All things, therefore, that they command you, observe and do. But do not act according to their works" (Matt. 23:2).

I should wish, therefore, that all of you would train yourselves to recognize Christ our Lord in any superior whomsoever, and with all devotion to reverence and obey the Divine Majesty in him.

I also desire that this be firmly fixed in your minds, that the first degree of obedience is very low, which consists in the execution of what is commanded, and that it does not deserve the name unless it attain the merit of obedience by rising to the second degree, which is to make the superior's will one's own, so that there will be not merely the effective fulfilling of the command, but an interior conformity in that both wish and do not wish the same. For this reason it is said in Scripture that "obedience is better than sacrifice" (1 Kings 15:22), for, according to St. Gregory, "In other sacrifices the flesh of another is slain, but in obedience our own will is sacrificed."

Now, since it is man's will that is of such great value, so too is the offering of it, when by obedience it is consecrated to his Creator and Lord. How great a deception it is, and how dangerous, for those who think it lawful to withdraw from the will of their superior—I do not mean only in those things pertaining to flesh and blood, but even in those which of their nature are spiritual and holy, such as fasts, prayers and other pious works! Let them hear Cassian's comment, in the *Conference of Daniel the Abbot*: "It is one and the selfsame kind of disobedience, whether in earnestness of labor or the desire of ease one breaks the command of the Superior, and as harmful to break the rules of the monastery to sleep as to remain awake. And, finally, it would be just as bad to fail to obey the command of the Abbot, whether you did it to read or to sleep."

TRY BELOVED BRETHREN, to make the surrender of your will complete. Offer freely to your Creator and Lord, through His ministers, the liberty He has bestowed upon you. Do not think it a slight advantage of your free will that in obedience you are able to restore it entirely to Him who gave it to you. You do not lose it by doing so, but rather perfect it by conforming your will to the surest rule of all rectitude, the will of God, the interpreter of which is the superior who governs you in place of God.

HE WHO AIMS at making an entire and perfect oblation of himself, besides his will, must offer his understanding, which is a distinct degree and the highest degree of obedience. He should not only wish the same as the superior, but think the same, submitting his own judgment to the superior's, so far as a devout will can incline the understanding.

... THE OBEDIENT MAN is a living holocaust, most acceptable to His Divine Majesty, as he keeps nothing for himself.

THE FIRST MEANS to attain to the perfection of the obedience of the understanding is, as I said in the beginning, that you do not behold in the person of your superior a man subject to error and distress, but rather Him whom you obey in man, Christ, highest Wisdom, immeasurable Goodness, and infinite Charity, who you know cannot be deceived and will not deceive you. Now, because you are certain that you have taken this yoke of obedience upon your shoulders for the love of God, submitting yourself to the will of the superior in order to be more conformed to God's will, rest assured that His most faithful charity will never fail to guide you by the means which you yourselves have chosen. Consequently, when the superior gives you a command do not take his voice to be any other than the voice of Christ. In this sense St. Paul speaks to the Colossians, when he exhorts subjects to obey their superiors: "Whatever you do, work at it from the heart, as for the Lord and not for men, knowing that from the Lord you will receive the inheritance, as your reward. Serve the Lord Christ" (Col. 3:23-24). And St. Bernard: "Whether it be God, or man His vicar, who commands anything, we must obey with equal diligence and show equal reverence—when, however, man commands nothing that is contrary to God." Thus, if you do not look upon man with the eyes of the body, but upon God with those of the soul, you will find no difficulty in conforming your will and judgment to the rule of conduct which you yourselves have chosen.

The second means is that you be quick to look for reasons to defend that which the superior commands, or to which he is inclined, rather than to disapprove of it. A help to this will be to love whatever obedience enjoins. Obedience will in this way become cheerful and unperturbed; for, as St. Leo says, "It is not hard to serve when we love what is commanded."

There is a third means of subjecting the understanding, which is easier and was much used by the holy Fathers. It is to presuppose and believe, very much as we are accustomed to do in matters of faith, that what the superior enjoins is the command of God our Lord and His holy will. Then proceed blindly, without enquiry of any kind to the carrying out of the command, with a kind of passion to obey.

This manner of subjecting one's own judgment without further enquiry, supposing that the command is holy and in conformity with God's will, is in use among the saints and ought to be imitated by anyone who wishes to obey perfectly in all things—where it is manifest, of course, that there is no sin.

Letter on Obedience

LET ONE WHO is about to enter religious life understand that he will not find a lasting, peaceful home unless he crosses the threshold with both feet at once—that is with both will and judgment.

MY SON, I want you to be happy and to rejoice in the Lord. The religious has no reason to be sad and many reasons for rejoicing. If you want to be joyful and cheerful always, be always humble and obedient.

THE OBEDIENT PERSON surpasses the level of his human condition and daringly launches out toward the highest grade of glory and dignity. Shaking off the ties of his human nature, he binds himself to God with strong bonds and in the most intimate manner—to God, the Supreme Good. God being the only one who can fill the soul of man, He does so to the degree that He finds it free of whatever could oppose His gifts, that is, of self-will. Hence, it follows that whoever attains to perfect obedience can make his own those words of the Apostle that are really the formula of sanctity: "It is no longer I who live, but Christ lives in me."

WE HAVE TO SET ASIDE all our own judgment, and keep our minds ever willing and quick to obey in all things the spouse of Christ our Lord, our holy mother the hierarchical Church.

We ought to be more quick to give our approval and praise to the commands, recommendations and mode of action of our superiors rather than to criticize them. Granted that some of the commands and so forth might not have been deserving of praise, still to speak out against them, while preaching publicly or speaking in public, would be to give rise to faultfinding and scandal rather than to do good. The result would be anger on the part of the people toward those in authority, be they secular or spiritual superiors. However, while speaking evil of superiors in their absence is harmful, it may be beneficial to speak of their improper conduct with those who can remedy the situation.

IF WE WANT to progress securely in all things, we have to hold firmly to this principle: What appears to me to be white, I will believe to be black if the hierarchical Church so declares. For I must be convinced that in Christ our Lord, the bridegroom, and in the Church, His spouse, only one Spirit reigns, which governs and rules for the salvation of souls. Indeed, it is by the same Spirit and Lord who gave the Ten Commandments that our holy mother Church is governed and ruled.

ST. JEROME

YOU WILL ADVANCE in proportion as you deny your own will.

RESPECT YOUR SUPERIOR as your master, and love him as your father.

ST. JOHN CLIMACUS

IF EVER FEELINGS, thoughts and judgments against obedience should come to you, even though they may seem good and holy, disregard them and promptly reject them as you would thoughts against chastity and against the faith.

BLESSED JOHN NEUMANN, C.SS.R. *

I BEG OF YOU to introduce the spiritual exercises and to maintain community life as strictly as possible. I desire that your house be a model of observance. . . . I am not afraid the necessaries of life will be wanting for you, for God and St. Joseph will always send something in time if the sisters will deserve such protection by their regularity and mutual condescension. *To a mother superior*

LET YOUR FIRST study be your rules. If you be faithful to them, Our Lord will bless your labors,

---

* From *Venerable John Neumann*, C.SS.R., by Rev. Michael J. Curley, C.SS.R. Used by permission of the Redemptorist Fathers of the Baltimore Province, holders of the copyright.

and it is only the blessing of God and not your own endeavors that puts the crown upon your work. I firmly believe that a sister, with comparatively-speaking few educational advantages, yet faithful to her duties to God, will be more successful in her teaching than one with more extensive learning, yet less exact in the fulfillment of her rule.

To a group of nuns

... My dear Father, whenever we feel a great desire to help the most abandoned, let us be ready to go to their aid if we are sent, but in the meantime let us pray that the Lord may help them in a more ordinary way. Since we cannot do more than pray and do penance for them, let us take things easy and leave the rest to God.... The principles of faith fade out of our hearts in proportion as we allow the principles of the world to come in. We place our confidence, not in God but in our own intelligence, experience, and so on. We seek not what is least or most difficult or most despised but what is easiest and what redounds most to our own glory. If only we loved God alone and from our whole heart, how easy it would be for our superiors to lead us according to the prescriptions of the rule. God would then urge us on and we would not resist. This, my dear Father, in my opinion, is the cause of all the unhappiness that seems to reign here. I believe that what is most necessary is that we should pray for one another daily with great confidence: *Spiritum rectum innova in visceribus meis. Adveniat regnum tuum.* *To his one-time mission partner*

ST. JOHN OF THE CROSS

IT MUST BE NOTED that among the many wiles the devil uses to deceive spiritual persons, the most common is to deceive them under an appearance of a good and not under an appearance of an evil. For he knows that if they recognize evil they are not likely to touch it. Therefore you must ever have misgivings concerning what seems good if it is not commanded by obedience. Security and success in this regard come from taking due counsel about it.

GOD PREFERS obedience to sacrifice, and the actions of a religious are not his own—they belong to obedience. If you withdraw them from obedience, you will have to account them as lost.

NEVER CONSIDER your superior as less than if he were God, no matter who the superior is, because to you he stands in the place of God. And realize that the devil, the enemy of humility, interferes herein greatly. If you consider your superior in the way that has been said, you gain and profit greatly. Otherwise, your loss and harm are great. With great vigilance, therefore, refrain from considering his character, his ways, his habits, or any of his other characteristics, for, if you do this, you will do yourself the harm of exchanging divine obedience for human, being moved, or unmoved, only by the observable characteristics of your superior, instead of by the invisible God whom you serve in his person. And your obedience will be vain. It will be more unfruitful if you take offense at any unpleasant characteristic of your superior, or if you rejoice when you discover him to be good and pleasant. For I tell you that the devil has ruined the perfection of a great multitude of religious by causing them to consider these characteristics. Their obedience is of very little value in God's eyes, for they have considered these things and not paid respect to obedience alone. If you do not strive until you come to regard it as indifferent to you, in so far as your own feelings are concerned, whether this person or that person be your superior, in no way can you become a spiritual person or keep your vows well.

ST. LAWRENCE JUSTINIAN

HE THAT HAS consecrated himself to God by the immolation of self-will will receive all that he shall ask for.

VEN. LIBERMANN *

... A MAN WHO desires nothing upon earth fears nothing either; and a man who desires nothing

---

* From *The Spirit of Venerable Libermann*, by Jean Gay, C.S.Sp. Used by permission of Alba House, a division of St. Paul Publications.

and fears nothing, must necessarily have his mind and heart in perfect freedom. For, where do pains, troubles, worry and embarrassment of mind and heart come from, especially in those who wish to serve God? They arise from the fact that such persons do not give themselves entirely to Him, or do not leave to Him the entire care of their spiritual progress. They propose to themselves the acquisition of such a virtue, or the possession of such a sentiment. They wish to serve God in such or such a manner, and they imagine that they cannot sanctify themselves in any other way than according to these ideas. A man of perfect self-denial, on the contrary, places himself entirely in the hands of God; and never seeks himself; and, on this account, his heart is always in profound peace and great freedom. You doubtlessly know the words of St. Augustine: "Love and do what you will."

LET THE GRACE of God be your guide, and do not imagine you are able to lead yourself. Be like a man who is blind and dead before God; let Him conduct and carry you wherever He pleases. Do not go and ask Him: "Lord, why do you make me blind?" This is not your business, it is His right to do with you as He pleases, and it is your duty to be overjoyed with everything that He decides.

I have noticed that you endeavor to find out what is wanting to you; you say that it is simplicity of intention, tranquillity of soul, etc., which you need. What advantage do you hope to gain from all these researches? You know what you are expected to do. Well, accomplish it in peace, and do not waste your time in seeking if this or that is wanting to you. . . .

WHAT HAVE WE TO DO on this earth except to put ourselves body and soul into the hands of God, that He may dispose of us according to His good pleasure, that He may sacrifice us entirely for His glory?

Our one and only thought should be to walk in the way Divine Providence has traced for us. Now, if we want to be faithful instruments in His hand, we should never be troubled about ourselves. Let us go on with simplicity. Let us not be concerned about the future, nor be tormented about the past. Let us accomplish the work of God with peace and confidence. In the present, in each moment of our lives, let us place our souls in the hands of God peacefully, humbly and gently. We should never want, or desire anything, but cast ourselves into His hands, and sacrifice ourselves to His holy will every moment of our lives.

The divine goodness will frequently put us to the test. Let us be docile, peaceful, humble. Let us never give way to sadness, nor ever allow our imagination to dominate over us. Besides doing wrong thereby, we harm our souls and those of others, and often we compromise God's work. As a general rule, every movement of our soul which tends to discouragement and trouble is displeasing to God. If we yield to it, we shall open all the avenues of our souls to the demon, who misses no opportunity to work our destruction.

Put everything into the hands of God. It is not our work we are doing; it is His. We are looking not after our own but His interests in the souls we want to save for Him. He is powerful enough to insure success; if He sees fit to oppose our efforts, that concerns Him alone. We ought to pray and wait, and not to judge or fathom the conduct of our divine Master. Dear friend, for the love of God, be more courageous, more detached and more calm.

ST. PASCAL BAYLON

Obedience comes first; devotion must take second place.

ST. TERESA OF AVILA

My daughters, what do you think is the will of our Lord? It is for us to become quite perfect and thus be made one with Him and His Father, as He prayed that we might be.... It is not necessary for us to receive any special gifts from God so as to attain to conformity with His will; by giving us His Son to teach us the way, He has done enough.... Only two things does our Lord ask of us: love of Him and of our neighbor. These we must strive to acquire. Let us make an effort to do His will perfectly; then shall we be united to Him.

WHAT A LOSS we suffer when we withhold from God what we offer Him in the "Our Father"! ... We can promise lightly enough to relinquish our will to somebody else, but when the time of the test arrives, we shall discover it to be the hardest thing in the world to do thoroughly.... Let not the promises you made to a Lord so great be merely empty words of compliment. Rather, force yourselves to suffer whatever God disposes. Any other manner of surrendering Him our will could be compared to offering someone a jewel, pleading with him to accept it, and then holding it tightly when he stretches forth his hand to take it. These mockeries must not be for Him, who was so mocked for us! Even if there were no other reason, it would be wrong so to mock Him again and again, with every repetition of the "Our Father." Once and forever, let us give Him the precious jewel we have so often offered Him.... Sometimes, we not only offer our jewel to God, but we actually place it in His hand, and then we turn right around and take it back. So generous at first, we are so miserly afterwards that it would have almost been better to have been more cautious when giving....

Oh, sisters, what power there is in this gift of the will! If it is made with proper determination, it cannot help but induce the Almighty to become one with our lowliness, to transform us into Himself, and to unite the creature with the Creator. Will you not be well recompensed? How kind your Master is—He knows how to gain the good will of His Father and He shows us how and by what means we may serve Him. The more determined we are and the more clearly our actions witness to the fact that our vows are not empty, the closer does God draw us to Himself, lifting us above all earthly things and even above ourselves. In this way, He prepares us to receive tremendous favors even in this life.

In obedience we find serenity, which is so greatly treasured by souls who want to please God. For if they have really resigned themselves to this holy obedience, and if they have surrendered their understanding to it and are ready to follow no opinion but their confessor's (if they are men or women religious, their superior's), the devil stops attacking them by constantly upsetting them, for he sees that instead of gaining he is losing.

It is a great comfort to me when I am in choir to look at these pure souls, occupied in praising God, and I cannot help but feel the same way, too, concerning many other things, such as obedience, noting how happy cloister and solitude make the sisters as well as occasions for mortification. The more grace the Lord gives to superiors for testing them in this regard, the happier I find them. And the superiors frequently tire more of testing them than they do of obeying, for in that regard, their desires are never satisfied. . . .

I BELIEVE that since satan sees there is no road that leads more quickly to the highest perfection than this of obedience, he suggests many difficulties under the color of some good, and makes it distasteful; let people look well into it and they will see plainly that I am telling the truth. Wherein lies the highest perfection? It is clear that it does not lie in interior delights, not in great raptures, not in visions, not in the spirit of prophecy, but in the conformity of our will to the will of God, so that there shall be nothing we know He wills that we do not will ourselves with our whole will, and accept the bitter as joyfully as the sweet, knowing it to be His Majesty's will.

. . . I WAS ONCE CONSIDERING the great penitential life lived by Doña Catalina de Cardona. I reflected, too, that judging by the desires which the Lord has sometimes given me, I might have done more than I do if it were not for the obedience owed my confessors. I was wondering if it would be better not to obey them in this regard, but the Lord said to me: 'No, daughter. You are on the straight, secure road. Do you see what a life of great penitence she lives? Yet, I prize your obedience even more.'

IT IS OBVIOUS that one cannot give what he does not have: he must possess the thing first. And, let me tell you, there is no better way of obtaining this treasure than to dig and labor to get it from this mine of obedience. The more we dig, the more we shall find; and the more we submit ourselves to human beings, and have no other will but our superior's, the more totally shall we become masters of our wills, the more completely shall we bring them into conformity with God's will. Reflect, then, sisters, whether our renunciation of the joys of solitude is not well repaid. I assure you that there is no reason for lack of solitude to prevent you from preparing to achieve this genuine union of which I have spoken—this union which consists in making our will one with God's. It is this union which I desire and would wish to see in you all: I do not covet for you those delightful types of absorption which one may experience and which are called by the name of union. They may amount to union if the effect of them is what I have described; but if this suspension leaves behind it much self-will and little obedience, it seems to me that it will be a union with self-love, not with God's will. May His Majesty grant that I myself may act in accord with my belief. . . .

ST. VINCENT DE PAUL

OBEDIENCE CONSISTS not only in doing what we are commanded at the present, but also in the constant disposition to do everything that may be asked of us on any occasion whatsoever.

Section 7

Not My Will but Yours

"GOD'S WILL, NOT MINE BE DONE" *
Richard Cardinal Cushing

ALWAYS TRY TO ENJOY the liberty which God the Father has given you. I propose to offer a few thoughts on the manner in which a true son of God should live. The purpose of your religious life is to come close to your Eternal Father. What is the one thing necessary if you are to come close to God? Can we sum it up in one single word? Yes—detachment. Put out of your life everything that is not God. Detach yourself first from your own will, putting in its place God's will. Is not this Our Lord's meaning when in the Our Father He has us say: "Hallowed be Thy Name, Thy Kingdom come, Thy will be done,"—in my life first of all and then in the lives of others? Let this truth impress itself well into your mind.

If you wish to grow in sanctity, if you wish to be a favored child of God, give up everything that your conscience tells you is holding you back from union with Him. Then there will be no limit to His graces. Give Him your will in its entirety. Say: "Whatever there is in my life at this present mo-

* From *Meditations for Religious,* by His Eminence, Richard Cardinal Cushing. St. Paul Editions, Boston, 1959.

ment which is keeping me back from You, that may interfere with my union with You, no matter how innocent, take it out of my life." We must have this frame of mind. God will not permit any restrictions on His love. God has given us Himself, He has given us everything; there is nothing that He could have done that He has not done, but He expects a return worthy of that generosity. Are you prepared to give it to Him? Are you prepared to detach yourself from all creatures, including your own will?

Sometimes a thought like that frightens us, and makes us a little timid. That is where the Fatherhood of God comes into play. St. Paul said: "For those who love God all things work together unto good" (Rom. 8:28). Almighty God will not permit anything that is not good for us. We must trust Him. Throw yourself entirely on the mercy of God, and you will fear nothing. This is what He wants, this confidence, this spirit of faith. Tell Him in childlike simplicity: "O my God, what is there in my life that is keeping me back from that degree of union You desire? Is it my pride? My own will? Some conceit of heart of which I am only half conscious?" It is necessary, this leaving of all things, and after all, is not this the religious life? The leaving of all things is not completed when you leave the world. You will be leaving things all your life. You constantly leave everything behind. God is always asking. Be sure you never say no, always say yes. This is detachment and, after all, is it not the most logical thing in the world? Why are you here at all? You are here to give glory to God. The love and the service He desires we cannot give Him unless in His own way.

Some have a desire to be holy but they inject too much of their own will into it. You must grow holy according to God's way, not according to your own way. You will never reach holiness on that plan; you must give it up, cast it aside. Throw yourself completely on God's providence. As St. Francis de Sales said: "Ask nothing, refuse nothing." Let God direct your life; He knows, after all, what is good for us. It is a strange thing that even in our prayers, sometimes, instead of bringing our will into conformity with the will of God, we try to bend the will of God to our requirements. We are not reconciled to the sweet, adorable and gracious will of God.

You have many devotions. I recommend this one to you: devotion to the holy will of God. That was our Blessed Mother's devotion: "Behold the handmaid of the Lord; be it done to me according to Thy word" (Luke 1:38)—according to Thy will, not mine, Thy way, not mine. We say that, too, in the Angelus, and ten minutes later we complain because God has taken us at our word. It is the devotion of Our Lord, also: "I seek not My own will, but the will of Him Who sent Me" (John 5:30). You must take that text for your own or this one: "My food is to do the will of Him who sent Me" (John

4:34). This is very fundamental in the religious life. You can leave many things outside, you may leave wealth, friends, and relatives behind, but you take yourself, and the religious life is the leaving of self. The first is easy: to enter the sacred walls of the monastery, but the second is the perpetual and real sacrifice. I want you at this point to ask yourself honestly: "Am I detached? Am I seriously striving to take everything out of my life that is not God? My own desires, inclinations, likes and dislikes? Anything and everything?"

(The question is: "Am I striving?" not "Have I succeeded?" Sometimes, you know, you may be a little severe with yourself. Any soul that is trying to be holy is growing holy.)

Examine yourself to see whether you are willing to seek God alone, to abandon yourself to the entire will of God, to take each day as it comes, to have no desires except that the will of God may be accomplished in your regard. Oh, if you strive to practice it through life you will, unquestionably, grow in holiness. The religious who abandons himself to God's holy will enjoys the true liberty of the children of God. Why? Because his will is in God and everything that happens is God's will. The element of fear is thus removed from religious life.

Religious are in God's blessed house, living a religion of love, serving a God of love, and yet, is it not strange how much fear, anxiety or timidity enters the lives of some? Why? The only reason can be that they are afraid something may happen to them which they do not want. In other words, they have quite a bit of self-love in their souls.

They, instead, who have abandoned their will once and for all have the true liberty of the children of God. Whatever comes—joy or sorrow, success or failure, trial or praise—it is God's will, therefore they fear nothing.

That is a very comforting thought, and you will have a comforting headline for the rest of your lives. Now I want you to try to lay that foundation stone of the spiritual edifice you are building. Lay it carefully, permanently. Tell God that if there is anything that is keeping you back, you want to lay it aside forever. You will have struggles, trials, and temptations; sometimes you may even fail. Our inclinations and feelings mean nothing to God, but you must have written on your soul: "God's will, not mine, be done."

After all, is not that the logical relationship that should exist between father and child? What greater pleasure should the child find than in conforming himself to the will of his father? What could be a greater joy? Tell God: "Here is my soul; it is not mine but Yours. Form it and fashion it according to Thy will; it is You Who supplied the means of sanctifying it." Remember that everything that happens from this hour to the hour you die is designed by God for your good, to sanctify your soul. Thank Him for all that.

Often say this little prayer: "Welcome be the will of God." Is it welcome to you? Yes, but sometimes we forget that. "May the beautiful, adorable and gracious will of God be accomplished in all hearts forever." Say that prayer or something like it. Pray that God's will may be done in others, pray for the world. Pray that God's will may be accomplished in everyone's heart and in your own. In the morning, pray that His will may be done in every human heart that day. If you start this apostolate, it will bring your own heart into conformity with His. Ask Almighty God that His will may be done particularly by priests, religious and all souls belonging to Him in a special manner.

A prayer of this kind will mean much. It will teach you the love that God expects from you. It will remove obstacles that stand between you and God. When these are removed, God's light and love have free play. That is what sanctity is: union between God and your soul. Self-will is like the shades on a window. We pull down the shades of self-will over our souls and we cannot see the will of God. Let up those shades and God will show Himself to you. What a beautiful thought that is! How happy the religious who throws everything aside and says: "I want God, that is all." How happy the religious who makes that plunge into the will of God. He fears nothing and has no anxieties. Whatever happens makes no difference. Why? Because it is God's will and that is his will, too.

How simple these things are if we would get down to bedrock! Sometimes we see this world going around, see men doing their own will, nations and peoples separating themselves from God and we think: Where is the will of God? It is there and if people will not follow the will of God, if they insist on following their own desires, they will fall into the will of God in another way. We must follow God's will, but He gives us the privilege of following it freely and of our own desire, by His grace. How thankful I ought to be that I, a sinner, have been called by Him to unite this tiny will of mine with His omnipotent will; that I have been called to this union with God, Who moves heaven and earth! Ask Him for this now; mean what you say. Do not do things by halves, make no limitations or restrictions. A test of a good religious is docility to the will of God.

What is the use of saying a great many prayers while separating yourself from God? If you have done this in the past, however, do not be afraid. God is too good to hold things against people. Sometimes we inject our own ways into our ideas of God, and because we are inclined to hold grudges, we think God is that way. God is not like that. No matter what you have been in the past, just be sorry and tell Him you want to change. That is all He wants. Past failings will never keep a soul back from a close union with God.

Meditate now on these thoughts. Follow your own natural inclinations with the aid of grace. The workings of the Holy Spirit in each soul constitute a world of grace. Follow the inspirations of grace; pray that everyone will cooperate. Pray that everyone will give obedience to the will of God. Praying for others has a wonderful effect on us. If I pray for others I am immediately ashamed. I like that word "ashamed;" it is a good word to use. We are children before God, and children are ashamed when they are naughty. Let us use that word in praying to God; it shames us into the wholesome, humble attitude we ought to take towards our Heavenly Father. If we could get a glimpse into the depths of that infinitely good God, no words would be needed. We cannot do it by vision but by faith.

Ask God to show you His will that you may follow it. "He who follows Me does not walk in the darkness" (John 8:12). The will of God will light up your soul as the sunlight lights up your way on this earth.

OBEDIENCE—
A GREAT SECRET OF SUCCESS [*]
Servant of God, Timothy Giaccardo, S.S.P.

WITH THE VIRTUE of obedience, we offer God the homage of our will, which is the principal faculty.

Obedience is, therefore, a great source of merit and of glory, for to serve God is to reign with Him.

OBEDIENCE is the simple, short and secure way to sanctity. It is the secret of peace, and the guarantee of success in the apostolate. The cry of *"I will not serve,"* is the devil's. The declaration, *"Behold I come* to do the will of Him who sent me," is Christ's, our Divine Master.

Whereas disobedience is ruinous, obedience is constructive and saving!

THE DIVINE MASTER left the bosom of the Father and came on earth to do His Father's will. From the first instant of His virginal Incarnation, He offered Himself as a Host to His Father's every desire.

[*] From *Dai Tetti in Su* by the Servant of God, Rev. Timothy Giaccardo. St. Paul Editions, Rome, 1956.

With His obedience, Christ atoned for the disobedience of the first man and became the Cause of justification and eternal salvation for us all.

OBEDIENCE is an act of faith in God. And God becomes obliged to bless those who have obeyed.

OBEDIENCE OVERTURNS PRIDE even in its very roots. It places the soul, as a victim, on the altar of the will of God.

BECAUSE OBEDIENCE is the most personal and most costly sacrifice of the ego, if the will and the heart are to look for it and love it, we must be convinced that by obeying we do something very valuable.

THROUGH OBEDIENCE WE ADHERE to the divine will: we desire something because it is the will of God and we do our duty in order to please God. Obedience, therefore, confirms us in love that is true and pure, for observance of the commandments is the proof of love.

IN AUTHORITY, it is necessary to see the Divine Master, to follow Him and listen to Him with faith, docility and love! One is to cooperate with his superiors, not resist them.

OBEDIENCE OUGHT TO BE perfectly human, which is to say, a moral act. It should be both effective—that is, exterior—and affective—that is, rational, worthy of an intelligent being.

He who obeys is a *person* and ought, therefore, to give *service* with the mind, will and heart.

It is not perfect obedience when the command is merely *executed*.

THE LITTLE ACTS of obedience are the nourishment, the mark and the exercise of humility. Through these little acts of obedience, one gives more proof of fidelity than through greater ones. And Jesus reveals Himself to "little ones." Obeying even when there is no obligation in conscience greatly glorifies God!

THROUGH OBEDIENCE, WE CHOOSE what is objectively more perfect, since nothing could surpass God's choice. What we do through obedience might not be the most perfect in itself, but obedience makes it such.

BY OBEYING, ONE always pleases God and meets with His approval. To want to act contrary to obedience is to be greatly deceived. Rather than sacrifice obedience, it is better to sacrifice any undertaking.

TO STAY CALM amid doubts that arise concerning directives given by superiors, it is necessary first of all to dispose one's self to agree in judgment with their decision, and then to practice patience, trust and prayer.

GOD TAKES OBEDIENT SOULS as His instruments. There are people of great and even exceptional gifts who, nevertheless, accomplish nothing in life because they are not obedient to their superiors.

SUPERIORS ARE AIDED in a negative manner when subjects refrain from thinking evil, from judging or criticizing, from dwelling on difficulties, from creating obstacles and from manifesting reluctance or disdain. But they are helped more through positive means, that is, through the ready, constant, all-embracing disposition to obey always, in everything and everywhere.

REAL ADVICE AND HELP is given superiors when we express our personal problems simply, freely, and trustingly. Of special value is prayer that they may carry out their duty in strength and gentleness. Good government by superiors is the source of joy and peace.

OBEDIENCE TO PARENTS is filial piety. As long as you are a son and your father is a father, you owe him reverence, respect, filial love, gratitude, and prayer.

Religious life does not neglect relations and natural affections. Instead, it strengthens them, reconsecrates them, elevates them.

Natural affections are to be disciplined so that they do not gain the upper hand and place themselves in opposition to God. They should be cultivated as a human personality is cultivated—elevated, purified, and supernaturalized. Thus, they become more intimate, more efficacious and more lasting.

IN ORDER TO LIVE in union with the Divine Master, it is essential to follow Him in the mystery of His obedience, too. Throughout life, He never did what He wanted. Rather, only and always He did what was pleasing to His Father. "He became obedient to death, even to death on a cross" (Phil. 2:8).

OBEDIENCE is a great secret of success.

A WISE SUPERIOR does not ordinarily command in an imperative manner. Rather he adapts the form of his commands to the matter at hand and to the character of the person. Often, therefore, he uses the form of a request, a favor, an exhortation, or an appeal to one's good will. A wise religious considers the value of a precept even when it is given in a friendly manner, and he faithfully carries it out.

THE WISDOM OF OBEDIENCE *

Thomas à Kempis

IT IS A VERY GREAT THING to stand in obedience, to live under a superior, and not be at one's own disposal.

It is much more secure to be in a state of subjection than in authority.

Many are under obedience, more out of necessity than for love; and these suffer and easily murmur.

Nor will they gain freedom of mind, unless they submit themselves, with their whole heart, for God's sake.

Run here or there, you will find no rest, but in humble subjection under the government of a superior.

The illusion of changing places has deceived many.

It is true, every one is desirous of acting according to his own liking; and is more inclined to such as are of his own mind.

But if God be among us, we must sometimes give up our own opinion for the sake of peace.

* From *The Imitation of Christ* by Thomas à Kempis. Copyright by the Daughters of St. Paul, 1962.

Who is so wise as to be able fully to know all things?

Therefore trust not too much in your own opinion; but be willing also to hear that of others.

Although your opinion be good, yet if for God's sake you leave it to follow that of another, it will be more profitable to you.

SON, HE WHO STRIVES to withdraw himself from obedience, withdraws himself from grace. If a man does not spontaneously and willingly submit himself to his superior, it is a sign that his flesh does not, as yet, perfectly obey him, but often rebels and complains.

Learn, therefore, to submit yourself promptly to your superior, if you desire to subjugate your flesh.

It is necessary that you conceive a true contempt of yourself if you want to triumph over flesh and blood.

And since you still love yourself too inordinately, therefore, you hesitate to resign yourself in all to the will of others.

But what great matter is it if you, who are but dust and a mere nothing, submit yourself for God's love to a man, when I, the Omnipotent and the Most High, who created all things out of nothing, for love of you humbly submitted myself to man?

I became the most humble and most abject of all, so that you might overcome your pride through my humility.

OBEDIENCE—
CONSTANT COMMUNION WITH CHRIST *

Arcadio Cardinal Larraona
PREFECT OF THE SACRED CONGREGATION OF RITES

WHEN IT COMES to an election in religion, we must have recourse to faith, to a joyous faith, as we find it in the Gospel: "Blessed are they who have not seen and yet have believed," and again, "Blessed are you who have believed." The joy of faith! The Christian feels it always and everywhere: "This is the victory that has overcome the world, your faith."

This is enlightened faith that becomes a way of life, and touches not only the mind, but the will and every action. Faith means to view things through God's eyes, judge things from His standards, love with His love, and carry out His works. It is a whole life lived close to this source of light, heat and energy.

In speaking of the Abbot, St. Benedict makes a marvellous point: "We believe that Christ lives in the Abbot!" The fact that Christ lives in superiors is the foundation of all authority, because "all authority comes from God." I do not surrender to a man. I am not a weak man or one seeking his

* Address of His Eminence, Cardinal Arcadio M. Larraona, Prefect of the Sacred Congregation of Rites, to the General Chapter of the Daughters of St. Paul, on the occasion of the election of their second Mother General, M. Ignatius Balla, 1964.

own interests. I see God and submit to Him. And the clearer, deeper and more complete this vision is, the more God comes in contact with me through His representative. As in the Eucharist, Jesus is present but hidden beneath the veils of bread and wine, so in religious life, He is hidden, but present, beneath the veils of the Superior. And as we have the real, true, active presence of Jesus beneath the Eucharistic veils, so also we have Christ's active presence in the superior. Whether he be older or younger, taller or shorter, brilliant or average in intelligence—all these are veils. And we are not interested in the veils. Through them we must see Jesus living in our midst. He ascended into heaven, but He remained with us: "I shall be with you." In this manner, too, He is with us. The superior's is not just any authority whatsoever. In him we follow Christ. Through the superior we are in continual contact with Jesus.

Religious life is the most demanding of lives.

Jesus gives Himself to us but He expects us to give ourselves to Him. St. Teresa used to repeat a phrase worthy of her: "God forces no one; He takes what you give Him. But He gives Himself fully only to the soul who gives herself fully to Him." He gives Himself in Communion to us, and we must give ourselves in Communion to Him—and through Him, to our neighbor.

Religious life demands special correspondence, in the most total manner. The Lord imposes his

Commandments on all the faithful, but He does not impose the evangelical counsels—He suggests them to the more generous souls: "If you wish. . ."

This total dedication must consist in a full, continual, special correspondence, so that no step is taken which does *not* follow the example of Jesus and no view is held that does not reflect His divine, eternal light.

The secret of the religious life—if it is to be what it ought to be—is first of all communion with Jesus. Our soul is a temple, and every temple requires an altar. On the altar the host is immolated, offered by the priest. In a certain sense, we are all priests, for ourselves and for others, too. Offer the Mass in your heart, offer it continually, so that the altar will never be empty and the priest never inactive.

Religious life must be identical with constant communion with Christ, who is with us, and with the superior, who represents Him, who speaks for Him, just as the priest speaks for Jesus when he says: "This is My Body."

Let us remind ourselves of the principles of faith, which are never to be neglected. In our superiors we have to see God, with simplicity and clear vision: obedience will then truly be the dominant virtue of the religious.

At times, there are inexact, incomplete ideas about the vows. A vow concerns a moral virtue, but above all, it is an evangelical counsel, backed up by the virtue of religion, which is the greatest of the moral virtues. In Christian life, it is not simply a moral virtue. Rather, it leads us to look on God as our Father and Creator; it brings us to perfect imitation of Jesus Christ: it leads to charity. We love Christ when we strive to be like Him, to think like Him, to act as He acted, to suffer as He suffered, to pray as He prayed—for our whole lives. This is sanctity. It is what makes the vow, when it is observed; it renders everything sacred, and transforms everything into a work of religion. We could really do our duties in ceremonial garb, like a priest in surplice and stole, for all that we do is elevated to a sacred action through the vow of obedience.

With obedience, the will gets exercise, because it bows to the will of others. This is good for it, since thus character is built up and a way of life is formed through the acceptance of another's will. But I do more than that, for faith tells me that God is in the superior, and so by obeying, I do His will. I am not doing the will of a man; I am doing the will of God.

If I obey my superior and my rule, my life is always in line with the will of God. This is my strength. In it I sanctify myself and give the greatest proof of my love for God. The vow of obedience leads to this, and gives me great faith—not in my own strength, but in the strength that comes from God.

Some think that to be under obedience is to be always caught in a press. This is completely false! The obedient man enjoys great liberty. "I do what

God wants and because God wants it. The superior is nothing but His representative." What could be greater, nobler or higher than to carry out the will of God?

So, forward in the Lord!

The theology of religious life has great beauty and depth. We must try to understand it. Clear ideas about religious life make us strong even in the face of hardship. They give us courage. Clear ideas are always of great help. Sentiment can grow weak, but the idea remains. For this reason, the most fervent religious orders are always those who have clear teachings as their foundation.

Section 8

Obedience
in the Plan of Salvation

OBEDIENCE
IN THE PLAN OF SALVATION *

The Old Testament

The fall of our first parents is presented as an act of disobedience to God, as is every sin:

AND THE LORD GOD commanded the man thus, "From every tree of the garden you may eat; but from the tree of the knowledge of good and evil you must not eat; for the day you eat of it, you must die."

Genesis 2:16-17

NOW THE SERPENT was more cunning than any beast of the field which the Lord God had made. He said to the woman, "Did God say, 'You shall not eat of any tree of the garden'?" The woman answered the serpent, "Of the fruit of all the trees in the garden we may eat; but 'Of the fruit of the tree in the middle of the garden,' God said, 'you shall not eat, neither shall you touch it, lest you die.'"

But the serpent said to the woman, "No, you shall not die; for God knows that when you eat of it, your eyes will be opened and you will be like God, knowing good and evil." Now the woman saw

---

* The following excerpts from Sacred Scripture are reprinted with the kind permission of the Confraternity of Christian Doctrine, Washington, D.C., holders of the copyright.

that the tree was good for food, pleasing to the eyes, and desirable for the knowledge it would give. She took of its fruit and ate it, and also gave some to her husband and he ate. . . . Then the Lord God said, "You have eaten of the tree of which I commanded you not to eat." The man said, "The woman you placed at my side gave me fruit from the tree and I ate." Then the Lord God said to the woman, "Why have you done this?" The woman said, "The serpent deceived me and I ate."

Then the Lord God said to the serpent: "Because you have done this, cursed are you among all animals, and among all beasts of the field; on your belly shall you crawl, dust shall you eat, all the days of your life. I will put enmity between you and the woman, between your seed and her seed; he shall crush your head, and you shall lie in wait for his heel." To the woman he said: "I will make great your distress in child-bearing; in pain shall you bring forth children; for your husband shall be your longing, though he have dominion over you." And to Adam he said, "Because you have listened to your wife, and have eaten of the tree of which I commanded you not to eat: cursed be the ground because of you; in toil shall you eat of it all the days of your life; thorns and thistles shall it bring forth to you, and you shall eat the plants of the field. In the sweat of your brow you shall eat bread, till you return to the ground, since out of it you were taken; for dust you are and unto dust you shall return." . . . The Lord God put him out of the garden of Eden to till the ground from which he was taken. He drove out the man; and at the east of the garden of Eden he placed the Cherubim, and the flaming sword, which turned every way, to guard the way to the tree of life. *Genesis* 3

Obedience demands self-renunciation in faith, as is clear from the call of the Patriarch Abraham.

THE LORD SAID to Abram: "Leave your country your kinsfolk and your father's house, for the land which I will show you; I will make a great nation of you. . . . In you shall all the nations of the earth be blessed."

Abram went away as the Lord had commanded him, and Lot went with him. Abram was seventy-five years old when he left Haran. Abram took Sarai his wife, Lot his brother's son, all the property they had acquired and the persons they had got in Haran; and they departed for the land of Chanaan. *Genesis* 12:1-5

The covenant obligated the Israelites to observe God's law. Obedience was their loving response to Yahweh for having chosen them as His people.

WHEN MOSES CAME to the people and related all the words and ordinances of the Lord, they all answered with one voice, "We will do everything that the Lord has told us." Moses then wrote down all the words of the Lord and, rising early the next day, he erected at the foot of the mountain an altar and twelve pillars for the twelve tribes of Israel. Then, having sent certain young men of the Israelites to offer holocausts and sacrifice young bulls as peace offerings to the Lord, Moses took half of the blood and put it in large bowls; the other half he splashed on the altar. Taking the Book of the Covenant, he read it aloud to the people, who answered, "All that the Lord has said, we will heed and do." Then he took the blood and sprinkled it on the people, saying, "This is the blood of the covenant which the Lord has made with you in accordance with all these words of his."

Exodus 24:3-8

"THE LORD HEARD your words as you were speaking to me and said to me, 'I have heard the words these people have spoken to you, which are all well said. Would that they might always be of such a mind, to fear me and to keep all my commandments! Then they and their descendants would prosper forever. Go, tell them to return to their tents. Then you wait here near me and I will give you all the commandments, the statutes and decrees you must teach them, that they may observe them in the land which I am giving them to possess.'

"Be careful, therefore, to do as the Lord, your God, has commanded you, not turning aside to the right or to the left, but following exactly the way prescribed for you by the Lord, your God, that you may live and prosper, and may have long life in the land which you are to occupy."

Deuteronomy 5:28-32

"THESE THEN ARE the commandments, the statutes and decrees which the Lord, your God, has ordered that you be taught to observe in the land into which you are crossing for conquest, so that you and your son and your grandson may fear the Lord, your God, and keep, throughout the days of your lives, all his statutes and commandments which I enjoined on you, and thus have long life. Hear then, Israel, and be careful to observe them, that you may grow and prosper the more, in keeping with the promise of the Lord, the God of your fathers, to give you a land flowing with milk and honey.

Deuteronomy 6:1-3

"LATER ON, WHEN your son asks you what these ordinances, statutes and decrees mean which the Lord, our God, has enjoined on you, you shall say to your son, 'We were once slaves of Pharao in Egypt, but the Lord brought us out of Egypt with his strong hand and wrought before our eyes signs and wonders, great and dire, against Egypt and against Pharao and his whole house. He brought us from there to lead us into the land he promised on oath to our fathers, and to give it to us. Therefore, the Lord commanded us to observe all these statutes in fear of the Lord, our God, that we may always have as prosperous and happy a life as we have today;

and our justice before the Lord, our God, is to consist in carefully observing all these commandments he has enjoined on us."

Deuteronomy 6:20-25

"BE CAREFUL to observe all the commandments I enjoin on you today, that you may live and increase, and may enter in and possess the land which the Lord promised on oath to your fathers."

Deuteronomy 8:1

"AND NOW, ISRAEL, what does the Lord, your God, ask of you but to fear the Lord, your God, and follow his ways exactly, to love and serve the Lord, your God, with all your heart and all your soul, to keep the commandments and statutes of the Lord which I enjoin on you today for your own good? Think! The heavens, even the highest heavens, belong to the Lord, your God, as well as the earth and everything on it. Yet in his love for your fathers the Lord was so attached to them as to choose you, their descendants, in preference to all other peoples, as indeed he has now done. Circumcise your hearts, therefore, and be no longer stiff-necked. For the Lord, your God, is the God of gods, the Lord of lords, the great God, mighty and awesome, who has no favorites, accepts no bribes; who executes justice for the orphan and the widow, and befriends the alien, feeding and clothing him. So you too must befriend the alien, for you were once aliens yourselves in the land of Egypt. The Lord, your God, shall you fear, and him shall you serve; hold fast to him and swear by his name."

Deuteronomy 10:12-20

Obedience was the condition for gaining possession of the Promised Land.

"KEEP ALL THE commandments, then, which I enjoined on you today, that you may be strong enough to enter in and take possession of the land into which you are crossing, and that you may have long life on the land which the Lord swore to your fathers he would give to them and their descendants, a land flowing with milk and honey.

" ... If, then, you truly heed the commandments which I enjoin on you today, loving and serving the Lord, your God, with all your heart and all your soul, I will give the seasonal rain to your land, the early rain and the late rain, that you may have your grain, wine and oil to gather in; and I will bring forth grass in your fields for your animals. Thus you may eat your fill. But be careful lest your heart be so lured away that you serve other gods and worship them. For then the wrath of the Lord will flare up against you and he will close up the heavens, so that no rain will fall, and the soil will not yield its crops, and you will soon perish from the good land he is giving you." *Deuteronomy* 11:8-17

Israel's obedience will be blessed; its disobedience, cursed.

"I SET BEFORE you here, this day, a blessing and a curse: a blessing for obeying the commandments of the Lord, your God, which I enjoin on you today; a curse if you do not obey the commandments of the Lord, your God, but turn aside from the way I ordain for you today, to follow other gods."

Deuteronomy 11:26-27

Blessings for Obedience

"THUS, THEN, SHALL it be: if you continue to heed the voice of the Lord, your God, and are careful to observe all his commandments which I enjoin on you today, the Lord, your God, will raise you high above all the nations of the earth. When you hearken to the voice of the Lord, your God, all these blessings will come upon you and overwhelm you:

"May you be blessed in the city, and blessed in the country! Blessed be the fruit of your womb, the produce of your soil and the offspring of your livestock, the issue of your herds and the young of your flocks! Blessed be your grain bin and your kneading bowl! May you be blessed in your coming in, and blessed in your going out!

Curses for Disobedience

"BUT IF YOU DO NOT hearken to the voice of the Lord, your God, and are not careful to observe all his commandments which I enjoin on you today, all these curses shall come upon you and overwhelm you:

"May you be cursed in the city, and cursed in the country! Cursed be your grain bin and your kneading bowl! Cursed be the fruit of your womb, the produce of your soil and the offspring of your livestock, the issue of your herds and the young of your flocks! May you be cursed in your coming in, and cursed in your going out!

"ALL THESE CURSES will come upon you, pursuing you and overwhelming you, until you are destroyed, because you would not hearken to the voice of the Lord, your God, nor keep the commandments and statutes he gave you. They will light on you and your descendants as a sign and a wonder for all time. Since you would not serve the Lord, your God, with joy and gratitude for abundance of every kind, therefore in hunger and thirst, in nakedness and utter poverty, you will serve the enemies whom the Lord will send against you. He will put an iron yoke on your neck, until he destroys you.

"IF YOU ARE NOT careful to observe every word of the Law which is written in this book, and to revere the glorious and awesome name of the Lord, your God, he will smite you and your descendants with severe and constant blows, malignant and lasting maladies. He will again afflict you with all the diseases of Egypt which you dread, and they will persist among you. Should there be any kind of sickness or calamity not mentioned in this Book of the Law, that too the Lord will bring upon you until you are destroyed. Of you who are numerous as the stars in the sky, only a few will be left, because you would not hearken to the voice of the Lord, your God.

"Just as the Lord once took delight in making you grow and prosper, so will he now take delight in ruining and destroying you, and you will be plucked out of the land you are now entering to occupy. The Lord will scatter you among all the nations from one end of the earth to the other, and there you will serve strange gods of wood and stone, such as you and your fathers have not known. Among these nations you will find no repose, not a foot of ground to stand upon, for there the Lord will give you an anguished heart and wasted eyes and a dismayed spirit. You will live in constant suspense and stand in dread both day and night, never sure of your existence. In the morning you will say, 'Would that it were evening!' and in the evening you will say, 'Would that it were morning!' for the dread that your heart must feel and the sight that your eyes must see. The Lord will send you back in galleys to Egypt, to the region I told you that you were never to see again; and there you will offer yourselves for sale to your enemies as male and female slaves, but there will be no buyer."

These are the words of the covenant which the Lord ordered Moses to make with the Israelites in the land of Moab, in addition to the covenant which he made with them at Horeb.

Deuteronomy 28

"EVERY COMMAND that I enjoin on you, you shall be careful to observe, neither adding to it nor subtracting from it.

"If there arises among you a prophet or a dreamer who promises you a sign or wonder, urging you to follow other gods, whom you have not known, and to serve them: even though the sign or wonder he has foretold you comes to pass, pay no attention to the words of that prophet or that dreamer; for the Lord, your God, is testing you to learn whether you really love him with all your heart and with all your soul. The Lord, your God, shall you follow, and him shall you fear; his commandment shall you observe, and his voice shall you heed, serving him and holding fast to him alone. But that prophet or that dreamer shall be put to death, because, in order to lead you astray from the way which the Lord, your God, has directed you to take, he has preached apostasy from the Lord, your God, who brought you out of the land of Egypt and ransomed you from that place of slavery. Thus shall you purge the evil from your midst.

Deuteronomy 13:1-6

Obedience is given to superiors, since the Lord vests them with His authority.

THEN MOSES SAID to the Lord, "May the Lord, the God of the spirits of all mankind, set over the community a man who shall act as their leader in all things, to guide them in all their actions; that the Lord's community may not be like sheep without a shepherd." And the Lord replied to Moses, "Take Josue, son of Nun, a man of spirit, and lay your hand upon him. Have him stand in the presence of the priest Eleazar and of the whole community, and commission him before their eyes. Invest him with some of your own dignity, that the whole Israelite community may obey him. He shall present himself to the priest Eleazar, to have him seek out for him the decisions of the Urim in the Lord's presence; and as he directs, Josue, all the Israelites with him, and the community as a whole shall perform all their actions." Moses did as the Lord had commanded him. Taking Josue and having him stand in the presence of the priest Eleazar and of the whole community, he laid his hands on him and gave him his commission, as the Lord had directed through Moses. *Numbers* 27:15-23

"WE WILL DO all you have commanded us," they answered Josue, "and we will go wherever you send us. We will obey you as completely as we obeyed Moses. But may the Lord, your God, be with you as he was with Moses. If anyone rebels against your orders and does not obey every command you give him, he shall be put to death. But be firm and steadfast."

Josue 1:16-18

Josue exhorts the Chosen People to serve Yahweh alone, who is holy and wills to be served in a holy manner. The people solemnly renew their promise of obedience and fidelity to the Lord.

"Now, THEREFORE, fear the Lord and serve him completely and sincerely. Cast out the gods your fathers served beyond the River and in Egypt, and serve the Lord. If it does not please you to serve the Lord, decide today whom you will serve, the gods your fathers served beyond the River or the gods of the Amorrites in whose country you are dwelling. As for me and my household, we will serve the Lord."

But the people answered, "Far be it from us to forsake the Lord for the service of other gods. For it was the Lord, our God, who brought us and our fathers up out of the land of Egypt, out of a state of slavery. He performed those great miracles before our very eyes and protected us along our entire journey and among all the peoples through whom we passed. At our approach the Lord drove out (all the peoples, including) the Amorrites who dwelt in the land. Therefore we also will serve the Lord, for he is our God."

Josue in turn said to the people, "You may not be able to serve the Lord, for he is a holy God;

he is a jealous God who will not forgive your transgressions or your sins. If, after the good he has done for you, you forsake the Lord and serve strange gods, he will do evil to you and destroy you."

But the people answered Josue, "We will still serve the Lord." Josue therefore said to the people, "You are your own witnesses that you have chosen to serve the Lord." They replied, "We are, indeed!" "Now, therefore, put away the strange gods that are among you and turn your hearts to the Lord, the God of Israel." Then the people promised Josue, "We will serve the Lord our God, and obey his voice."

So Josue made a covenant with the people that day and made statutes and ordinances for them at Sichem, which he recorded in the Book of the Law of God. Then he took a large stone and set it up there under the oak that was in the sanctuary of the Lord. And Josue said to all the people, "This stone shall be our witness, for it has heard all the words which the Lord spoke to us. It shall be a witness against you, should you wish to deny your God." Then Josue dismissed the people, each to his own heritage.

Josue 24:14-28

God does not want religion to be reduced to mere external rites. He teaches that the essence of religion lies in the interior giving of self to God through knowledge and love.

AND SAMUEL SAID: Doth the Lord desire holocausts and victims, and not rather that the voice of the Lord should be obeyed? For obedience is better than sacrifices: and to hearken rather than to offer the fat of rams. Because it is like the sin of witchcraft, to rebel; and like the crime of idolatry, to refuse to obey.   I *Kings* 15:22-23

SACRIFICE OR oblation you wished not, but ears open to obedience you gave me. Holocausts or sin-offerings you sought not; then said I, "Behold I come; in the written scroll it is prescribed for me, to do your will, O my God, is my delight, and your law is within my heart!" I announced your justice in the vast assembly; I did not restrain my lips, as you, O Lord, know.   *Psalm* 39:7-10

THE LORD SAID: Since this people draws near with words only and honors me with their lips alone, though their hearts are far from me, and their reverence for me has become routine observance of the precepts of men, therefore I will again deal with this people in surprising and wondrous fashion: the wisdom of its wise men shall perish and the understanding of its prudent men be hid.

Isaia 29:13-14

THUS SAYS THE Lord of hosts, the God of Israel: Heap your holocausts upon your sacrifices; eat up the flesh! In speaking to your fathers on the day I brought them out of the land of Egypt, I gave them no command concerning holocaust or sacrifice. This rather is what I commanded them: Listen to my voice; then I will be your God and you shall be my people. Walk in all the ways that I command you, so that you may prosper.

But they obeyed not, nor did they pay heed. They walked in the hardness of their evil hearts and turned their backs, not their faces, to me. From the day that your fathers left the land of Egypt even to this day, I have sent you untiringly all my servants the prophets. Yet they have not obeyed me nor paid heed; they have stiffened their necks and done worse than their fathers. When you speak all these words to them, they will not listen to you either; when you call to them, they will not answer you. Say to them: This is the nation which does not listen to the voice of the Lord, its God, or take correction. Faithfulness has disappeared; the word itself is banished from their speech.
Jeremia 7:21-28

IN THEIR AFFLICTION, they shall look for me: "Come, let us return to the Lord, for it is he who has rent, but he will heal us; he has struck us, but he will bind our wounds. He will revive us after two days; on the third day he will raise us up, to live in his presence. Let us know, let us strive to know the Lord; as certain as the .dawn is his coming, and his judgment shines forth like the light of day! He will come to us like the rain, like spring rain waters the earth."

What can I do with you, Ephraim? What can I do with you, Juda? Your piety is like a morning cloud, like the dew that early passes away. For this reason I smote them through the prophets, I slew them by the words of my mouth; for it is love that I desire, not sacrifice, and knowledge of God rather than holocausts. *Osee* 6:1-6

WITH WHAT SHALL I come before the Lord, and bow before God most high? Shall I come before him with holocausts, with calves a year old? Will the Lord be pleased with thousands of rams, with myriad streams of oil? Shall I give my first-born for my crime, the fruit of my body for the sin of my soul? You have been told, O man, what is good, and what the Lord requires of you: Only to do the right and to love goodness, and to walk humbly with your God. *Michea* 6:6-8

I HATE, I spurn your feasts, I take no pleasure in your solemnities; your cereal offerings I will not accept, nor consider your stall-fed peace offerings. Away with your noisy songs! I will not listen to the melodies of your harps. But if you would offer me holocausts, then let justice surge like water, and goodness like an unfailing stream. *Amos* 5:21-23

In Psalm 118 the psalmist sings the praises of the divine Law
and, with increasing anxiety, invokes help to remain faithful to
it even in the midst of trials.

Happy are they whose way is blameless,
who walk in the law of the Lord.
Happy are they who observe his decrees,
who seek him with all their heart,
And do no wrong
but walk in his ways.
You have commanded that your precepts
be diligently kept.
Oh, that I might be firm in the ways
of keeping your statutes!
Then should I not be put to shame
when I beheld all your commands.
I will give you thanks with an upright heart,
when I have learned your just ordinances.
I will keep your statutes;
do not utterly forsake me.

How SHALL A YOUNG MAN be faultless
    in his way?
By keeping to your words.
With all my heart I seek you;
let me not stray from your commands.
Within my heart I treasure your promise,
that I may not sin against you.
Blessed are you, O Lord;
teach me your statutes.
With lips I declare
all the ordinances of your mouth.

In the way of your decrees I rejoice,
as much as in all riches.
I will meditate on your precepts,
and consider your ways.
In your statutes I will delight;
I will not forget your words.

BE GOOD TO YOUR SERVANT, that I may live
and keep your words.
Open my eyes, that I may consider
the wonders of your law.
I am a wayfarer of earth;
hide not your commands from me.
My soul is consumed with longing
for your ordinances at all times.
You rebuke the accursed proud,
who turn away from your commands.
Take away from me reproach and contempt,
for I observe your decrees.
Though princes meet and talk against me,
your servant meditates on your statutes.
Yes, your decrees are my delight;
they are my counselors.

I LIE PROSTRATE in the dust;
give me life according to your word.
I declared my ways, and you answered me;
teach me your statutes.
Make me understand the way of your precepts,
and I will meditate on your wondrous deeds.
My soul weeps for sorrow;

strengthen me according to your words.
Remove from me the way of falsehood,
and favor me with your law.
The way of truth I have chosen;
I have set your ordinances before me.
I cling to your decrees;
O Lord, let me not be put to shame.
I will run the way of your commands
when you give me a docile heart.

INSTRUCT ME, O Lord, in the way of your
  statutes,
that I may exactly observe them.
Give me discernment, that I may observe your
  law
and keep it with all my heart.
Lead me in the path of your commands,
for in it I delight.
Incline my heart to your decrees
and not to gain.
Turn away my eyes from seeing what is vain;
by your way give me life.
Fulfill for your servant
your promise to those who fear you.
Turn away from me the reproach which I dread,
for your ordinances are good.
Behold, I long for your precepts;
in your justice give me life.

LET YOUR KINDNESS come to me, O Lord,
your salvation according to your promise.

So shall I have an answer for those who reproach me,
for I trust in your words.
Take not the word of truth from my mouth,
for in your ordinances is my hope;
And I will keep your law continually,
forever and ever.
And I will walk at liberty,
because I seek your precepts.
I will speak of your decrees before kings
without being ashamed.
And I will delight in your commands,
which I love.
And I will lift up my hands to your commands
and meditate on your statutes.

REMEMBER YOUR WORD to your servant
since you have given me hope.
My comfort in my affliction is
that your promise gives me life.
Though the proud scoff bitterly at me,
I turn not away from your law.
I remember your ordinances of old, O Lord,
and I am comforted.
Indignation seizes me because of the wicked
who forsake your law.
Your statutes are the theme of my song
in the place of my exile.
By night I remember your name, O Lord,
and I will keep your law.

This has been mine,
that I have observed your precepts.

I HAVE SAID, O Lord, that my part
is to keep your words.
I entreat you with all my heart,
have pity on me according to your promise.
I considered my ways
and turned my feet to your decrees.
I was prompt and did not hesitate
in keeping your commands.
Though the snares of the wicked are twined
about me,
your law I have not forgotten.
At midnight I rise to give you thanks
because of your just ordinances.
I am the companion of all who fear you
and keep your precepts.
Of your kindness, O Lord, the earth is full;
teach me your statutes.

YOU HAVE DONE GOOD to your servant,
O Lord, according to your word.
Teach me wisdom and knowledge,
for in your commands I trust.
Before I was afflicted I went astray,
but now I hold to your promise.
You are good and bountiful;
teach me your statutes.
Though the proud forge lies against me,
with all my heart I will observe your precepts.

Their heart has become gross and fat;
as for me, your law is my delight.
It is good for me that I have been afflicted,
that I may learn your statutes.
The law of your mouth is to me more precious
than thousands of gold and silver pieces.

YOUR HANDS HAVE MADE ME and fashioned me;
give me discernment that I may learn your
    commands.
Those who fear you shall see me and be glad,
because I hope in your word.
I know, O Lord, that your ordinances are just,
and in your faithfulness you have afflicted me.
Let your kindness comfort me
according to your promise to your servants.
Let your compassion come to me that I
    may live,
for your law is my delight.
Let the proud be put to shame for oppressing
    me unjustly;
I will meditate on your precepts.
Let those turn to me who fear you
and acknowledge your decrees.
Let my heart be perfect in your statutes,
that I be not put to shame.

MY SOUL PINES for your salvation;
I hope in your word.
My eyes strain after your promise;
when will you comfort me?

Though I am shriveled like a leathern flask
  in the smoke,
I have not forgotten your statutes.
How many are the days of your servant?
When will you do judgment on my persecutors?
The proud have dug pits for me;
this is against your law.
All your commands are steadfast;
they persecute me wrongfully; help me!
They have all but put an end to me
  on the earth,
but I have not forsaken your precepts.
In your kindness give me life,
that I may keep the decrees of your mouth.

YOUR WORD, O LORD, endures forever;
it is firm as the heavens.
Through all generations your truth endures;
you have established the earth,
  and it stands firm.
According to your ordinances
  they still stand firm:
all things serve you.
Had not your law been my delight,
I should have perished in my affliction.
Never will I forget your precepts,
for through them you give me life.
I am yours; save me,
for I have sought your precepts.
Sinners wait to destroy me,
but I pay heed to your decrees.

I see that all fulfillment has its limits;
broad indeed is your command.

How I LOVE YOUR LAW, O Lord!
It is my meditation all the day.
Your command has made me
    wiser than my enemies,
for it is ever with me.
I have more understanding than all my teachers
when your decrees are my meditation.
I have more discernment than the elders,
because I observe your precepts.
From every evil way I withhold my feet
that I may keep your words.
From your ordinances I turn not away,
for you have instructed me.
How sweet to my palate are your promises,
sweeter than honey to my mouth!
Through your precepts I gain discernment;
therefore I hate every false way.

A LAMP TO MY FEET is your word,
a light to my path.
I resolve and swear
to keep your just ordinances.
I am very much afflicted;
O Lord, give me life according to your word.
Accept, O Lord, the free homage of my mouth,
and teach me your decrees.
Though constantly I take my life in my hands,
yet I forget not your law.

The wicked have laid a snare for me,
but from your precepts I have not strayed.
Your decrees are my inheritance forever;
the joy of my heart they are.
I intend in my heart to fulfill your statutes
always, to the letter.

I HATE MEN of divided heart,
but I love your law.
You are my refuge and my shield;
in your word I hope.
Depart from me, you wrongdoers,
and I will observe the commands of my God.
Sustain me as you have promised,
    that I may live;
disappoint me not in my hope.
Help me, that I may be safe
and ever delight in your statutes.
You despise all who stray from your statutes,
for their deceitfulness is in vain.
You account all the wicked of the earth as dross;
therefore I love your decrees.
My flesh shudders with dread of you,
and I fear your ordinances.

I HAVE FULFILLED just ordinances;
leave me not to my oppressors.
Be surety for the welfare of your servant;
let not the proud oppress me.
My eyes strain after your salvation
and your just promise.

Deal with your servant according to your
  kindness,
and teach me your statutes.
I am your servant; give me discernment
that I may know your decrees.
It is time for the Lord to act:
they have broken your law.
For I love your command
more than gold, however fine.
For in all your precepts I go forward;
every false way I hate.

WONDERFUL ARE your decrees;
therefore I observe them.
The revelation of your words sheds light,
giving understanding to the simple.
I gasp with open mouth
in my yearning for your commands.
Turn to me in pity
as you turn to those who love your name.
Steady my footsteps according to your promise,
and let no iniquity rule over me.
Redeem me from the oppression of men,
that I may keep your precepts.
Let your countenance shine upon your servant,
and teach me your statutes.
My eyes shed streams of tears
because your law has not been kept.

YOU ARE JUST, O Lord,
and your ordinance is right.

You have pronounced your decrees in justice
and in perfect faithfulness.
My zeal consumes me,
because my foes forget your words.
Your promise is very sure,
and your servant loves it.
I am mean and contemptible,
but your precepts I have not forgotten.
Your justice is everlasting justice,
and your law is permanent.
Though distress and anguish have come
    upon me,
your commands are my delight.
Your decrees are forever just;
give me discernment that I may live.

I CALL OUT WITH all my heart; answer me,
    O Lord;
I will observe your statutes.
I call upon you; save me,
and I will keep your decrees.
Before dawn I come and cry out;
I hope in your words.
My eyes greet the night watches
in meditation on your promise.
Hear my voice according to your kindness, O
    Lord;
according to your ordinance give me life.
I am attacked by malicious persecutors
who are far from your law.
You, O Lord, are near,

and all your commands are permanent.
Of old I know from your decrees,
that you have established them forever.

BEHOLD MY AFFLICTION, and rescue me,
for I have not forgotten your law.
Plead my cause and redeem me;
for the sake of your promise give me life.
Far from sinners is salvation
because they seek not your statutes.
Your compassion is great, O Lord;
according to your ordinances give me life.
Though my persecutors and my foes are many,
I turn not away from your decrees.
I beheld the apostates with loathing,
because they kept not to your promise.
See how I love your precepts, O Lord;
in your kindness give me life.
Permanence is your word's chief trait;
each of your just ordinances is everlasting.

PRINCES PERSECUTE ME without cause
but my heart stands in awe of your word.
I rejoice at your promise,
as one who has found rich spoil.
Falsehood I hate and abhor;
your law I love.
Seven times a day I praise you
for your just ordinances.

Those who love your law have great peace,
and for them there is no stumbling block.
I wait for your salvation, O Lord,
and your commands I fulfill.
I keep your decrees
and love them deeply.
I keep your precepts and your decrees,
for all my ways are before you.

LET MY CRY COME before you, O Lord;
in keeping with your word, give me
    discernment.
Let my supplication reach you;
rescue me according to your promise.
My lips pour forth your praise,
because you teach me your statutes.
May my tongue sing of your promise,
for all your commands are just.
Let your hand be ready to help me,
for I have chosen your precepts.
I long for your salvation, O Lord,
and your law is my delight.
Let my soul live to praise you,
and may your ordinances help me.
I have gone astray (like a lost sheep);
    seek your servant,
because your commands I do not forget.

Psalm 118

According to the sapiential authors, to obey is to yield to the word of God and of His representatives.

MY SON, FORGET not my teaching, keep in mind my commands; for many days, and years of life, and peace, will they bring you. *Proverbs* 3:1-2

HEAR, MY SON, your father's instruction, and reject not your mother's teaching; a graceful diadem will they be for your head; a torque for your neck. *Proverbs* 1:8-9

MY SON, IF YOU receive my words and treasure my commands, turning your ear to wisdom, inclining your heart to understanding; yes, if you call to intelligence, and to understanding raise your voice; if you seek her like silver, and like hidden treasures search her out: then will you understand the fear of the Lord; the knowledge of God you will find; for the Lord gives wisdom, from his mouth come knowledge and understanding; he has counsel in store for the upright, he is the shield of those who walk honestly, guarding the paths of justice, protecting the way of his pious ones. *Proverbs* 2:1-8

Now, O CHILDREN, listen to me; instruction and wisdom do not reject! Happy the man who obeys me, and happy those who keep my ways, happy the man watching daily at my gates, waiting at my doorposts; for he who finds me finds life, and wins favor from the Lord. *Proverbs* 8:32-35

The New Testament

As soon as Mary manifests her absolute submission to the will of God, the Word takes flesh in her womb.

NOW IN THE SIXTH month the angel Gabriel was sent from God to a town of Galilee called Nazareth to a virgin betrothed to a man named Joseph of the house of David, and the virgin's name was Mary. And when the angel had come to her, he said, "Hail, full of grace, the Lord is with thee. Blessed art thou among women." When she had heard him she was troubled at his word, and kept pondering what manner of greeting this might be.

And the angel said to her, "Do not be afraid, Mary, for thou hast found grace with God. Behold, thou shalt conceive in thy womb and shalt bring forth a son; and thou shalt call his name Jesus. He shall be great, and shall be called the Son of the Most High; and the Lord God will give him the throne of David his father and he shall be king over the house of Jacob forever; and of his kingdom there shall be no end." But Mary said to the angel, "How shall this happen since I do not know man?"

And the angel answered and said to her, "The Holy Spirit shall come upon thee and the power of the Most High shall overshadow thee; and therefore the Holy One to be born shall be called the Son of God. And behold, Elizabeth thy kinswoman also has conceived a son in her old age, and she who was called barren is now in her sixth month, for nothing shall be impossible with God."

But Mary said, "Behold the handmaid of the Lord; be it done to me according to thy word." And the angel departed from her. *Luke* 1:26-38

Christ stresses obedience to the will of God as proof of love.

"NOT EVERYONE WHO says to me, 'Lord, Lord,' shall enter the kingdom of heaven; but he who does the will of my Father in heaven shall enter the kingdom of heaven. Many will say to me in that day, 'Lord, Lord, did we not prophesy in thy name, and cast out devils in thy name, and work many miracles in thy name?' And then I will declare to them, 'I never knew you. Depart from me, you workers of iniquity!'

"Everyone therefore who hears these my words and acts upon them, shall be likened to a wise man who built his house on rock. And the rain fell, and the floods came, and the winds blew and beat against that house, but it did not fall, because it was founded on rock. And everyone who hears these my words and does not act upon them, shall be likened to a foolish man who built his house on sand. And the rain fell, and the floods came, and the winds blew and beat against that house, and it fell, and was utterly ruined." *Matthew* 7:21-27

"HE WHO HAS my commandments and keeps them, he it is who loves me. But he who loves me will be loved by my Father, and I will love him and manifest myself to him,"

Judas, not the Iscariot, said to him, "Lord, how is it that thou art about to manifest thyself to us, and not to the world?" Jesus answered and said to him, "If anyone love me, he will keep my word, and my Father will love him, and we will come to him and make our abode with him. He who does not love me does not keep my words. And the word that you have heard is not mine, but the Father's who sent me."

John 14:21-24

Christ teaches us to pray thus:

"THY KINGDOM COME, thy will be done on earth, as it is in heaven."

Matthew 6:10

The will of God is that the world should be saved by His Son. And the law of the Son's mission, as well as His dominant thought, is to carry out the merciful will of His Father.

"FOR I HAVE come down from heaven, not to do my own will, but the will of him who sent me. Now this is the will of him who sent me, the Father, that I should lose nothing of what he has given me, but that I should raise it up on the last day. For this is the will of my Father who sent me, that whoever beholds the Son, and believes in him, shall have everlasting life, and I will raise him up on the last day." John 6:38-40

"OF MYSELF I can do nothing. As I hear, I judge, and my judgment is just because I seek not my own will, but the will of him who sent me." John 5:30

THESE THINGS JESUS spoke; and raising his eyes to heaven, he said, "Father, the hour has come! Glorify thy Son, that thy Son may glorify thee, even as thou hast given him power over all flesh, in order that to all thou hast given him he may give everlasting life. Now this is everlasting life, that they may know thee, the only true God, and him whom thou hast sent, Jesus Christ. I have glorified thee on earth; I have accomplished the work that thou hast given me to do." John 17:1-4

MEANWHILE, HIS DISCIPLES besought him, saying, "Rabbi, eat." But he said to them, "I have food to eat of which you do not know." The disciples therefore said to one another, "Has someone brought him something to eat?"

Jesus said to them, "My food is to do the will of him who sent me, to accomplish his work." John 4:31-34

In His agony, Christ will not let the will of His human nature prevail, and He teaches us to pray that the will of God may be done (ORIGEN).

THEN JESUS CAME with them to a country place called Gethsemani, and he said to his disciples, "Sit down here, while I go over yonder and pray." And he took with him Peter and the two sons of Zebedee, and he began to be saddened and exceedingly troubled. Then he said to them, "My soul is sad, even unto death. Wait here and watch with me." And going forward a little, he fell prostrate and prayed, saying, "Father, if it is possible, let this cup pass away from me; yet not as I will, but as thou willest."

Then he came to the disciples and found them sleeping. And he said to Peter, "Could you not, then, watch one hour with me? Watch and pray, that you may not enter into temptation. The spirit indeed is willing, but the flesh is weak." Again a second time he went away and prayed, saying, "My Father, if this cup cannot pass away unless I drink it, thy will be done." And he came again and found them sleeping, for their eyes were heavy. And leaving them he went back again, and prayed a third time, saying the same words over.   *Matthew* 26:36-44

FOR JESUS, IN the days of his earthly life, with a loud cry and tears, offered up prayers and supplications to him who was able to save him from death, and was heard because of his reverent submission. And he, Son though he was, learned obedience from the things that he suffered; and when perfected, he became to all who obey him the cause of eternal salvation, called by God a high priest according to the order of Melchisedech.

Hebrews 5:7-10

Sin entered into the world through the disobedience of Adam, but by His obedience, Christ triumphed over it.

THEREFORE AS THROUGH one man sin entered into the world and through sin death, and thus death has passed unto all men because all have sinned—for until the Law sin was in the world, but sin is not imputed when there is no law; yet death reigned from Adam until Moses even over those who did not sin after the likeness of the transgression of Adam, who is a figure of him who was to come.

But not like the offense is the gift. For if by the offense of the one the many died, much more has the grace of God, and the gift in the grace of the one man Jesus Christ, abounded unto the many. Nor is the gift as it was in the case of one man's sin, for the judgment was from one man unto condemnation, but grace is from many offenses unto justification. For if by reason of the one man's offense death reigned through the one man, much more will they who receive the abundance of the grace and of the gift of justice reign in life through the one Jesus Christ. Therefore as from the offense of the one man the result was unto condemnation to all men, so from the justice of the one the result is unto justification of life to all men. For just as by the disobedience of the one man the many were constituted sinners, so also by the obedience of the one the many will be constituted just.

Romans 5:12-19

The best exhortation to obedience is the example of Christ.

HAVE THIS MIND in you which was also in Christ Jesus, who though he was by nature God, did not consider being equal to God a thing to be clung to, but emptied himself, taking the nature of a slave and being made like unto men. And appearing in the form of man, he humbled himself, becoming obedient to death, even to death on a cross. Therefore God also has exalted him and has bestowed upon him the name that is above every name, so that at the name of Jesus every knee should bend of those in heaven, on earth and under the earth, and every tongue should confess that the Lord Jesus Christ is in the glory of God the Father.

Philippians 2:5-11

Like the Apostles and their disciples we must ever obey Christ and His Gospel, rather than men.

SUMMONING THEM, they charged them not to speak or to teach at all in the name of Jesus.

But Peter and John answered and said to them, "Whether it is right in the sight of God to listen to you rather than to God, decide for yourselves. For we cannot but speak of what we have seen and heard."

Acts 4:18-20

HAVING BROUGHT THEM, they set them before the Sanhedrin. And the high priest questioned them, saying, "We strictly charged you not to teach in this name, and behold, you have filled Jerusalem with your teaching, and want to bring this man's blood upon us."

But Peter and the apostles answered and said, "We must obey God rather than men. The God of our fathers raised Jesus, whom you put to death, hanging him on a tree. Him God exalted with his right hand to be Prince and Savior, to grant repentance to Israel and forgiveness of sins. And we are witnesses of these things, and so is the Holy Spirit, whom God has given to all who obey him."

Acts 5:27-32

For a man to obey a man is absurd inasmuch as they are equals as men. But it is supreme nobility and great security to obey God, who manifests His will through legitimate authority.

LET EVERYONE BE subject to the higher authorities, for there exists no authority except from God, and those who exist have been appointed by God. Therefore he who resists the authority resists the ordinance of God; and they that resist bring on themselves condemnation. For rulers are a terror not to the good work but to the evil. Dost thou wish, then, not to fear the authority? Do what is good and thou wilt have praise from it. For it is God's minister to thee for good. But if thou dost what is evil, fear, for not without reason does it carry the sword. For it is God's minister, an avenger to execute wrath on him who does evil. Wherefore you must needs be subject, not only because of the wrath, but also for conscience' sake. *Romans* 13:1-5

OBEY YOUR SUPERIORS and be subject to them, for they keep watch as having to render an account of your souls; so that they may do this with joy, and not with grief, for that would not be expedient for you. *Hebrews* 13:17

NOW WE BESEECH you, brethren, to appreciate those who labor among you, and who are over you in the Lord and admonish you. Esteem them with a more abundant love on account of their work. Be at peace with them. 1 *Thessalonians* 5:12-13

The Christian obeys his superior as Christ obeyed His Father.

As THE FATHER has loved me, I also have loved you. Abide in my love. If you keep my commandments you will abide in my love, as I also have kept my Father's commandments, and abide in his love. These things I have spoken to you that my joy may be in you, and that your joy may be made full.

You are my friends if you do the things I command you. No longer do I call you servants, because the servant does not know what his master does. But I have called you friends, because all things that I have heard from my Father I have made known to you. *John* 15:9-11; 14-15

DAUGHTERS OF ST. PAUL

IN MASSACHUSETTS
    50 St. Paul's Ave.
      Jamaica Plain
      Boston, Mass. 02130
    172 Tremont St.
      Boston, Mass. 02111
    381 Dorchester St.
      So. Boston, Mass. 02127
    325 Main St.
      Fitchburg, Mass.
IN NEW YORK
    78 Fort Place
      Staten Island, N.Y. 10301
    625 East 187th St.
      Bronx, N.Y.
    39 Erie St.
      Buffalo, N.Y. 14202
IN CONNECTICUT
    202 Fairfield Ave.
      Bridgeport, Conn. 06603
IN OHIO
    141 West Rayen Ave.
      Youngstown, Ohio 44503
    Daughters of St. Paul
      Cleveland, Ohio
IN TEXAS
    114 East Main Plaza
      San Antonio, Texas 78205
IN CALIFORNIA
    1570 Fifth Ave.
      San Diego, Calif. 92101
    278 - 17th Street
      Oakland, California 94612
IN LOUISIANA
    86 Bolton Ave.
      Alexandria, La. 71301
IN FLORIDA
    2700 Biscayne Blvd.
      Miami, Florida 33137
IN CANADA
    8885 Blvd. Lacordaire
      St. Leonard Deport-Maurice
      Montreal, Canada
      1063 St. Clair Ave. West
      Toronto, Canada
IN ENGLAND
    29 Beauchamp Place
      London, S.W. 3, England
IN AFRICA
    Box 4392
      Kampala, Uganda
IN INDIA
    Water Field Road Extension
    Plot No. 143
      Bandra, India
IN THE PHILIPPINE ISLANDS
    2650 F.B. Harrison St.
    Pasay City
      Philippine Islands
IN AUSTRALIA
    58 Abbotsford Rd.
      Homebush N.S.W., Australia
    226 Victoria Square
      Adelaide, South-Australia
    6 Muir Street
      Hawthorn, Victoria, Australia